DICTIONARY

THEME-BASED

British English Collection

ENGLISH-BULGARIAN

The most useful words
To expand your lexicon and sharpen
your language skills

9000 words

Theme-based dictionary British English-Bulgarian - 9000 words
By Andrey Taranov

T&P Books vocabularies are intended for helping you learn, memorize and review foreign words. The dictionary is divided into themes, covering all major spheres of everyday activities, business, science, culture, etc.

The process of learning words using T&P Books' theme-based dictionaries gives you the following advantages:

- Correctly grouped source information predetermines success at subsequent stages of word memorization
- Availability of words derived from the same root allowing memorization of word units (rather than separate words)
- Small units of words facilitate the process of establishing associative links needed for consolidation of vocabulary
- Level of language knowledge can be estimated by the number of learned words

T&P Books Publishing
www.tpbooks.com

This book is also available in E-book formats.
Please visit www.tpbooks.com or the major online bookstores.

BULGARIAN THEME-BASED DICTIONARY
British English collection

T&P Books vocabularies are intended to help you learn, memorize, and review foreign words. The vocabulary contains over 9000 commonly used words arranged thematically.

- Vocabulary contains the most commonly used words
- Recommended as an addition to any language course
- Meets the needs of beginners and advanced learners of foreign languages
- Convenient for daily use, revision sessions, and self-testing activities
- Allows you to assess your vocabulary

Special features of the vocabulary

- Words are organized according to their meaning, not alphabetically
- Words are presented in three columns to facilitate the reviewing and self-testing processes
- Words in groups are divided into small blocks to facilitate the learning process
- The vocabulary offers a convenient and simple transcription of each foreign word

The vocabulary has 256 topics including:

Basic Concepts, Numbers, Colors, Months, Seasons, Units of Measurement, Clothing & Accessories, Food & Nutrition, Restaurant, Family Members, Relatives, Character, Feelings, Emotions, Diseases, City, Town, Sightseeing, Shopping, Money, House, Home, Office, Working in the Office, Import & Export, Marketing, Job Search, Sports, Education, Computer, Internet, Tools, Nature, Countries, Nationalities and more ...

TABLE OF CONTENTS

PRONUNCIATION GUIDE

T&P phonetic alphabet	Bulgarian example	English example
[a]	**сладък** [sládək]	shorter than in 'ask'
[e]	**череша** [ʧeréʃa]	elm, medal
[i]	**килим** [kilím]	shorter than in 'feet'
[o]	**отломка** [otlómka]	pod, John
[u]	**улуча** [ulúʧa]	book
[ə]	**въже** [vəʒə́]	Schwa, reduced 'e'
[ja], [ʲa]	**вечеря** [veʧérʲa]	royal
[ʲu]	**ключ** [klʲuʧ]	cued, cute
[ʲo]	**фризьор** [frizʲór]	New York
[ja], [ʲa]	**история** [istórija]	royal
[b]	**събота** [sə́bota]	baby, book
[d]	**пладне** [pládne]	day, doctor
[f]	**парфюм** [parfʲúm]	face, food
[g]	**гараж** [garáʒ]	game, gold
[ʒ]	**мрежа** [mréʒa]	forge, pleasure
[j]	**двубой** [dvubój]	yes, New York
[h]	**храбър** [hrábər]	huge, hat
[k]	**колело** [koleló]	clock, kiss
[l]	**паралел** [paralél]	lace, people
[m]	**мяукам** [mʲaúkam]	magic, milk
[n]	**фонтан** [fontán]	name, normal
[p]	**пушек** [púʃek]	pencil, private
[r]	**крепост** [krépost]	rice, radio
[s]	**каса** [kása]	city, boss
[t]	**тютюн** [tʲutʲún]	tourist, trip
[v]	**завивам** [zavívam]	very, river
[ʦ]	**църква** [tsə́rkva]	cats, tsetse fly
[ʃ]	**шапка** [ʃápka]	machine, shark
[ʧ]	**чорапи** [ʧorápi]	church, French
[w]	**уиски** [wíski]	vase, winter
[z]	**зарзават** [zarzavát]	zebra, please

ABBREVIATIONS used in the dictionary

English abbreviations

ab. - about
adj - adjective
adv - adverb
anim. - animate
as adj - attributive noun used as adjective
e.g. - for example
etc. - et cetera
fam. - familiar
fem. - feminine
form. - formal
inanim. - inanimate
masc. - masculine
math - mathematics
mil. - military
n - noun
pl - plural
pron. - pronoun
sb - somebody
sing. - singular
sth - something
v aux - auxiliary verb
vi - intransitive verb
vi, vt - intransitive, transitive verb
vt - transitive verb

Bulgarian abbreviations

ж - feminine noun
ж мн - feminine plural
м - masculine noun
м мн - masculine plural
м, ж - masculine, feminine
мн - plural
с - neuter
с мн - neuter plural

BASIC CONCEPTS

Basic concepts. Part 1

1. Pronouns

I, me	**аз**	[az]
you	**ти**	[ti]
he	**той**	[toj]
she	**тя**	[tʲa]
it	**то**	[to]
we	**ние**	[níe]
you (to a group)	**вие**	[víe]
they	**те**	[te]

2. Greetings. Salutations. Farewells

Hello! (fam.)	**Здравей!**	[zdravéj]
Hello! (form.)	**Здравейте!**	[zdravéjte]
Good morning!	**Добро утро!**	[dobró útro]
Good afternoon!	**Добър ден!**	[dóbər den]
Good evening!	**Добър вечер!**	[dóbər vétʃer]
to say hello	**поздравявам**	[pozdravʲávam]
Hi! (hello)	**Здрасти!**	[zdrásti]
greeting (n)	**поздрав** (м)	[pózdrav]
to greet (vt)	**приветствувам**	[privétstvuvam]
How are you?	**Как си?**	[kak si]
What's new?	**Какво ново?**	[kakvó nóvo]
Bye-Bye! Goodbye!	**Довиждане!**	[dovíʒdane]
See you soon!	**До скора среща!**	[do skóra sréʃta]
Farewell!	**Сбогом!**	[zbógom]
to say goodbye	**сбогувам се**	[sbogúvam se]
Cheers!	**До скоро!**	[do skóro]
Thank you! Cheers!	**Благодаря!**	[blagodarʲá]
Thank you very much!	**Много благодаря!**	[mnógo blagodarʲá]
My pleasure!	**Моля.**	[mólʲa]
Don't mention it!	**Няма нищо.**	[nʲáma níʃto]
It was nothing	**Няма за какво.**	[nʲáma za kakvó]
Excuse me! (fam.)	**Извинявай!**	[izvinʲávaj]
Excuse me! (form.)	**Извинявайте!**	[izvinʲávajte]
to excuse (forgive)	**извинявам**	[izvinʲávam]

to apologize (vi)	**извинявам се**	[izvinʲávam se]
My apologies	**Моите извинения.**	[móite izvinénija]
I'm sorry!	**Прощавайте!**	[proʃtávajte]
please (adv)	**моля**	[mólʲa]
Don't forget!	**Не забравяйте!**	[ne zabrávʲajte]
Certainly!	**Разбира се!**	[razbíra se]
Of course not!	**Разбира се, не!**	[razbíra se ne]
Okay! (I agree)	**Съгласен!**	[səglásen]
That's enough!	**Стига!**	[stíga]

3. How to address

mister, sir	**Господине**	[gospodíne]
madam	**Госпожо**	[gospóʒo]
miss	**Госпожице**	[gospóʒitse]
young man	**Младежо**	[mladéʒo]
young man (little boy)	**Момче**	[momtʃé]
miss (little girl)	**Момиче**	[momítʃe]

4. Cardinal numbers. Part 1

0 zero	**нула** (ж)	[núla]
1 one	**едно**	[ednó]
2 two	**две**	[dve]
3 three	**три**	[tri]
4 four	**четири**	[tʃétiri]
5 five	**пет**	[pet]
6 six	**шест**	[ʃest]
7 seven	**седем**	[sédem]
8 eight	**осем**	[ósem]
9 nine	**девет**	[dévet]
10 ten	**десет**	[déset]
11 eleven	**единадесет**	[edinádeset]
12 twelve	**дванадесет**	[dvanádeset]
13 thirteen	**тринадесет**	[trinádeset]
14 fourteen	**четиринадесет**	[tʃetirinádeset]
15 fifteen	**петнадесет**	[petnádeset]
16 sixteen	**шестнадесет**	[ʃesnádeset]
17 seventeen	**седемнадесет**	[sedemnádeset]
18 eighteen	**осемнадесет**	[osemnádeset]
19 nineteen	**деветнадесет**	[devetnádeset]
20 twenty	**двадесет**	[dvádeset]
21 twenty-one	**двадесет и едно**	[dvádeset i ednó]
22 twenty-two	**двадесет и две**	[dvádeset i dve]
23 twenty-three	**двадесет и три**	[dvádeset i tri]
30 thirty	**тридесет**	[trídeset]
31 thirty-one	**тридесет и едно**	[trídeset i ednó]

32 thirty-two	**тридесет и две**	[trídeset i dve]
33 thirty-three	**тридесет и три**	[trídeset i tri]
40 forty	**четиридесет**	[ʧetírideset]
41 forty-one	**четиридесет и едно**	[ʧetírideset i ednó]
42 forty-two	**четиридесет и две**	[ʧetírideset i dve]
43 forty-three	**четиридесет и три**	[ʧetírideset i tri]
50 fifty	**петдесет**	[petdesét]
51 fifty-one	**петдесет и едно**	[petdesét i ednó]
52 fifty-two	**петдесет и две**	[petdesét i dve]
53 fifty-three	**петдесет и три**	[petdesét i tri]
60 sixty	**шестдесет**	[ʃestdesét]
61 sixty-one	**шестдесет и едно**	[ʃestdesét i ednó]
62 sixty-two	**шестдесет и две**	[ʃestdesét i dve]
63 sixty-three	**шестдесет и три**	[ʃestdesét i tri]
70 seventy	**седемдесет**	[sedemdesét]
71 seventy-one	**седемдесет и едно**	[sedemdesét i ednó]
72 seventy-two	**седемдесет и две**	[sedemdesét i dve]
73 seventy-three	**седемдесет и три**	[sedemdesét i tri]
80 eighty	**осемдесет**	[osemdesét]
81 eighty-one	**осемдесет и едно**	[osemdesét i ednó]
82 eighty-two	**осемдесет и две**	[osemdesét i dve]
83 eighty-three	**осемдесет и три**	[osemdesét i tri]
90 ninety	**деветдесет**	[devetdesét]
91 ninety-one	**деветдесет и едно**	[devetdesét i ednó]
92 ninety-two	**деветдесет и две**	[devetdesét i dve]
93 ninety-three	**деветдесет и три**	[devetdesét i tri]

5. Cardinal numbers. Part 2

100 one hundred	**сто**	[sto]
200 two hundred	**двеста**	[dvésta]
300 three hundred	**триста**	[trísta]
400 four hundred	**четиристотин**	[ʧétiri·stótin]
500 five hundred	**петстотин**	[pét·stótin]
600 six hundred	**шестстотин**	[ʃést·stótin]
700 seven hundred	**седемстотин**	[sédem·stótin]
800 eight hundred	**осемстотин**	[ósem·stótin]
900 nine hundred	**деветстотин**	[dévet·stótin]
1000 one thousand	**хиляда** (ж)	[hilʲáda]
2000 two thousand	**две хиляди**	[dve hílʲadi]
3000 three thousand	**три хиляди**	[tri hílʲadi]
10000 ten thousand	**десет хиляди**	[déset hílʲadi]
one hundred thousand	**сто хиляди**	[sto hílʲadi]
million	**милион** (м)	[milión]
billion	**милиард** (м)	[miliárt]

6. Ordinal numbers

first (adj)	**първи**	[pərvi]
second (adj)	**втори**	[ftóri]
third (adj)	**трети**	[tréti]
fourth (adj)	**четвърти**	[ʧetvərti]
fifth (adj)	**пети**	[péti]
sixth (adj)	**шести**	[ʃésti]
seventh (adj)	**седми**	[sédmi]
eighth (adj)	**осми**	[ósmi]
ninth (adj)	**девети**	[devéti]
tenth (adj)	**десети**	[deséti]

7. Numbers. Fractions

fraction	**дроб** (м)	[drop]
one half	**една втора**	[edná ftóra]
one third	**една трета**	[edná tréta]
one quarter	**една четвърта**	[edná ʧetvərta]
one eighth	**една осма**	[edná ósma]
one tenth	**една десета**	[edná deséta]
two thirds	**две трети**	[dve tréti]
three quarters	**три четвърти**	[tri ʧetvərti]

8. Numbers. Basic operations

subtraction	**изваждане** (с)	[izváʒdane]
to subtract (vi, vt)	**изваждам**	[izváʒdam]
division	**деление** (с)	[delénie]
to divide (vt)	**деля**	[delʲá]
addition	**събиране** (с)	[səbírane]
to add up (vt)	**събера**	[səberá]
to add (vi)	**прибавям**	[pribávʲam]
multiplication	**умножение** (с)	[umnoʒénie]
to multiply (vt)	**умножавам**	[umnoʒávam]

9. Numbers. Miscellaneous

digit, figure	**цифра** (ж)	[tsífra]
number	**число** (с)	[ʧisló]
numeral	**числително име** (с)	[ʧislítelno íme]
minus sign	**минус** (м)	[mínus]
plus sign	**плюс** (м)	[plʲus]
formula	**формула** (ж)	[fórmula]
calculation	**изчисление** (с)	[isʧislénie]
to count (vi, vt)	**броя**	[brojá]

to count up	**преброявам**	[prebrojávam]
to compare (vt)	**сравнявам**	[sravnʲávam]
How much?	**Колко?**	[kólko]
sum, total	**сума** (ж)	[súma]
result	**резултат** (м)	[rezultát]
remainder	**остатък** (м)	[ostátək]
a few (e.g., ~ years ago)	**няколко**	[nʲákolko]
little (I had ~ time)	**малко …**	[málko]
the rest	**остатък** (м)	[ostátək]
one and a half	**един и половина**	[edín i polovína]
dozen	**дузина** (ж)	[duzína]
in half (adv)	**наполовина**	[napolovína]
equally (evenly)	**поравно**	[porávno]
half	**половина** (ж)	[polovína]
time (three ~s)	**път** (м)	[pət]

10. The most important verbs. Part 1

to advise (vt)	**съветвам**	[səvétvam]
to agree (say yes)	**съгласявам се**	[səglasʲávam se]
to answer (vi, vt)	**отговарям**	[otgovárʲam]
to arrive (vi)	**пристигам**	[pristígam]
to ask (~ oneself)	**питам**	[pítam]
to ask (~ sb to do sth)	**моля**	[mólʲa]
to be (vi)	**съм, бъда**	[səm], [bə́da]
to be afraid	**страхувам се**	[strahúvam se]
to be hungry	**искам да ям**	[ískam da jam]
to be interested in …	**интересувам се**	[interesúvam se]
to be needed	**трябвам**	[trʲábvam]
to be surprised	**удивлявам се**	[udivlʲávam se]
to be thirsty	**искам да пия**	[ískam da píja]
to begin (vt)	**започвам**	[zapóʧvam]
to belong to …	**принадлежа …**	[prinadleʒá]
to boast (vi)	**хваля се**	[hválʲa se]
to break (split into pieces)	**чупя**	[ʧúpʲa]
to call (~ for help)	**викам**	[víkam]
can (v aux)	**мога**	[móga]
to catch (vt)	**ловя**	[lovʲá]
to change (vt)	**сменям**	[sménʲam]
to choose (select)	**избирам**	[izbíram]
to come down (the stairs)	**слизам**	[slízam]
to compare (vt)	**сравнявам**	[sravnʲávam]
to complain (vi, vt)	**оплаквам се**	[oplákvam se]
to confuse (mix up)	**обърквам**	[obə́rkvam]
to continue (vt)	**продължавам**	[prodəlʒávam]
to control (vt)	**контролирам**	[kontrolíram]

to cook (dinner)	**готвя**	[gótvʲa]
to cost (vt)	**струвам**	[strúvam]
to count (add up)	**броя**	[brojá]
to count on ...	**разчитам на ...**	[rastʃítam na]
to create (vt)	**създам**	[səzdám]
to cry (weep)	**плача**	[plátʃa]

11. The most important verbs. Part 2

to deceive (vi, vt)	**лъжа**	[ləʒa]
to decorate (tree, street)	**украсявам**	[ukrasʲávam]
to defend (a country, etc.)	**защитавам**	[zaʃtitávam]
to demand (request firmly)	**изисквам**	[izískvam]
to dig (vt)	**ровя**	[róvʲa]
to discuss (vt)	**обсъждам**	[obsə́ʒdam]
to do (vt)	**правя**	[právʲa]
to doubt (have doubts)	**съмнявам се**	[səmnʲávam se]
to drop (let fall)	**изтървавам**	[istərvávam]
to enter (room, house, etc.)	**влизам**	[vlízam]
to excuse (forgive)	**извинявам**	[izvinʲávam]
to exist (vi)	**съществувам**	[səʃtestvúvam]
to expect (foresee)	**предвиждам**	[predvíʒdam]
to explain (vt)	**обяснявам**	[obʲasnʲávam]
to fall (vi)	**падам**	[pádam]
to fancy (vt)	**харесвам**	[harésvam]
to find (vt)	**намирам**	[namíram]
to finish (vt)	**приключвам**	[priklʲútʃvam]
to fly (vi)	**летя**	[letʲá]
to follow ... (come after)	**вървя след ...**	[varvʲá slet]
to forget (vi, vt)	**забравям**	[zabrávʲam]
to forgive (vt)	**прощавам**	[proʃtávam]
to give (vt)	**давам**	[dávam]
to give a hint	**намеквам**	[namékvam]
to go (on foot)	**вървя**	[vərvʲá]
to go for a swim	**къпя се**	[kə́pʲa se]
to go out (for dinner, etc.)	**излизам**	[izlízam]
to guess (the answer)	**отгатна**	[otgátna]
to have (vt)	**имам**	[ímam]
to have breakfast	**закусвам**	[zakúsvam]
to have dinner	**вечерям**	[vetʃérʲam]
to have lunch	**обядвам**	[obʲádvam]
to hear (vt)	**чувам**	[tʃúvam]
to help (vt)	**помагам**	[pomágam]
to hide (vt)	**крия**	[kríja]
to hope (vi, vt)	**надявам се**	[nadʲávam se]
to hunt (vi, vt)	**ловувам**	[lovúvam]
to hurry (vi)	**бързам**	[bə́rzam]

12. The most important verbs. Part 3

to inform (vt)	**информирам**	[informíram]
to insist (vi, vt)	**настоявам**	[nastojávam]
to insult (vt)	**оскърбявам**	[oskərbʲávam]
to invite (vt)	**каня**	[kánʲa]
to joke (vi)	**шегувам се**	[ʃegúvam se]
to keep (vt)	**съхранявам**	[səhranʲávam]
to keep silent, to hush	**мълча**	[məltʃá]
to kill (vt)	**убивам**	[ubívam]
to know (sb)	**познавам**	[poznávam]
to know (sth)	**знам**	[znam]
to laugh (vi)	**смея се**	[sméja se]
to liberate (city, etc.)	**освобождавам**	[osvoboʒdávam]
to look for ... (search)	**търся**	[tə́rsʲa]
to love (sb)	**обичам**	[obítʃam]
to make a mistake	**греша**	[greʃá]
to manage, to run	**ръководя**	[rəkovódʲa]
to mean (signify)	**означавам**	[oznatʃávam]
to mention (talk about)	**споменавам**	[spomenávam]
to miss (school, etc.)	**пропускам**	[propúskam]
to notice (see)	**забелязвам**	[zabelʲázvam]
to object (vi, vt)	**възразявам**	[vəzrazʲávam]
to observe (see)	**наблюдавам**	[nablʲudávam]
to open (vt)	**отварям**	[otvárʲam]
to order (meal, etc.)	**поръчвам**	[porə́tʃvam]
to order (mil.)	**заповядвам**	[zapovʲádvam]
to own (possess)	**владея**	[vladéja]
to participate (vi)	**участвам**	[utʃástvam]
to pay (vi, vt)	**плащам**	[pláʃtam]
to permit (vt)	**разрешавам**	[razreʃávam]
to plan (vt)	**планирам**	[planíram]
to play (children)	**играя**	[igrája]
to pray (vi, vt)	**моля се**	[mólʲa se]
to prefer (vt)	**предпочитам**	[pretpotʃítam]
to promise (vt)	**обещавам**	[obeʃtávam]
to pronounce (vt)	**произнасям**	[proiznásʲam]
to propose (vt)	**предлагам**	[predlágam]
to punish (vt)	**наказвам**	[nakázvam]

13. The most important verbs. Part 4

to read (vi, vt)	**чета**	[tʃeta]
to recommend (vt)	**съветвам**	[səvétvam]
to refuse (vi, vt)	**отказвам се**	[otkázvam se]
to regret (be sorry)	**съжалявам**	[səʒalʲávam]
to rent (sth from sb)	**наемам**	[naémam]

to repeat (say again)	**повтарям**	[poftárʲam]
to reserve, to book	**резервирам**	[rezervíram]
to run (vi)	**бягам**	[bʲágam]
to save (rescue)	**спасявам**	[spasʲávam]
to say (~ thank you)	**кажа**	[káʒa]
to scold (vt)	**ругая**	[rugája]
to see (vt)	**виждам**	[víʒdam]
to sell (vt)	**продавам**	[prodávam]
to send (vt)	**изпращам**	[ispráʃtam]
to shoot (vi)	**стрелям**	[strélʲam]
to shout (vi)	**викам**	[víkam]
to show (vt)	**показвам**	[pokázvam]
to sign (document)	**подписвам**	[potpísvam]
to sit down (vi)	**сядам**	[sʲádam]
to smile (vi)	**усмихвам се**	[usmíhvam se]
to speak (vi, vt)	**говоря**	[govórʲa]
to steal (money, etc.)	**крада**	[kradá]
to stop (for pause, etc.)	**спирам се**	[spíram se]
to stop (please ~ calling me)	**прекратявам**	[prekratʲávam]
to study (vt)	**изучавам**	[izuʧávam]
to swim (vi)	**плувам**	[plúvam]
to take (vt)	**взимам**	[vzímam]
to think (vi, vt)	**мисля**	[míslʲa]
to threaten (vt)	**заплашвам**	[zapláʃvam]
to touch (with hands)	**пипам**	[pípam]
to translate (vt)	**превеждам**	[prevéʒdam]
to trust (vt)	**доверявам**	[doverʲávam]
to try (attempt)	**опитвам се**	[opítvam se]
to turn (e.g., ~ left)	**завивам**	[zavívam]
to underestimate (vt)	**недооценявам**	[nedootsenʲávam]
to understand (vt)	**разбирам**	[razbíram]
to unite (vt)	**обединявам**	[obedinʲávam]
to wait (vt)	**чакам**	[ʧákam]
to want (wish, desire)	**искам**	[ískam]
to warn (vt)	**предупреждавам**	[predupreʒdávam]
to work (vi)	**работя**	[rabótʲa]
to write (vt)	**пиша**	[píʃa]
to write down	**записвам**	[zapísvam]

14. Colours

colour	**цвят** (м)	[tsvʲat]
shade (tint)	**оттенък** (м)	[otténək]
hue	**тон** (м)	[ton]
rainbow	**небесна дъга** (ж)	[nebésna dəgá]
white (adj)	**бял**	[bʲal]
black (adj)	**черен**	[ʧéren]

grey (adj)	**сив**	[siv]
green (adj)	**зелен**	[zelén]
yellow (adj)	**жълт**	[ʒəlt]
red (adj)	**червен**	[ʧervén]
blue (adj)	**син**	[sin]
light blue (adj)	**небесносин**	[nebesnosín]
pink (adj)	**розов**	[rózov]
orange (adj)	**оранжев**	[oránʒev]
violet (adj)	**виолетов**	[violétov]
brown (adj)	**кафяв**	[kafʲáv]
golden (adj)	**златен**	[zláten]
silvery (adj)	**сребрист**	[srebríst]
beige (adj)	**бежов**	[béʒov]
cream (adj)	**кремав**	[krémaf]
turquoise (adj)	**тюркоазен**	[tʲurkoázen]
cherry red (adj)	**вишнев**	[víʃnev]
lilac (adj)	**лилав**	[liláf]
crimson (adj)	**малинов**	[malínov]
light (adj)	**светъл**	[svétəl]
dark (adj)	**тъмен**	[témen]
bright, vivid (adj)	**ярък**	[járək]
coloured (pencils)	**цветен**	[tsvéten]
colour (e.g. ~ film)	**цветен**	[tsvéten]
black-and-white (adj)	**черно-бял**	[ʧérno-bʲal]
plain (one-coloured)	**едноцветен**	[edno·tsvéten]
multicoloured (adj)	**многоцветен**	[mnogo·tsvéten]

15. Questions

Who?	**Кой?**	[koj]
What?	**Какво?**	[kakvó]
Where? (at, in)	**Къде?**	[kədé]
Where (to)?	**Къде?**	[kədé]
From where?	**Откъде?**	[otkədé]
When?	**Кога?**	[kogá]
Why? (What for?)	**За какво?**	[za kakvó]
Why? (~ are you crying?)	**Защо?**	[zaʃtó]
What for?	**За какво?**	[za kakvó]
How? (in what way)	**Как?**	[kak]
Which?	**Кой?**	[koj]
To whom?	**На кого?**	[na kogó]
About whom?	**За кого?**	[za kogó]
About what?	**За какво?**	[za kakvó]
With whom?	**С кого?**	[s kogó]
How many? How much?	**Колко?**	[kólko]
Whose?	**Чий?**	[ʧij]

16. Prepositions

with (accompanied by)	**с ...**	[s]
without	**без**	[bez]
to (indicating direction)	**в, във**	[v], [vəf]
about (talking ~ ...)	**за**	[za]
before (in time)	**преди**	[predí]
in front of ...	**пред ...**	[pret]
under (beneath, below)	**под**	[pot]
above (over)	**над**	[nat]
on (atop)	**върху**	[vərhú]
from (off, out of)	**от**	[ot]
of (made from)	**от**	[ot]
in (e.g. ~ ten minutes)	**след**	[slet]
over (across the top of)	**през**	[pres]

17. Function words. Adverbs. Part 1

Where? (at, in)	**Къде?**	[kədé]
here (adv)	**тук**	[tuk]
there (adv)	**там**	[tam]
somewhere (to be)	**някъде**	[nʲákəde]
nowhere (not in any place)	**никъде**	[níkəde]
by (near, beside)	**до ...**	[do]
by the window	**до прозореца**	[do prozóretsa]
Where (to)?	**Къде?**	[kədé]
here (e.g. come ~!)	**тук**	[tuk]
there (e.g. to go ~)	**нататък**	[natátək]
from here (adv)	**оттук**	[ottúk]
from there (adv)	**оттам**	[ottám]
close (adv)	**близо**	[blízo]
far (adv)	**далече**	[dalétʃe]
near (e.g. ~ Paris)	**до**	[do]
nearby (adv)	**редом**	[rédom]
not far (adv)	**недалече**	[nedalétʃe]
left (adj)	**ляв**	[lʲav]
on the left	**отляво**	[otlʲávo]
to the left	**вляво**	[vlʲávo]
right (adj)	**десен**	[désen]
on the right	**отдясно**	[otdʲásno]
to the right	**вдясно**	[vdʲásno]
in front (adv)	**отпред**	[otprét]
front (as adj)	**преден**	[préden]

ahead (the kids ran ~)	**напред**	[naprét]
behind (adv)	**отзад**	[otzát]
from behind	**отзад**	[otzát]
back (towards the rear)	**назад**	[nazát]
middle	**среда** (ж)	[sredá]
in the middle	**по средата**	[po sredáta]
at the side	**встрани**	[fstraní]
everywhere (adv)	**навсякъде**	[nafsʲákəde]
around (in all directions)	**наоколо**	[naókolo]
from inside	**отвътре**	[otvə́tre]
somewhere (to go)	**някъде**	[nʲákəde]
straight (directly)	**направо**	[naprávo]
back (e.g. come ~)	**обратно**	[obrátno]
from anywhere	**откъдето и да е**	[otkədéto i da e]
from somewhere	**отнякъде**	[otnʲákəde]
firstly (adv)	**първо**	[pə́rvo]
secondly (adv)	**второ**	[ftóro]
thirdly (adv)	**трето**	[tréto]
suddenly (adv)	**изведнъж**	[izvednə́ʃ]
at first (in the beginning)	**в началото**	[f natʃáloto]
for the first time	**за пръв път**	[za prəv pə́t]
long before ...	**много време преди ...**	[mnógo vréme predí]
anew (over again)	**наново**	[nanóvo]
for good (adv)	**завинаги**	[zavínagi]
never (adv)	**никога**	[níkoga]
again (adv)	**пак**	[pak]
now (at present)	**сега**	[segá]
often (adv)	**често**	[tʃésto]
then (adv)	**тогава**	[togáva]
urgently (quickly)	**срочно**	[srótʃno]
usually (adv)	**обикновено**	[obiknovéno]
by the way, ...	**между другото ...**	[mézdu drúgoto]
possibly	**възможно**	[vəzmóʒno]
probably (adv)	**вероятно**	[verojátno]
maybe (adv)	**може би**	[móʒe bi]
besides ...	**освен това, ...**	[osvén tová]
that's why ...	**затова**	[zatová]
in spite of ...	**въпреки че ...**	[və́preki tʃe]
thanks to ...	**благодарение на ...**	[blagodarénie na]
what (pron.)	**какво**	[kakvó]
that (conj.)	**че**	[tʃe]
something	**нещо**	[néʃto]
anything (something)	**нещо**	[néʃto]
nothing	**нищо**	[níʃto]
who (pron.)	**кой**	[koj]
someone	**някой**	[nʲákoj]

somebody	**някой**	[nʲákoj]
nobody	**никой**	[níkoj]
nowhere (a voyage to ~)	**никъде**	[níkəde]
nobody's	**ничий**	[nítʃij]
somebody's	**нечий**	[nétʃij]
so (I'm ~ glad)	**така**	[taká]
also (as well)	**също така**	[sə́ʃto taká]
too (as well)	**също**	[sə́ʃto]

18. Function words. Adverbs. Part 2

Why?	**Защо?**	[zaʃtó]
for some reason	**кой знае защо**	[koj znáe zaʃtó]
because ...	**защото ...**	[zaʃtóto]
for some purpose	**кой знае защо**	[koj znáe zaʃtó]
and	**и**	[i]
or	**или**	[ilí]
but	**но**	[no]
for (e.g. ~ me)	**за**	[za]
too (excessively)	**прекалено**	[prekaléno]
only (exclusively)	**само**	[sámo]
exactly (adv)	**точно**	[tótʃno]
about (more or less)	**около**	[ókolo]
approximately (adv)	**приблизително**	[priblizítelno]
approximate (adj)	**приблизителен**	[priblizítelen]
almost (adv)	**почти**	[potʃtí]
the rest	**остатък** (м)	[ostátək]
the other (second)	**друг**	[druk]
other (different)	**друг**	[druk]
each (adj)	**всеки**	[fséki]
any (no matter which)	**всеки**	[fséki]
many, much (a lot of)	**много**	[mnógo]
many people	**много**	[mnógo]
all (everyone)	**всички**	[fsítʃki]
in return for ...	**в обмяна на ...**	[v obmʲána na]
in exchange (adv)	**в замяна**	[v zamʲána]
by hand (made)	**ръчно**	[rə́tʃno]
hardly (negative opinion)	**едва ли**	[edvá li]
probably (adv)	**вероятно**	[verojátno]
on purpose (intentionally)	**специално**	[spetsiálno]
by accident (adv)	**случайно**	[slutʃájno]
very (adv)	**много**	[mnógo]
for example (adv)	**например**	[naprímer]
between	**между**	[meʒdú]
among	**сред**	[sret]
so much (such a lot)	**толкова**	[tólkova]
especially (adv)	**особено**	[osóbeno]

Basic concepts. Part 2

19. Opposites

rich (adj)	**богат**	[bogát]
poor (adj)	**беден**	[béden]
ill, sick (adj)	**болен**	[bólen]
well (not sick)	**здрав**	[zdrav]
big (adj)	**голям**	[golʲám]
small (adj)	**малък**	[málək]
quickly (adv)	**бързо**	[bə́rzo]
slowly (adv)	**бавно**	[bávno]
fast (adj)	**бърз**	[bərz]
slow (adj)	**бавен**	[báven]
glad (adj)	**весел**	[vésel]
sad (adj)	**тъжен**	[tə́ʒen]
together (adv)	**заедно**	[záedno]
separately (adv)	**поотделно**	[pootdélno]
aloud (to read)	**на глас**	[na glás]
silently (to oneself)	**на ум**	[na úm]
tall (adj)	**висок**	[visók]
low (adj)	**нисък**	[nísək]
deep (adj)	**дълбок**	[dəlbók]
shallow (adj)	**плитък**	[plítək]
yes	**да**	[da]
no	**не**	[ne]
distant (in space)	**далечен**	[dalétʃen]
nearby (adj)	**близък**	[blízək]
far (adv)	**далече**	[dalétʃe]
nearby (adv)	**близо**	[blízo]
long (adj)	**дълъг**	[dələk]
short (adj)	**къс**	[kəs]
good (kindhearted)	**добър**	[dobə́r]
evil (adj)	**зъл**	[zəl]

married (adj)	**женен**	[ʒénen]
single (adj)	**ерген**	[ergén]
to forbid (vt)	**забранявам**	[zabranʲávam]
to permit (vt)	**разрешавам**	[razreʃávam]
end	**край** (м)	[kraj]
beginning	**начало** (с)	[natʃálo]
left (adj)	**ляв**	[lʲav]
right (adj)	**десен**	[désen]
first (adj)	**първи**	[pérvi]
last (adj)	**последен**	[posléden]
crime	**престъпление** (с)	[prestəplénie]
punishment	**наказание** (с)	[nakazánie]
to order (vt)	**заповядвам**	[zapovʲádvam]
to obey (vi, vt)	**подчиня се**	[podtʃinʲá se]
straight (adj)	**прав**	[prav]
curved (adj)	**крив**	[kriv]
paradise	**рай** (м)	[raj]
hell	**ад** (м)	[at]
to be born	**родя се**	[rodʲá se]
to die (vi)	**умра**	[umrá]
strong (adj)	**силен**	[sílen]
weak (adj)	**слаб**	[slap]
old (adj)	**стар**	[star]
young (adj)	**млад**	[mlat]
old (adj)	**стар**	[star]
new (adj)	**нов**	[nov]
hard (adj)	**твърд**	[tvərt]
soft (adj)	**мек**	[mek]
warm (tepid)	**топъл**	[tópəl]
cold (adj)	**студен**	[studén]
fat (adj)	**дебел**	[debél]
thin (adj)	**слаб**	[slap]
narrow (adj)	**тесен**	[tésen]
wide (adj)	**широк**	[ʃirók]
good (adj)	**добър**	[dobér]
bad (adj)	**лош**	[loʃ]
brave (adj)	**храбър**	[hrábər]
cowardly (adj)	**страхлив**	[strahlíf]

20. Weekdays

Monday	**понеделник** (м)	[ponedélnik]
Tuesday	**вторник** (м)	[ftórnik]
Wednesday	**сряда** (ж)	[srʲáda]
Thursday	**четвъртък** (м)	[ʧetvártək]
Friday	**петък** (м)	[pétək]
Saturday	**събота** (ж)	[sábota]
Sunday	**неделя** (ж)	[nedélʲa]
today (adv)	**днес**	[dnes]
tomorrow (adv)	**утре**	[útre]
the day after tomorrow	**вдругиден**	[vdrugidén]
yesterday (adv)	**вчера**	[vʧéra]
the day before yesterday	**завчера**	[závʧera]
day	**ден** (м)	[den]
working day	**работен ден** (м)	[rabóten den]
public holiday	**празничен ден** (м)	[prázniʧen den]
day off	**почивен ден** (м)	[poʧíven dén]
weekend	**почивни дни** (м мн)	[poʧívni dni]
all day long	**цял ден**	[tsʲal den]
the next day (adv)	**на следващия ден**	[na slédvaʃtija den]
two days ago	**преди два дена**	[predí dva déna]
the day before	**в навечерието**	[v naveʧérieto]
daily (adj)	**всекидневен**	[fsekidnéven]
every day (adv)	**всекидневно**	[fsekidnévno]
week	**седмица** (ж)	[sédmitsa]
last week (adv)	**през миналата седмица**	[pres mínalata sédmitsa]
next week (adv)	**през следващата седмица**	[pres slédvaʃtata sédmitsa]
weekly (adj)	**седмичен**	[sédmiʧen]
every week (adv)	**седмично**	[sédmiʧno]
twice a week	**два пъти на седмица**	[dva pətí na sédmitsa]
every Tuesday	**всеки вторник**	[fséki ftórnik]

21. Hours. Day and night

morning	**сутрин** (ж)	[sútrin]
in the morning	**сутринта**	[sutrintá]
noon, midday	**пладне** (с)	[pládne]
in the afternoon	**следобед**	[sledóbet]
evening	**вечер** (ж)	[véʧer]
in the evening	**вечер**	[véʧer]
night	**нощ** (ж)	[noʃt]
at night	**нощем**	[nóʃtem]
midnight	**полунощ** (ж)	[polunóʃt]
second	**секунда** (ж)	[sekúnda]
minute	**минута** (ж)	[minúta]
hour	**час** (м)	[ʧas]

half an hour	**половин час** (м)	[polovín ʧas]
a quarter-hour	**четвърт** (ж) **час**	[ʧétvərt ʧas]
fifteen minutes	**петнадесет минути**	[petnádeset minúti]
24 hours	**денонощие** (с)	[denonóʃtie]
sunrise	**изгрев слънце** (с)	[ízgrev sléntsə]
dawn	**разсъмване** (с)	[rassémvane]
early morning	**ранна сутрин** (ж)	[ránna sútrin]
sunset	**залез** (м)	[zález]
early in the morning	**рано сутрин**	[ráno sútrin]
this morning	**тази сутрин**	[tázi sútrin]
tomorrow morning	**утре сутрин**	[útre sútrin]
this afternoon	**днес през деня**	[dnes pres denʲá]
in the afternoon	**следобед**	[sledóbet]
tomorrow afternoon	**утре следобед**	[útre sledóbet]
tonight (this evening)	**довечера**	[dovéʧera]
tomorrow night	**утре вечер**	[útre véʧer]
at 3 o'clock sharp	**точно в три часа**	[tóʧno v tri ʧasá]
about 4 o'clock	**около четири часа**	[ókolo ʧétiri ʧasá]
by 12 o'clock	**към дванадесет часа**	[kəm dvanádeset ʧasá]
in 20 minutes	**след двадесет минути**	[slet dvádeset minúti]
in an hour	**след един час**	[slet edín ʧas]
on time (adv)	**навреме**	[navréme]
a quarter to …	**без четвърт …**	[bes ʧétvərt]
within an hour	**в течение на един час**	[v teʧénie na edín ʧas]
every 15 minutes	**на всеки петнадесет минути**	[na fséki petnádeset minúti]
round the clock	**цяло денонощие**	[tsʲálo denonóʃtie]

22. Months. Seasons

January	**януари** (м)	[januári]
February	**февруари** (м)	[fevruári]
March	**март** (м)	[mart]
April	**април** (м)	[apríl]
May	**май** (м)	[maj]
June	**юни** (м)	[júni]
July	**юли** (м)	[júli]
August	**август** (м)	[ávgust]
September	**септември** (м)	[septémvri]
October	**октомври** (м)	[októmvri]
November	**ноември** (м)	[noémvri]
December	**декември** (м)	[dekémvri]
spring	**пролет** (ж)	[prólet]
in spring	**през пролетта**	[prez prolettá]
spring (as adj)	**пролетен**	[próleten]

summer	**лято** (с)	[lʲáto]
in summer	**през лятото**	[prez lʲátoto]
summer (as adj)	**летен**	[léten]
autumn	**есен** (ж)	[ésen]
in autumn	**през есента**	[prez esentá]
autumn (as adj)	**есенен**	[ésenen]
winter	**зима** (ж)	[zíma]
in winter	**през зимата**	[prez zímata]
winter (as adj)	**зимен**	[zímen]
month	**месец** (м)	[mésets]
this month	**през този месец**	[pres tózi mésets]
next month	**през следващия месец**	[prez slédvaʃtija mésets]
last month	**през миналия месец**	[prez mínalija mésets]
a month ago	**преди един месец**	[predí edín mésets]
in a month (a month later)	**след един месец**	[slet edín mésets]
in 2 months (2 months later)	**след два месеца**	[slet dva mésetsa]
the whole month	**цял месец**	[tsʲal mésets]
all month long	**цял месец**	[tsʲal mésets]
monthly (~ magazine)	**месечен**	[méseʧen]
monthly (adv)	**месечно**	[méseʧno]
every month	**всеки месец**	[fséki mésets]
twice a month	**два пъти на месец**	[dva pəti na məsets]
year	**година** (ж)	[godína]
this year	**тази година**	[tázi godína]
next year	**през следващата година**	[prez slédvaʃtata godína]
last year	**през миналата година**	[prez mínalata godína]
a year ago	**преди една година**	[predí edná godína]
in a year	**след една година**	[slet edná godína]
in two years	**след две години**	[slet dve godíni]
the whole year	**цяла година**	[tsʲála godína]
all year long	**цяла година**	[tsʲála godína]
every year	**всяка година**	[fsʲáka godína]
annual (adj)	**ежегоден**	[eʒegóden]
annually (adv)	**ежегодно**	[eʒegódno]
4 times a year	**четири пъти годишно**	[ʧétiri pəti godíʃno]
date (e.g. today's ~)	**число** (с)	[ʧisló]
date (e.g. ~ of birth)	**дата** (ж)	[dáta]
calendar	**календар** (м)	[kalendár]
half a year	**половин година**	[polovín godína]
six months	**полугодие** (с)	[polugódie]
season (summer, etc.)	**сезон** (м)	[sezón]
century	**век** (м)	[vek]

23. Time. Miscellaneous

time	**време** (с)	[vréme]
moment	**миг** (м)	[mik]
instant (n)	**мигновение** (с)	[mignovénie]
instant (adj)	**мигновен**	[mignovén]
lapse (of time)	**отрязък** (м)	[otrʲázək]
life	**живот** (м)	[ʒivót]
eternity	**вечност** (ж)	[vétʃnost]
epoch	**епоха** (ж)	[epóha]
era	**ера** (ж)	[éra]
cycle	**цикъл** (м)	[tsíkəl]
period	**период** (м)	[períot]
term (short-~)	**срок** (м)	[srok]
the future	**бъдеще** (с)	[bədeʃte]
future (as adj)	**бъдещ**	[bədeʃt]
next time	**следващия път**	[slédvaʃtija pət]
the past	**минало** (с)	[mínalo]
past (recent)	**минал**	[mínal]
last time	**миналия път**	[mínalija pət]
later (adv)	**по-късно**	[po-késno]
after (prep.)	**след това**	[slet tová]
nowadays (adv)	**сега**	[segá]
now (at this moment)	**сега**	[segá]
immediately (adv)	**незабавно**	[nezabávno]
soon (adv)	**скоро**	[skóro]
in advance (beforehand)	**предварително**	[predvarítelno]
a long time ago	**отдавна**	[otdávna]
recently (adv)	**неотдавна**	[neotdávna]
destiny	**съдба** (ж)	[sədbá]
recollections	**памет** (ж)	[pámet]
archives	**архив** (м)	[arhív]
during ...	**по времето на ...**	[po vrémeto na]
long, a long time (adv)	**дълго**	[dəlgo]
not long (adv)	**недълго**	[nedəlgo]
early (in the morning)	**рано**	[ráno]
late (not early)	**късно**	[késno]
forever (for good)	**завинаги**	[zavínagi]
to start (begin)	**започвам**	[zapótʃvam]
to postpone (vt)	**отложа**	[otlóʒa]
at the same time	**едновременно**	[ednovrémenno]
permanently (adv)	**постоянно**	[postojánno]
constant (noise, pain)	**постоянен**	[postojánen]
temporary (adj)	**временен**	[vrémenen]
sometimes (adv)	**понякога**	[ponʲákoga]
rarely (adv)	**рядко**	[rʲátko]
often (adv)	**често**	[tʃésto]

24. Lines and shapes

square	**квадрат** (м)	[kvadrát]
square (as adj)	**квадратен**	[kvadráten]
circle	**кръг** (м)	[krək]
round (adj)	**кръгъл**	[krəgəl]
triangle	**триъгълник** (м)	[triəgəlnik]
triangular (adj)	**триъгълен**	[triəgəlen]
oval	**овал** (м)	[ovál]
oval (as adj)	**овален**	[oválen]
rectangle	**правоъгълник** (м)	[pravoəgəlnik]
rectangular (adj)	**правоъгълен**	[pravoəgəlen]
pyramid	**пирамида** (ж)	[piramída]
rhombus	**ромб** (м)	[romp]
trapezium	**трапец** (м)	[trapéts]
cube	**куб** (м)	[kup]
prism	**призма** (ж)	[prízma]
circumference	**окръжност** (ж)	[okrəʒnost]
sphere	**сфера** (ж)	[sféra]
ball (solid sphere)	**кълбо** (с)	[kəlbó]
diameter	**диаметър** (м)	[diámetər]
radius	**радиус** (м)	[rádius]
perimeter (circle's ~)	**периметър** (м)	[perímetər]
centre	**център** (м)	[tséntər]
horizontal (adj)	**хоризонтален**	[horizontálen]
vertical (adj)	**вертикален**	[vertikálen]
parallel (n)	**паралел** (м)	[paralél]
parallel (as adj)	**паралелно**	[paralélno]
line	**линия** (ж)	[línija]
stroke	**черта** (ж)	[ʧertá]
straight line	**права** (ж)	[práva]
curve (curved line)	**крива** (ж)	[kríva]
thin (line, etc.)	**тънък**	[tənək]
contour (outline)	**контур** (м)	[kóntur]
intersection	**пресичане** (с)	[presíʧane]
right angle	**прав ъгъл** (м)	[prav əgəl]
segment	**сегмент** (м)	[segmént]
sector (circular ~)	**сектор** (м)	[séktor]
side (of a triangle)	**страна** (ж)	[straná]
angle	**ъгъл** (м)	[əgəl]

25. Units of measurement

weight	**тегло** (с)	[tegló]
length	**дължина** (ж)	[dəlʒiná]
width	**широчина** (ж)	[ʃiroʧiná]
height	**височина** (ж)	[visoʧiná]

depth	**дълбочина** (ж)	[dəlbotʃiná]
volume	**обем** (м)	[obém]
area	**площ** (ж)	[ploʃt]
gram	**грам** (м)	[gram]
milligram	**милиграм** (м)	[miligrám]
kilogram	**килограм** (м)	[kilográm]
ton	**тон** (м)	[ton]
pound	**фунт** (м)	[funt]
ounce	**унция** (ж)	[úntsija]
metre	**метър** (м)	[métər]
millimetre	**милиметър** (м)	[milimétər]
centimetre	**сантиметър** (м)	[santimétər]
kilometre	**километър** (м)	[kilométər]
mile	**миля** (ж)	[míl^ja]
inch	**дюйм** (м)	[d^jujm]
foot	**фут** (м)	[fut]
yard	**ярд** (м)	[jart]
square metre	**квадратен метър** (м)	[kvadráten métər]
hectare	**хектар** (м)	[hektár]
litre	**литър** (м)	[lítər]
degree	**градус** (м)	[grádus]
volt	**волт** (м)	[volt]
ampere	**ампер** (м)	[ampér]
horsepower	**конска сила** (ж)	[kónska síla]
quantity	**количество** (с)	[kolítʃestvo]
a little bit of …	**малко …**	[málko]
half	**половина** (ж)	[polovína]
dozen	**дузина** (ж)	[duzína]
piece (item)	**брой** (м)	[broj]
size	**размер** (м)	[razmér]
scale (map ~)	**мащаб** (м)	[maʃtáp]
minimal (adj)	**минимален**	[minimálen]
the smallest (adj)	**най-малък**	[naj-málək]
medium (adj)	**среден**	[sréden]
maximal (adj)	**максимален**	[maksimálen]
the largest (adj)	**най-голям**	[naj-gol^jám]

26. Containers

canning jar (glass ~)	**буркан** (м)	[burkán]
tin, can	**тенекия** (ж)	[tenekíja]
bucket	**кофа** (ж)	[kófa]
barrel	**бъчва** (ж)	[bə́tʃva]
wash basin (e.g., plastic ~)	**леген** (м)	[legén]
tank (100L water ~)	**резервоар** (м)	[rezervoár]

hip flask	**манерка** (ж)	[manérka]
jerrycan	**туба** (ж)	[túba]
tank (e.g., tank car)	**цистерна** (ж)	[tsistérna]
mug	**чаша** (ж)	[ʧáʃa]
cup (of coffee, etc.)	**чаша** (ж)	[ʧáʃa]
saucer	**чинийка** (ж)	[ʧiníjka]
glass (tumbler)	**стакан** (м)	[stakán]
wine glass	**чаша** (ж) **за вино**	[ʧáʃa za víno]
stock pot (soup pot)	**тенджера** (ж)	[téndʒera]
bottle (~ of wine)	**бутилка** (ж)	[butílka]
neck (of the bottle, etc.)	**гърло** (с) **на бутилка**	[gə́rlo na butílka]
carafe (decanter)	**гарафа** (ж)	[garáfa]
pitcher	**кана** (ж)	[kána]
vessel (container)	**съд** (м)	[sət]
pot (crock, stoneware ~)	**гърне** (с)	[gərné]
vase	**ваза** (ж)	[váza]
flacon, bottle (perfume ~)	**шишенце** (с)	[ʃiʃéntse]
vial, small bottle	**шишенце** (с)	[ʃiʃéntse]
tube (of toothpaste)	**тубичка** (ж)	[túbiʧka]
sack (bag)	**чувал** (м)	[ʧuvál]
bag (paper ~, plastic ~)	**плик** (м)	[plik]
packet (of cigarettes, etc.)	**кутия** (ж)	[kutíja]
box (e.g. shoebox)	**кутия** (ж)	[kutíja]
crate	**щайга** (ж)	[ʃtájga]
basket	**кошница** (ж)	[kóʃnitsa]

27. Materials

material	**материал** (м)	[materiál]
wood (n)	**дърво** (с)	[dərvó]
wood-, wooden (adj)	**дървен**	[də́rven]
glass (n)	**стъкло** (с)	[stəkló]
glass (as adj)	**стъклен**	[stə́klen]
stone (n)	**камък** (м)	[kámək]
stone (as adj)	**каменен**	[kámenen]
plastic (n)	**пластмаса** (ж)	[plastmása]
plastic (as adj)	**пластмасов**	[plastmásov]
rubber (n)	**гума** (ж)	[gúma]
rubber (as adj)	**гумен**	[gúmen]
cloth, fabric (n)	**плат** (м)	[plat]
fabric (as adj)	**от плат**	[ot plát]
paper (n)	**хартия** (ж)	[hartíja]
paper (as adj)	**хартиен**	[hartíen]

cardboard (n)	**картон** (м)	[kartón]
cardboard (as adj)	**картонен**	[kartónen]
polyethylene	**полиетилен** (м)	[polietilén]
cellophane	**целофан** (м)	[tselofán]
plywood	**шперплат** (м)	[ʃperplát]
porcelain (n)	**порцелан** (м)	[portselán]
porcelain (as adj)	**порцеланов**	[portselánof]
clay (n)	**глина** (ж)	[glína]
clay (as adj)	**глинен**	[glínen]
ceramic (n)	**керамика** (ж)	[kerámika]
ceramic (as adj)	**керамичен**	[kerámitʃen]

28. Metals

metal (n)	**метал** (м)	[metál]
metal (as adj)	**метален**	[metálen]
alloy (n)	**сплав** (м)	[splav]
gold (n)	**злато** (с)	[zláto]
gold, golden (adj)	**златен**	[zláten]
silver (n)	**сребро** (с)	[srebró]
silver (as adj)	**сребърен**	[srébəren]
iron (n)	**желязо** (с)	[ʒelʲázo]
iron-, made of iron (adj)	**железен**	[ʒelézen]
steel (n)	**стомана** (ж)	[stomána]
steel (as adj)	**стоманен**	[stománen]
copper (n)	**мед** (ж)	[met]
copper (as adj)	**меден**	[méden]
aluminium (n)	**алуминий** (м)	[alumínij]
aluminium (as adj)	**алуминиев**	[alumíniev]
bronze (n)	**бронз** (м)	[bronz]
bronze (as adj)	**бронзов**	[brónzov]
brass	**месинг** (м)	[mésink]
nickel	**никел** (м)	[níkel]
platinum	**платина** (ж)	[platína]
mercury	**живак** (м)	[ʒivák]
tin	**калай** (м)	[kaláj]
lead	**олово** (с)	[olóvo]
zinc	**цинк** (м)	[tsink]

HUMAN BEING

Human being. The body

29. Humans. Basic concepts

human being	**човек** (м)	[ʧovék]
man (adult male)	**мъж** (м)	[məʒ]
woman	**жена** (ж)	[ʒená]
child	**дете** (с)	[deté]
girl	**момиче** (с)	[momíʧe]
boy	**момче** (с)	[momʧé]
teenager	**тинейджър** (м)	[tinéjdʒər]
old man	**старец** (м)	[stárets]
old woman	**старица** (ж)	[stáritsa]

30. Human anatomy

organism (body)	**организъм** (м)	[organízəm]
heart	**сърце** (с)	[sərtsé]
blood	**кръв** (ж)	[krəv]
artery	**артерия** (ж)	[artérija]
vein	**вена** (ж)	[véna]
brain	**мозък** (м)	[mózək]
nerve	**нерв** (м)	[nerv]
nerves	**нерви** (м мн)	[nérvi]
vertebra	**прешлен** (м)	[préʃlen]
spine (backbone)	**гръбнак** (м)	[grəbnák]
stomach (organ)	**стомах** (м)	[stomáh]
intestines, bowels	**стомашно-чревен тракт** (м)	[stomáʃno-ʧréven trakt]
intestine (e.g. large ~)	**черво** (с)	[ʧervó]
liver	**черен дроб** (м)	[ʧéren drop]
kidney	**бъбрек** (м)	[bə́brek]
bone	**кост** (ж)	[kost]
skeleton	**скелет** (м)	[skélet]
rib	**ребро** (с)	[rebró]
skull	**череп** (м)	[ʧérep]
muscle	**мускул** (м)	[múskul]
biceps	**бицепс** (м)	[bítseps]
triceps	**трицепс** (м)	[trítseps]
tendon	**сухожилие** (с)	[suhoʒílie]
joint	**става** (ж)	[stáva]

lungs	**бели дробове** (м мн)	[béli dróbove]
genitals	**полови органи** (м мн)	[pólovi órgani]
skin	**кожа** (ж)	[kóʒa]

31. Head

head	**глава** (ж)	[glavá]
face	**лице** (с)	[litsé]
nose	**нос** (м)	[nos]
mouth	**уста** (ж)	[ustá]
eye	**око** (с)	[okó]
eyes	**очи** (с мн)	[otʃí]
pupil	**зеница** (ж)	[zénitsa]
eyebrow	**вежда** (ж)	[véʒda]
eyelash	**мигла** (ж)	[mígla]
eyelid	**клепач** (м)	[klepátʃ]
tongue	**език** (м)	[ezík]
tooth	**зъб** (м)	[zəp]
lips	**устни** (ж мн)	[ústni]
cheekbones	**скули** (ж мн)	[skúli]
gum	**венец** (м)	[venéts]
palate	**небце** (с)	[nebtsé]
nostrils	**ноздри** (ж мн)	[nózdri]
chin	**брадичка** (ж)	[bradítʃka]
jaw	**челюст** (ж)	[tʃélʲust]
cheek	**буза** (ж)	[búza]
forehead	**чело** (с)	[tʃeló]
temple	**слепоочие** (с)	[slepoótʃie]
ear	**ухо** (с)	[uhó]
back of the head	**тил** (м)	[til]
neck	**шия** (ж)	[ʃíja]
throat	**гърло** (с)	[gərlo]
hair	**коса** (ж)	[kosá]
hairstyle	**прическа** (ж)	[pritʃéska]
haircut	**подстригване** (с)	[potstrígvane]
wig	**перука** (ж)	[perúka]
moustache	**мустаци** (м мн)	[mustátsi]
beard	**брада** (ж)	[bradá]
to have (a beard, etc.)	**нося**	[nósʲa]
plait	**коса** (ж)	[kosá]
sideboards	**бакенбарди** (мн)	[bakenbárdi]
red-haired (adj)	**червенокос**	[tʃervenokós]
grey (hair)	**беловлас**	[belovlás]
bald (adj)	**плешив**	[pleʃív]
bald patch	**плешивина** (ж)	[pleʃiviná]
ponytail	**опашка** (ж)	[opáʃka]
fringe	**бретон** (м)	[bretón]

32. Human body

hand	**китка** (ж)	[kítka]
arm	**ръка** (ж)	[rəká]
finger	**пръст** (м)	[prəst]
toe	**пръст** (м) **на крак**	[prəst na krak]
thumb	**палец** (м)	[pálets]
little finger	**кутре** (с)	[kutré]
nail	**нокът** (м)	[nókət]
fist	**юмрук** (м)	[jumrúk]
palm	**длан** (ж)	[dlan]
wrist	**китка** (ж)	[kítka]
forearm	**предмишница** (ж)	[predmíʃnitsa]
elbow	**лакът** (м)	[lákət]
shoulder	**рамо** (с)	[rámo]
leg	**крак** (м)	[krak]
foot	**ходило** (с)	[hodílo]
knee	**коляно** (с)	[kolʲáno]
calf	**прасец** (м)	[praséts]
hip	**бедро** (с)	[bedró]
heel	**пета** (ж)	[petá]
body	**тяло** (с)	[tʲálo]
stomach	**корем** (м)	[korém]
chest	**гръд** (ж)	[grəd]
breast	**женска гръд** (ж)	[ʒénska grəd]
flank	**страна** (ж)	[straná]
back	**гръб** (м)	[grəp]
lower back	**кръст** (м)	[krəst]
waist	**талия** (ж)	[tálija]
navel (belly button)	**пъп** (м)	[pəp]
buttocks	**седалище** (с)	[sedáliʃte]
bottom	**задник** (м)	[zádnik]
beauty spot	**бенка** (ж)	[bénka]
birthmark (café au lait spot)	**родилно петно** (с)	[rodílno petnó]
tattoo	**татуировка** (ж)	[tatuirófka]
scar	**белег** (м)	[bélek]

Clothing & Accessories

33. Outerwear. Coats

clothes	**облекло** (с)	[oblekló]
outerwear	**горни дрехи** (ж мн)	[górni dréhi]
winter clothing	**зимни дрехи** (ж мн)	[zímni dréhi]
coat (overcoat)	**палто** (с)	[paltó]
fur coat	**кожено палто** (с)	[kóʒeno paltó]
fur jacket	**полушубка** (ж)	[poluʃúpka]
down coat	**пухено яке** (с)	[púheno jáke]
jacket (e.g. leather ~)	**яке** (с)	[jáke]
raincoat (trenchcoat, etc.)	**шлифер** (м)	[ʃlífer]
waterproof (adj)	**непромокаем**	[nepromokáem]

34. Men's & women's clothing

shirt (button shirt)	**риза** (ж)	[ríza]
trousers	**панталон** (м)	[pantalón]
jeans	**дънки, джинси** (мн)	[dənki], [dʒínsi]
suit jacket	**сако** (с)	[sakó]
suit	**костюм** (м)	[kostʲúm]
dress (frock)	**рокля** (ж)	[róklʲa]
skirt	**пола** (ж)	[polá]
blouse	**блуза** (ж)	[blúza]
knitted jacket (cardigan, etc.)	**жилетка** (ж)	[ʒilétka]
jacket (of a woman's suit)	**сако** (с)	[sakó]
T-shirt	**тениска** (ж)	[téniska]
shorts (short trousers)	**къси панталони** (м мн)	[kəsi pantalóni]
tracksuit	**анцуг** (м)	[ántsuk]
bathrobe	**хавлиен халат** (м)	[havlíen halát]
pyjamas	**пижама** (ж)	[piʒáma]
jumper (sweater)	**пуловер** (м)	[pulóver]
pullover	**пуловер** (м)	[pulóver]
waistcoat	**елек** (м)	[elék]
tailcoat	**фрак** (м)	[frak]
dinner suit	**смокинг** (м)	[smóking]
uniform	**униформа** (ж)	[unifórma]
workwear	**работно облекло** (с)	[rabótno oblekló]
boiler suit	**гащеризон** (м)	[gaʃterizón]
coat (e.g. doctor's smock)	**бяла престилка** (ж)	[bʲála prestílka]

35. Clothing. Underwear

underwear	**бельо** (с)	[bel'ó]
pants	**боксер** (м)	[boksér]
panties	**прашка** (ж)	[práʃka]
vest (singlet)	**потник** (м)	[pótnik]
socks	**чорапи** (м мн)	[ʧorápi]
nightdress	**нощница** (ж)	[nóʃtnitsa]
bra	**сутиен** (м)	[sutién]
knee highs (knee-high socks)	**чорапи три четвърт** (м мн)	[ʧorápi tri ʧétvərt]
tights	**чорапогащник** (м)	[ʧorapogáʃtnik]
stockings (hold ups)	**чорапи** (м мн)	[ʧorápi]
swimsuit, bikini	**бански костюм** (м)	[bánski kost'úm]

36. Headwear

hat	**шапка** (ж)	[ʃápka]
trilby hat	**шапка** (ж)	[ʃápka]
baseball cap	**шапка** (ж) **с козирка**	[ʃápka s kozirká]
flatcap	**каскет** (м)	[kaskét]
beret	**барета** (ж)	[baréta]
hood	**качулка** (ж)	[katʃúlka]
panama hat	**панама** (ж)	[panáma]
knit cap (knitted hat)	**плетена шапка** (ж)	[plétena ʃápka]
headscarf	**кърпа** (ж)	[kərpa]
women's hat	**шапка** (ж)	[ʃápka]
hard hat	**каска** (ж)	[káska]
forage cap	**пилотка** (ж)	[pilótka]
helmet	**шлем** (м)	[ʃlem]
bowler	**бомбе** (с)	[bombé]
top hat	**цилиндър** (м)	[tsilíndər]

37. Footwear

footwear	**обувки** (ж мн)	[obúfki]
shoes (men's shoes)	**ботинки** (мн)	[botínki]
shoes (women's shoes)	**обувки** (ж мн)	[obúfki]
boots (e.g., cowboy ~)	**ботуши** (м мн)	[botúʃi]
carpet slippers	**чехли** (м мн)	[ʧéhli]
trainers	**маратонки** (ж мн)	[maratónki]
trainers	**кецове** (м мн)	[kétsove]
sandals	**сандали** (мн)	[sandáli]
cobbler (shoe repairer)	**обущар** (м)	[obuʃtár]
heel	**ток** (м)	[tok]

pair (of shoes)	**чифт** (м)	[ʧift]
lace (shoelace)	**връзка** (ж)	[vrəska]
to lace up (vt)	**връзвам**	[vrəzvam]
shoehorn	**обувалка** (ж)	[obuválka]
shoe polish	**крем** (м) **за обувки**	[krem za obúfki]

38. Textile. Fabrics

cotton (n)	**памук** (м)	[pamúk]
cotton (as adj)	**от памук**	[ot pamúk]
flax (n)	**лен** (м)	[len]
flax (as adj)	**от лен**	[ot len]
silk (n)	**коприна** (ж)	[koprína]
silk (as adj)	**копринен**	[koprínen]
wool (n)	**вълна** (ж)	[vəlna]
wool (as adj)	**вълнен**	[vəlnen]
velvet	**кадифе** (с)	[kadifé]
suede	**велур** (м)	[velúr]
corduroy	**кадифе** (с)	[kadifé]
nylon (n)	**найлон** (м)	[najlón]
nylon (as adj)	**от найлон**	[ot najlón]
polyester (n)	**полиестер** (м)	[poliéster]
polyester (as adj)	**полиестерен**	[poliésteren]
leather (n)	**кожа** (ж)	[kóʒa]
leather (as adj)	**кожен**	[kóʒen]
fur (n)	**кожа** (ж)	[kóʒa]
fur (e.g. ~ coat)	**кожен**	[kóʒen]

39. Personal accessories

gloves	**ръкавици** (ж мн)	[rəkavítsi]
mittens	**ръкавици** (ж мн) **с един пръст**	[rəkavítsi s edín pərst]
scarf (muffler)	**шал** (м)	[ʃal]
glasses	**очила** (мн)	[oʧilá]
frame (eyeglass ~)	**рамка** (ж) **за очила**	[rámka za oʧilá]
umbrella	**чадър** (м)	[ʧadər]
walking stick	**бастун** (м)	[bastún]
hairbrush	**четка** (ж) **за коса**	[ʧétka za kosá]
fan	**ветрило** (с)	[vetrílo]
tie (necktie)	**вратовръзка** (ж)	[vratovrəzka]
bow tie	**папийонка** (ж)	[papijónka]
braces	**тиранти** (мн)	[tiránti]
handkerchief	**носна кърпичка** (ж)	[nósna kərpiʧka]
comb	**гребен** (м)	[grében]
hair slide	**шнола** (ж)	[ʃnóla]

hairpin	**фиба** (ж)	[fíba]
buckle	**катарама** (ж)	[kataráma]
belt	**колан** (м)	[kolán]
shoulder strap	**ремък** (м)	[rémək]
bag (handbag)	**чанта** (ж)	[ʧánta]
handbag	**чантичка** (ж)	[ʧántiʧka]
rucksack	**раница** (ж)	[ránitsa]

40. Clothing. Miscellaneous

fashion	**мода** (ж)	[móda]
in vogue (adj)	**модерен**	[modéren]
fashion designer	**моделиер** (м)	[modeliér]
collar	**яка** (ж)	[jaká]
pocket	**джоб** (м)	[dʒop]
pocket (as adj)	**джобен**	[dʒóben]
sleeve	**ръкав** (м)	[rəkáv]
hanging loop	**закачалка** (ж)	[zakaʧálka]
flies (on trousers)	**копчелък** (м)	[kopʧelək]
zip (fastener)	**цип** (м)	[tsip]
fastener	**закопчалка** (ж)	[zakopʧálka]
button	**копче** (с)	[kópʧe]
buttonhole	**илик** (м)	[ilík]
to come off (ab. button)	**откъсна се**	[otkésna se]
to sew (vi, vt)	**шия**	[ʃíja]
to embroider (vi, vt)	**бродирам**	[brodíram]
embroidery	**бродерия** (ж)	[brodérija]
sewing needle	**игла** (ж)	[iglá]
thread	**конец** (м)	[konéts]
seam	**тегел** (м)	[tegél]
to get dirty (vi)	**изцапам се**	[istsápam se]
stain (mark, spot)	**петно** (с)	[petnó]
to crease, to crumple	**смачкам се**	[smáʧkam se]
to tear, to rip (vt)	**скъсам**	[skésam]
clothes moth	**молец** (м)	[moléts]

41. Personal care. Cosmetics

toothpaste	**паста** (ж) **за зъби**	[pásta za zébi]
toothbrush	**четка** (ж) **за зъби**	[ʧétka za zébi]
to clean one's teeth	**мия си зъбите**	[míja si zébite]
razor	**бръснач** (м)	[brəsnáʧ]
shaving cream	**крем** (м) **за бръснене**	[krem za brésnene]
to shave (vi)	**бръсна се**	[brésna se]
soap	**сапун** (м)	[sapún]

shampoo	**шампоан** (м)	[ʃampoán]
scissors	**ножица** (ж)	[nóʒitsa]
nail file	**пиличка** (ж) **за нокти**	[pílitʃka za nókti]
nail clippers	**ножичка** (ж) **за нокти**	[nóʒitʃka za nókti]
tweezers	**пинсета** (ж)	[pinséta]
cosmetics	**козметика** (ж)	[kozmétika]
face mask	**маска** (ж)	[máska]
manicure	**маникюр** (м)	[manikʲúr]
to have a manicure	**правя маникюр**	[právʲa manikʲúr]
pedicure	**педикюр** (м)	[pedikʲúr]
make-up bag	**козметична чантичка** (ж)	[kozmetítʃna tʃántitʃka]
face powder	**пудра** (ж)	[púdra]
powder compact	**пудриера** (ж)	[pudriéra]
blusher	**руж** (ж)	[ruʃ]
perfume (bottled)	**парфюм** (м)	[parfʲúm]
toilet water (lotion)	**тоалетна вода** (ж)	[toalétna vodá]
lotion	**лосион** (м)	[losión]
cologne	**одеколон** (м)	[odekolón]
eyeshadow	**сенки** (ж мн) **за очи**	[sénki za otʃí]
eyeliner	**молив** (м) **за очи**	[móliv za otʃí]
mascara	**спирала** (ж)	[spirála]
lipstick	**червило** (с)	[tʃervílo]
nail polish	**лак** (м) **за нокти**	[lak za nókti]
hair spray	**лак** (м) **за коса**	[lak za kosá]
deodorant	**дезодорант** (м)	[dezodoránt]
cream	**крем** (м)	[krem]
face cream	**крем** (м) **за лице**	[krem za litsé]
hand cream	**крем** (м) **за ръце**	[krem za rətsé]
anti-wrinkle cream	**крем** (м) **срещу бръчки**	[krem sreʃtú brətʃki]
day cream	**дневен крем** (м)	[dnéven krem]
night cream	**нощен крем** (м)	[nóʃten krem]
day (as adj)	**дневен**	[dnéven]
night (as adj)	**нощен**	[nóʃten]
tampon	**тампон** (м)	[tampón]
toilet paper (toilet roll)	**тоалетна хартия** (ж)	[toalétna hartíja]
hair dryer	**сешоар** (м)	[seʃoár]

42. Jewellery

jewellery, jewels	**скъпоценности** (ж мн)	[skəpotsénnosti]
precious (e.g. ~ stone)	**скъпоценен**	[skəpotsénen]
hallmark stamp	**проба** (ж)	[próba]
ring	**пръстен** (м)	[prə́sten]
wedding ring	**халка** (ж)	[halká]
bracelet	**гривна** (ж)	[grívna]
earrings	**обеци** (ж мн)	[obetsí]

necklace (~ of pearls)	**огърлица** (ж)	[ogərlítsa]
crown	**корона** (ж)	[koróna]
bead necklace	**гердан** (м)	[gerdán]
diamond	**диамант** (м)	[diamánt]
emerald	**изумруд** (м)	[izumrút]
ruby	**рубин** (м)	[rubín]
sapphire	**сапфир** (м)	[sapfír]
pearl	**бисер** (м)	[bíser]
amber	**кехлибар** (м)	[kehlibár]

43. Watches. Clocks

watch (wristwatch)	**часовник** (м)	[ʧasóvnik]
dial	**циферблат** (м)	[tsiferblát]
hand (clock, watch)	**стрелка** (ж)	[strelká]
metal bracelet	**гривна** (ж)	[grívna]
watch strap	**каишка** (ж)	[kaíʃka]
battery	**батерия** (ж)	[batérija]
to be flat (battery)	**батерията се изтощи**	[batérijata se istoʃtí]
to change a battery	**сменям батерия**	[smén'am batérija]
to run fast	**избързвам**	[izbərzvam]
to run slow	**изоставам**	[izostávam]
wall clock	**стенен часовник** (м)	[sténen ʧasóvnik]
hourglass	**пясъчен часовник** (м)	[p'ásəʧen ʧasóvnik]
sundial	**слънчев часовник** (м)	[slənʧev ʧasóvnik]
alarm clock	**будилник** (м)	[budílnik]
watchmaker	**часовникар** (м)	[ʧasovnikár]
to repair (vt)	**поправям**	[poprávʲam]

Food. Nutricion

44. Food

meat	**месо** (с)	[mesó]
chicken	**кокошка** (ж)	[kokóʃka]
poussin	**пиле** (с)	[píle]
duck	**патица** (ж)	[pátitsa]
goose	**гъска** (ж)	[gə́ska]
game	**дивеч** (ж)	[dívetʃ]
turkey	**пуйка** (ж)	[pújka]
pork	**свинско** (с)	[svínsko]
veal	**телешко месо** (с)	[téleʃko mesó]
lamb	**агнешко** (с)	[ágneʃko]
beef	**говеждо** (с)	[govéʒdo]
rabbit	**питомен заек** (м)	[pítomen záek]
sausage (bologna, etc.)	**салам** (м)	[salám]
vienna sausage (frankfurter)	**кренвирш** (м)	[krénvirʃ]
bacon	**бекон** (м)	[bekón]
ham	**шунка** (ж)	[ʃúnka]
gammon	**бут** (м)	[but]
pâté	**пастет** (м)	[pastét]
liver	**черен дроб** (м)	[tʃéren drop]
mince (minced meat)	**кайма** (ж)	[kajmá]
tongue	**език** (м)	[ezík]
egg	**яйце** (с)	[jajtsé]
eggs	**яйца** (с мн)	[jajtsá]
egg white	**белтък** (м)	[beltə́k]
egg yolk	**жълтък** (м)	[ʒəltə́k]
fish	**риба** (ж)	[ríba]
seafood	**морски продукти** (м мн)	[mórski prodúkti]
caviar	**хайвер** (м)	[hajvér]
crab	**морски рак** (м)	[mórski rak]
prawn	**скарида** (ж)	[skarída]
oyster	**стрида** (ж)	[strída]
spiny lobster	**лангуста** (ж)	[langústa]
octopus	**октопод** (м)	[oktopót]
squid	**калмар** (м)	[kalmár]
sturgeon	**есетра** (ж)	[esétra]
salmon	**сьомга** (ж)	[sʲómga]
halibut	**палтус** (м)	[páltus]
cod	**треска** (ж)	[tréska]
mackerel	**скумрия** (ж)	[skumríja]

tuna	**риба тон** (м)	[ríba ton]
eel	**змиорка** (ж)	[zmiórka]
trout	**пъстърва** (ж)	[pəstə́rva]
sardine	**сардина** (ж)	[sardína]
pike	**щука** (ж)	[ʃtúka]
herring	**селда** (ж)	[sélda]
bread	**хляб** (м)	[hlʲap]
cheese	**кашкавал** (м)	[kaʃkavál]
sugar	**захар** (ж)	[záhar]
salt	**сол** (ж)	[sol]
rice	**ориз** (м)	[oríz]
pasta (macaroni)	**макарони** (мн)	[makaróni]
noodles	**юфка** (ж)	[jufká]
butter	**краве масло** (с)	[kráve masló]
vegetable oil	**олио** (с)	[ólio]
sunflower oil	**слънчогледово масло** (с)	[sləntʃoglédovo máslo]
margarine	**маргарин** (м)	[margarín]
olives	**маслини** (ж мн)	[maslíni]
olive oil	**зехтин** (м)	[zehtín]
milk	**мляко** (с)	[mlʲáko]
condensed milk	**сгъстено мляко** (с)	[sgəsténo mlʲáko]
yogurt	**йогурт** (м)	[jógurt]
soured cream	**сметана** (ж)	[smetána]
cream (of milk)	**каймак** (м)	[kajmák]
mayonnaise	**майонеза** (ж)	[majonéza]
buttercream	**крем** (м)	[krem]
groats (barley ~, etc.)	**грис, булгур** (м)	[gris], [bulgúr]
flour	**брашно** (с)	[braʃnó]
tinned food	**консерви** (ж мн)	[konsérvi]
cornflakes	**царевичен флейкс** (м)	[tsárevitʃen flejks]
honey	**мед** (м)	[met]
jam	**конфитюр** (м)	[konfitʲúr]
chewing gum	**дъвка** (ж)	[də́fka]

45. Drinks

water	**вода** (ж)	[vodá]
drinking water	**питейна вода** (ж)	[pitéjna vodá]
mineral water	**минерална вода** (ж)	[minerálna vodá]
still (adj)	**негазирана**	[negazíran]
carbonated (adj)	**газирана**	[gazíran]
sparkling (adj)	**газирана**	[gazíran]
ice	**лед** (м)	[let]
with ice	**с лед**	[s let]

non-alcoholic (adj)	**безалкохолен**	[bezalkohólen]
soft drink	**безалкохолна напитка** (ж)	[bezalkohólna napítka]
refreshing drink	**разхладителна напитка** (ж)	[rashladítelna napítka]
lemonade	**лимонада** (ж)	[limonáda]
spirits	**спиртни напитки** (ж мн)	[spírtni napítki]
wine	**вино** (с)	[víno]
white wine	**бяло вино** (с)	[bʲálo víno]
red wine	**червено вино** (с)	[ʧervéno víno]
liqueur	**ликьор** (м)	[likʲór]
champagne	**шампанско** (с)	[ʃampánsko]
vermouth	**вермут** (м)	[vermút]
whisky	**уиски** (с)	[wíski]
vodka	**водка** (ж)	[vótka]
gin	**джин** (м)	[dʒin]
cognac	**коняк** (м)	[konʲák]
rum	**ром** (м)	[rom]
coffee	**кафе** (с)	[kafé]
black coffee	**черно кафе** (с)	[ʧérno kafé]
white coffee	**кафе** (с) **с мляко**	[kafé s mlʲáko]
cappuccino	**кафе** (с) **със сметана**	[kafé səs smetána]
instant coffee	**разтворимо кафе** (с)	[rastvorímo kafé]
milk	**мляко** (с)	[mlʲáko]
cocktail	**коктейл** (м)	[koktéjl]
milkshake	**млечен коктейл** (м)	[mléʧen koktéjl]
juice	**сок** (м)	[sok]
tomato juice	**доматен сок** (м)	[domáten sok]
orange juice	**портокалов сок** (м)	[portokálov sok]
freshly squeezed juice	**фреш** (м)	[freʃ]
beer	**бира** (ж)	[bíra]
lager	**светла бира** (ж)	[svétla bíra]
bitter	**тъмна бира** (ж)	[təmna bíra]
tea	**чай** (м)	[ʧaj]
black tea	**черен чай** (м)	[ʧéren ʧaj]
green tea	**зелен чай** (м)	[zelén ʧaj]

46. Vegetables

vegetables	**зеленчуци** (м мн)	[zelenʧútsi]
greens	**зарзават** (м)	[zarzavát]
tomato	**домат** (м)	[domát]
cucumber	**краставица** (ж)	[krástavitsa]
carrot	**морков** (м)	[mórkof]
potato	**картофи** (мн)	[kartófi]
onion	**лук** (м)	[luk]
garlic	**чесън** (м)	[ʧésən]

cabbage	**зеле** (с)	[zéle]
cauliflower	**карфиол** (м)	[karfiól]
Brussels sprouts	**брюкселско зеле** (с)	[brʲúkselsko zéle]
broccoli	**броколи** (с)	[brókoli]
beetroot	**цвекло** (с)	[tsvekló]
aubergine	**патладжан** (м)	[patladʒán]
courgette	**тиквичка** (ж)	[tíkvitʃka]
pumpkin	**тиква** (ж)	[tíkva]
turnip	**ряпа** (ж)	[rʲápa]
parsley	**магданоз** (м)	[magdanóz]
dill	**копър** (м)	[kópər]
lettuce	**салата** (ж)	[saláta]
celery	**целина** (ж)	[tsélina]
asparagus	**аспержа** (ж)	[aspérʒa]
spinach	**спанак** (м)	[spanák]
pea	**грах** (м)	[grah]
beans	**боб** (м)	[bop]
maize	**царевица** (ж)	[tsárevitsa]
kidney bean	**фасул** (м)	[fasúl]
sweet paper	**пипер** (м)	[pipér]
radish	**репичка** (ж)	[répitʃka]
artichoke	**ангинар** (м)	[anginár]

47. Fruits. Nuts

fruit	**плод** (м)	[plot]
apple	**ябълка** (ж)	[jábəlka]
pear	**круша** (ж)	[krúʃa]
lemon	**лимон** (м)	[limón]
orange	**портокал** (м)	[portokál]
strawberry (garden ~)	**ягода** (ж)	[jágoda]
tangerine	**мандарина** (ж)	[mandarína]
plum	**слива** (ж)	[slíva]
peach	**праскова** (ж)	[práskova]
apricot	**кайсия** (ж)	[kajsíja]
raspberry	**малина** (ж)	[malína]
pineapple	**ананас** (м)	[ananás]
banana	**банан** (м)	[banán]
watermelon	**диня** (ж)	[dínʲa]
grape	**грозде** (с)	[grózde]
sour cherry	**вишна** (ж)	[víʃna]
sweet cherry	**череша** (ж)	[tʃeréʃa]
melon	**пъпеш** (м)	[pəpeʃ]
grapefruit	**грейпфрут** (м)	[gréjpfrut]
avocado	**авокадо** (с)	[avokádo]
papaya	**папая** (ж)	[papája]
mango	**манго** (с)	[mángo]

pomegranate	**нар** (м)	[nar]
redcurrant	**червено френско грозде** (с)	[ʧervéno frénsko grózde]
blackcurrant	**черно френско грозде** (с)	[ʧérno frénsko grózde]
gooseberry	**цариградско грозде** (с)	[tsarigrátsko grózde]
bilberry	**боровинки** (ж мн)	[borovínki]
blackberry	**къпина** (ж)	[kəpína]
raisin	**стафиди** (ж мн)	[stafídi]
fig	**смокиня** (ж)	[smokínʲa]
date	**фурма** (ж)	[furmá]
peanut	**фъстък** (м)	[fəstək]
almond	**бадем** (м)	[badém]
walnut	**орех** (м)	[óreh]
hazelnut	**лешник** (м)	[léʃnik]
coconut	**кокосов орех** (м)	[kokósov óreh]
pistachios	**шамфъстъци** (м мн)	[ʃamfəstətsi]

48. Bread. Sweets

bakers' confectionery (pastry)	**сладкарски изделия** (с мн)	[slatkárski izdélija]
bread	**хляб** (м)	[hlʲap]
biscuits	**бисквити** (ж мн)	[biskvíti]
chocolate (n)	**шоколад** (м)	[ʃokolát]
chocolate (as adj)	**шоколадов**	[ʃokoládov]
candy (wrapped)	**бонбон** (м)	[bonbón]
cake (e.g. cupcake)	**паста** (ж)	[pásta]
cake (e.g. birthday ~)	**торта** (ж)	[tórta]
pie (e.g. apple ~)	**пирог** (м)	[pirók]
filling (for cake, pie)	**плънка** (ж)	[plənka]
jam (whole fruit jam)	**сладко** (с)	[slátko]
marmalade	**мармалад** (м)	[marmalát]
wafers	**вафли** (ж мн)	[váfli]
ice-cream	**сладолед** (м)	[sladolét]

49. Cooked dishes

course, dish	**ястие** (с)	[jástie]
cuisine	**кухня** (ж)	[kúhnʲa]
recipe	**рецепта** (ж)	[retsépta]
portion	**порция** (ж)	[pórtsija]
salad	**салата** (ж)	[saláta]
soup	**супа** (ж)	[súpa]
clear soup (broth)	**бульон** (м)	[buljón]
sandwich (bread)	**сандвич** (м)	[sándviʧ]
fried eggs	**пържени яйца** (с мн)	[pérʒeni jajtsá]

hamburger (beefburger)	**хамбургер** (м)	[hámburger]
beefsteak	**бифтек** (м)	[bifték]
side dish	**гарнитура** (ж)	[garnitúra]
spaghetti	**спагети** (мн)	[spagéti]
mash	**картофено пюре** (с)	[kartófeno pʲuré]
pizza	**пица** (ж)	[pítsa]
porridge (oatmeal, etc.)	**каша** (ж)	[káʃa]
omelette	**омлет** (м)	[omlét]
boiled (e.g. ~ beef)	**варен**	[varén]
smoked (adj)	**пушен**	[púʃen]
fried (adj)	**пържен**	[pərʒen]
dried (adj)	**сушен**	[suʃén]
frozen (adj)	**замразен**	[zamrazén]
pickled (adj)	**маринован**	[marinóvan]
sweet (sugary)	**сладък**	[sládək]
salty (adj)	**солен**	[solén]
cold (adj)	**студен**	[studén]
hot (adj)	**горещ**	[goréʃt]
bitter (adj)	**горчив**	[gortʃív]
tasty (adj)	**вкусен**	[fkúsen]
to cook in boiling water	**готвя**	[gótvʲa]
to cook (dinner)	**готвя**	[gótvʲa]
to fry (vt)	**пържа**	[pərʒa]
to heat up (food)	**затоплям**	[zatóplʲam]
to salt (vt)	**соля**	[solʲá]
to pepper (vt)	**слагам пипер**	[slágam pipér]
to grate (vt)	**стъргам**	[stərgam]
peel (n)	**кожа** (ж)	[kóʒa]
to peel (vt)	**беля**	[bélʲa]

50. Spices

salt	**сол** (ж)	[sol]
salty (adj)	**солен**	[solén]
to salt (vt)	**соля**	[solʲá]
black pepper	**черен пипер** (м)	[tʃéren pipér]
red pepper (milled ~)	**червен пипер** (м)	[tʃervén pipér]
mustard	**горчица** (ж)	[gortʃítsa]
horseradish	**хрян** (м)	[hrʲan]
condiment	**подправка** (ж)	[podpráfka]
spice	**подправка** (ж)	[podpráfka]
sauce	**сос** (м)	[sos]
vinegar	**оцет** (м)	[otsét]
anise	**анасон** (м)	[anasón]
basil	**босилек** (м)	[bosílek]
cloves	**карамфил** (м)	[karamfíl]

ginger	**джинджифил** (м)	[dʒindʒifíl]
coriander	**кориандър** (м)	[koriándər]
cinnamon	**канела** (ж)	[kanéla]
sesame	**сусам** (м)	[susám]
bay leaf	**дафинов лист** (м)	[dafínov list]
paprika	**червен пипер** (м)	[ʧervén pipér]
caraway	**черен тмин** (м)	[ʧéren tmin]
saffron	**шафран** (м)	[ʃafrán]

51. Meals

food	**храна** (ж)	[hraná]
to eat (vi, vt)	**ям**	[jam]
breakfast	**закуска** (ж)	[zakúska]
to have breakfast	**закусвам**	[zakúsvam]
lunch	**обяд** (м)	[obʲát]
to have lunch	**обядвам**	[obʲádvam]
dinner	**вечеря** (ж)	[veʧérʲa]
to have dinner	**вечерям**	[veʧérʲam]
appetite	**апетит** (м)	[apetít]
Enjoy your meal!	**Добър апетит!**	[dobər apetít]
to open (~ a bottle)	**отварям**	[otvárʲam]
to spill (liquid)	**излея**	[izléja]
to spill out (vi)	**излея се**	[izléja se]
to boil (vi)	**вря**	[vrʲa]
to boil (vt)	**варя до кипване**	[varʲá do kípvane]
boiled (~ water)	**преварен**	[prevarén]
to chill, cool down (vt)	**охладя**	[ohladʲá]
to chill (vi)	**изстудявам се**	[isstudʲávam se]
taste, flavour	**вкус** (м)	[fkus]
aftertaste	**привкус** (м)	[prífkus]
to slim down (lose weight)	**отслабвам**	[otslábvam]
diet	**диета** (ж)	[diéta]
vitamin	**витамин** (м)	[vitamín]
calorie	**калория** (ж)	[kalórija]
vegetarian (n)	**вегетарианец** (м)	[vegetariánets]
vegetarian (adj)	**вегетариански**	[vegetariánski]
fats (nutrient)	**мазнини** (ж мн)	[mazniní]
proteins	**белтъчини** (ж мн)	[beltəʧiní]
carbohydrates	**въглехидрати** (м мн)	[vəglehidráti]
slice (of lemon, ham)	**резенче** (с)	[rézenʧe]
piece (of cake, pie)	**парче** (с)	[parʧé]
crumb (of bread, cake, etc.)	**троха** (ж)	[trohá]

52. Table setting

spoon	**лъжица** (ж)	[ləʒítsa]
knife	**нож** (м)	[noʒ]
fork	**вилица** (ж)	[vílitsa]
cup (e.g., coffee ~)	**чаша** (ж)	[ʧáʃa]
plate (dinner ~)	**чиния** (ж)	[ʧiníja]
saucer	**чинийка** (ж)	[ʧiníjka]
serviette	**салфетка** (ж)	[salfétka]
toothpick	**клечка** (ж) **за зъби**	[klə́ʧka za zə́bi]

53. Restaurant

restaurant	**ресторант** (м)	[restoránt]
coffee bar	**кафене** (с)	[kafené]
pub, bar	**бар** (м)	[bar]
tearoom	**чаен салон** (м)	[ʧáen salón]
waiter	**сервитьор** (м)	[servitʲór]
waitress	**сервитьорка** (ж)	[servitʲórka]
barman	**барман** (м)	[bárman]
menu	**меню** (с)	[menʲú]
wine list	**карта** (ж) **на виното**	[kárta na vínoto]
to book a table	**резервирам масичка**	[rezervíram másiʧka]
course, dish	**ядене** (с)	[jádene]
to order (meal)	**поръчам**	[porə́ʧam]
to make an order	**правя поръчка**	[právʲa porə́ʧka]
aperitif	**аперитив** (м)	[aperitív]
starter	**мезе** (с)	[mezé]
dessert, pudding	**десерт** (м)	[desért]
bill	**сметка** (ж)	[smétka]
to pay the bill	**плащам сметка**	[pláʃtam smétka]
to give change	**връщам ресто**	[vrə́ʃtam résto]
tip	**бакшиш** (м)	[bakʃíʃ]

Family, relatives and friends

54. Personal information. Forms

name (first name)	**име** (с)	[íme]
surname (last name)	**фамилия** (ж)	[família]
date of birth	**дата** (ж) **на раждане**	[dáta na ráʒdane]
place of birth	**място** (с) **на раждане**	[mʲásto na ráʒdane]
nationality	**националност** (ж)	[natsionálnost]
place of residence	**местожителство** (с)	[mestoʒítelstvo]
country	**страна** (ж)	[straná]
profession (occupation)	**професия** (ж)	[profésija]
gender, sex	**пол** (м)	[pol]
height	**ръст** (м)	[rəst]
weight	**тегло** (с)	[tegló]

55. Family members. Relatives

mother	**майка** (ж)	[májka]
father	**баща** (м)	[baʃtá]
son	**син** (м)	[sin]
daughter	**дъщеря** (ж)	[dəʃterʲá]
younger daughter	**по-малка дъщеря** (ж)	[po-málka dəʃterʲá]
younger son	**по-малък син** (м)	[po-málək sin]
eldest daughter	**по-голяма дъщеря** (ж)	[po-golʲáma dəʃterʲá]
eldest son	**по-голям син** (м)	[po-golʲám sin]
brother	**брат** (м)	[brat]
sister	**сестра** (ж)	[sestrá]
cousin (masc.)	**братовчед** (м)	[bratovtʃét]
cousin (fem.)	**братовчедка** (ж)	[bratovtʃétka]
mummy	**мама** (ж)	[máma]
dad, daddy	**татко** (м)	[tátko]
parents	**родители** (м мн)	[rodíteli]
child	**дете** (с)	[deté]
children	**деца** (с мн)	[detsá]
grandmother	**баба** (ж)	[bába]
grandfather	**дядо** (м)	[dʲádo]
grandson	**внук** (м)	[vnuk]
granddaughter	**внучка** (ж)	[vnútʃka]
grandchildren	**внуци** (м мн)	[vnútsi]
uncle	**вуйчо** (м)	[vújtʃo]
aunt	**леля** (ж)	[lélʲa]

nephew	**племенник** (м)	[plémennik]
niece	**племенница** (ж)	[plémennitsa]
mother-in-law (wife's mother)	**тъща** (ж)	[təʃta]
father-in-law (husband's father)	**свекър** (м)	[svékər]
son-in-law (daughter's husband)	**зет** (м)	[zet]
stepmother	**мащеха** (ж)	[máʃteha]
stepfather	**пастрок** (м)	[pástrok]
infant	**кърмаче** (с)	[kərmáʧe]
baby (infant)	**бебе** (с)	[bébe]
little boy, kid	**момченце** (с)	[momʧéntse]
wife	**жена** (ж)	[ʒená]
husband	**мъж** (м)	[məʒ]
spouse (husband)	**съпруг** (м)	[səprúk]
spouse (wife)	**съпруга** (ж)	[səprúga]
married (masc.)	**женен**	[ʒénen]
married (fem.)	**омъжена**	[oméʒena]
single (unmarried)	**неженен**	[neʒénen]
bachelor	**ерген** (м)	[ergén]
divorced (masc.)	**разведен**	[razvéden]
widow	**вдовица** (ж)	[vdovítsa]
widower	**вдовец** (м)	[vdovéts]
relative	**роднина** (м, ж)	[rodnína]
close relative	**близък роднина** (м)	[blízək rodnína]
distant relative	**далечен роднина** (м)	[daléʧen rodnína]
relatives	**роднини** (мн)	[rodníni]
orphan (boy or girl)	**сирак** (м)	[sirák]
guardian (of a minor)	**опекун** (м)	[opekún]
to adopt (a boy)	**осиновявам**	[osinovʲávam]
to adopt (a girl)	**осиновявам момиче**	[osinovʲávam momíʧe]

56. Friends. Colleagues

friend (masc.)	**приятел** (м)	[prijátel]
friend (fem.)	**приятелка** (ж)	[prijátelka]
friendship	**приятелство** (с)	[prijátelstvo]
to be friends	**дружа**	[druʒá]
pal (masc.)	**приятел** (м)	[prijátel]
pal (fem.)	**приятелка** (ж)	[prijátelka]
partner	**партньор** (м)	[partnʲór]
chief (boss)	**шеф** (м)	[ʃef]
superior (n)	**началник** (м)	[naʧálnik]
subordinate (n)	**подчинен** (м)	[podʧinén]
colleague	**колега** (м, ж)	[koléga]

acquaintance (person)	**познат** (м)	[poznát]
fellow traveller	**спътник** (м)	[spǝ́tnik]
classmate	**съученик** (м)	[sǝutʃeník]
neighbour (masc.)	**съсед** (м)	[sǝsét]
neighbour (fem.)	**съседка** (ж)	[sǝsétka]
neighbours	**съседи** (м мн)	[sǝsédi]

57. Man. Woman

woman	**жена** (ж)	[ʒená]
girl (young woman)	**девойка** (ж)	[devójka]
bride	**годеница** (ж)	[godenítsa]
beautiful (adj)	**хубава**	[húbava]
tall (adj)	**висока**	[visóka]
slender (adj)	**стройна**	[strójna]
short (adj)	**невисок**	[nevisók]
blonde (n)	**блондинка** (ж)	[blondínka]
brunette (n)	**брюнетка** (ж)	[brʲunétka]
ladies' (adj)	**дамски**	[dámski]
virgin (girl)	**девственица** (ж)	[défstvenitsa]
pregnant (adj)	**бременна**	[brémenna]
man (adult male)	**мъж** (м)	[mǝʒ]
blonde haired man	**блондин** (м)	[blondín]
dark haired man	**брюнет** (м)	[brʲunét]
tall (adj)	**висок**	[visók]
short (adj)	**невисок**	[nevisók]
rude (rough)	**груб**	[grup]
stocky (adj)	**едър**	[édǝr]
robust (adj)	**як**	[jak]
strong (adj)	**силен**	[sílen]
strength	**сила** (ж)	[síla]
plump, fat (adj)	**пълен**	[pǝ́len]
swarthy (dark-skinned)	**мургав**	[múrgav]
slender (well-built)	**строен**	[stróen]
elegant (adj)	**елегантен**	[elegánten]

58. Age

age	**възраст** (ж)	[vǝ́zrast]
youth (young age)	**младост** (ж)	[mládost]
young (adj)	**млад**	[mlat]
younger (adj)	**по-малък**	[po-málǝk]
older (adj)	**по-голям**	[po-golʲám]
young man	**младеж** (м)	[mladéʒ]

teenager	**тийнейджър** (м)	[tinéjdʒər]
guy, fellow	**момък** (м)	[mómək]
old man	**старец** (м)	[stárets]
old woman	**старица** (ж)	[stáritsa]
adult (adj)	**възрастен**	[vəzrasten]
middle-aged (adj)	**на средна възраст**	[na srədna vəzrast]
elderly (adj)	**възрастен**	[vəzrasten]
old (adj)	**стар**	[star]
retirement	**пенсия** (ж)	[pénsija]
to retire (from job)	**пенсионирам се**	[pensioníram se]
retiree, pensioner	**пенсионер** (м)	[pensionér]

59. Children

child	**дете** (с)	[deté]
children	**деца** (с мн)	[detsá]
twins	**близнаци** (м мн)	[bliznátsi]
cradle	**люлка** (ж)	[lʲúlka]
rattle	**дрънкалка** (ж)	[drənkálka]
nappy	**памперс** (м)	[pámpers]
dummy, comforter	**биберон** (м)	[biberón]
pram	**детска количка** (ж)	[détska kolítʃka]
nursery	**детска градина** (ж)	[détska gradína]
babysitter	**детегледачка** (ж)	[detegledátʃka]
childhood	**детство** (с)	[détstvo]
doll	**кукла** (ж)	[kúkla]
toy	**играчка** (ж)	[igrátʃka]
construction set (toy)	**конструктор** (м)	[konstrúktor]
well-bred (adj)	**възпитан**	[vəspítan]
ill-bred (adj)	**невъзпитан**	[nevəspítan]
spoilt (adj)	**разглезен**	[razglézen]
to be naughty	**палувам**	[palúvam]
mischievous (adj)	**палав**	[pálav]
mischievousness	**лудория** (ж)	[ludoríja]
mischievous child	**палавник** (м)	[pálavnik]
obedient (adj)	**послушен**	[poslúʃen]
disobedient (adj)	**непослушен**	[neposlúʃen]
docile (adj)	**благоразумен**	[blagorazúmen]
clever (intelligent)	**умен**	[úmen]
child prodigy	**вундеркинд** (м)	[vúnderkint]

60. Married couples. Family life

to kiss (vt)	**целувам**	[tselúvam]
to kiss (vi)	**целувам се**	[tselúvam se]
family (n)	**семейство** (с)	[seméjstvo]
family (as adj)	**семеен**	[seméen]
couple	**двойка** (ж)	[dvójka]
marriage (state)	**брак** (м)	[brak]
hearth (home)	**семейно огнище** (с)	[seméjno ogníʃte]
dynasty	**династия** (ж)	[dinástija]
date	**среща** (ж)	[sréʃta]
kiss	**целувка** (ж)	[tselúfka]
love (for sb)	**обич** (ж)	[óbitʃ]
to love (sb)	**обичам**	[obítʃam]
beloved	**любим**	[lʲubím]
tenderness	**нежност** (ж)	[néʒnost]
tender (affectionate)	**нежен**	[néʒen]
faithfulness	**вярност** (ж)	[vʲárnost]
faithful (adj)	**верен**	[véren]
care (attention)	**грижа** (ж)	[gríʒa]
caring (~ father)	**грижлив**	[griʒlív]
newlyweds	**младоженци** (м мн)	[mladoʒéntsi]
honeymoon	**меден месец** (м)	[méden mésets]
to get married (ab. woman)	**омъжа се**	[oméʒa se]
to get married (ab. man)	**женя се**	[ʒénʲa se]
wedding	**сватба** (ж)	[svátba]
golden wedding	**златна сватба** (ж)	[zlátna svádba]
anniversary	**годишнина** (ж)	[godíʃnina]
lover (masc.)	**любовник** (м)	[lʲubóvnik]
mistress (lover)	**любовница** (ж)	[lʲubóvnitsa]
adultery	**изневяра** (ж)	[iznevʲára]
to cheat on ... (commit adultery)	**изневерявам**	[izneverʲávam]
jealous (adj)	**ревнив**	[revnív]
to be jealous	**ревнувам**	[revnúvam]
divorce	**развод** (м)	[razvót]
to divorce (vi)	**развеждам се**	[razvéʒdam se]
to quarrel (vi)	**карам се**	[káram se]
to be reconciled (after an argument)	**сдобрявам се**	[zdobrʲávam se]
together (adv)	**заедно**	[záedno]
sex	**секс** (м)	[seks]
happiness	**щастие** (с)	[ʃtástie]
happy (adj)	**щастлив**	[ʃtastlív]
misfortune (accident)	**нещастие** (с)	[neʃtástie]
unhappy (adj)	**нещастен**	[neʃtásten]

Character. Feelings. Emotions

61. Feelings. Emotions

feeling (emotion)	**чувство** (с)	[ʧúvstvo]
feelings	**чувства** (с мн)	[ʧúvstva]
to feel (vt)	**чувствам**	[ʧúfstvam]
hunger	**глад** (м)	[glat]
to be hungry	**искам да ям**	[ískam da jam]
thirst	**жажда** (ж)	[ʒáʒda]
to be thirsty	**искам да пия**	[ískam da píja]
sleepiness	**сънливост** (ж)	[sənlívost]
to feel sleepy	**искам да спя**	[ískam da spʲa]
tiredness	**умора** (ж)	[umóra]
tired (adj)	**изморен**	[izmorén]
to get tired	**уморя се**	[umorʲá se]
mood (humour)	**настроение** (с)	[nastroénie]
boredom	**скука** (ж)	[skúka]
to be bored	**скучая**	[skuʧája]
seclusion	**самота** (ж)	[samotá]
to seclude oneself	**уединявам се**	[uedinʲávam se]
to worry (make anxious)	**безпокоя**	[bespokojá]
to be worried	**безпокоя се**	[bespokojá se]
worrying (n)	**безпокойство** (с)	[bespokójstvo]
anxiety	**тревога** (ж)	[trevóga]
preoccupied (adj)	**загрижен**	[zagríʒen]
to be nervous	**нервирам се**	[nervíram se]
to panic (vi)	**паникьосвам се**	[panikʲósvam se]
hope	**надежда** (ж)	[nadéʒda]
to hope (vi, vt)	**надявам се**	[nadʲávam se]
certainty	**увереност** (ж)	[uvérenost]
certain, sure (adj)	**уверен**	[uvéren]
uncertainty	**неувереност** (ж)	[neuvérenost]
uncertain (adj)	**неуверен**	[neuvéren]
drunk (adj)	**пиян**	[piján]
sober (adj)	**трезвен**	[trézven]
weak (adj)	**слаб**	[slap]
happy (adj)	**щастлив**	[ʃtastlív]
to scare (vt)	**изплаша**	[ispláʃa]
fury (madness)	**бяс** (м)	[bʲas]
rage (fury)	**ярост** (ж)	[járost]
depression	**депресия** (ж)	[deprésija]
discomfort (unease)	**дискомфорт** (м)	[diskomfórt]

comfort	**комфорт** (м)	[komfórt]
to regret (be sorry)	**съжалявам**	[səʒalʲávam]
regret	**съжаление** (с)	[səʒalénie]
bad luck	**несполука** (ж)	[nespolúka]
sadness	**огорчение** (с)	[ogortʃénie]
shame (remorse)	**срам** (м)	[sram]
gladness	**веселба** (ж)	[veselbá]
enthusiasm, zeal	**ентусиазъм** (м)	[entusiázəm]
enthusiast	**ентусиаст** (м)	[entusiást]
to show enthusiasm	**ентусиазирам**	[entusiazíram]

62. Character. Personality

character	**характер** (м)	[harákter]
character flaw	**недостатък** (м)	[nedostátək]
mind	**ум** (м)	[um]
reason	**разум** (м)	[rázum]
conscience	**съвест** (ж)	[sə́vest]
habit (custom)	**навик** (м)	[návik]
ability (talent)	**способност** (ж)	[sposóbnost]
can (e.g. ~ swim)	**умея**	[uméja]
patient (adj)	**търпелив**	[tərpelív]
impatient (adj)	**нетърпелив**	[netərpelív]
curious (inquisitive)	**любопитен**	[lʲubopíten]
curiosity	**любопитство** (с)	[lʲubopítstvo]
modesty	**скромност** (ж)	[skrómnost]
modest (adj)	**скромен**	[skrómen]
immodest (adj)	**нескромен**	[neskrómen]
laziness	**мързел** (м)	[mə́rzel]
lazy (adj)	**мързелив**	[mərzelív]
lazy person (masc.)	**мързеливец** (м)	[mərzelívets]
cunning (n)	**хитрост** (ж)	[hítrost]
cunning (as adj)	**хитър**	[hítər]
distrust	**недоверие** (с)	[nedovérie]
distrustful (adj)	**недоверчив**	[nedovertʃív]
generosity	**щедрост** (ж)	[ʃtédrost]
generous (adj)	**щедър**	[ʃtédər]
talented (adj)	**талантлив**	[talantlív]
talent	**талант** (м)	[talánt]
courageous (adj)	**смел**	[smel]
courage	**смелост** (м)	[smélost]
honest (adj)	**честен**	[tʃésten]
honesty	**честност** (ж)	[tʃéstnost]
careful (cautious)	**предпазлив**	[predpazlív]
brave (courageous)	**храбър**	[hrábər]

serious (adj)	**сериозен**	[seriózen]
strict (severe, stern)	**строг**	[strok]
decisive (adj)	**решителен**	[reʃítelen]
indecisive (adj)	**нерешителен**	[nereʃítelen]
shy, timid (adj)	**свенлив**	[svenlív]
shyness, timidity	**свенливост** (ж)	[svenlívost]
confidence (trust)	**доверие** (с)	[dovérie]
to believe (trust)	**вярвам**	[v^járvam]
trusting (credulous)	**доверчив**	[dovertʃív]
sincerely (adv)	**искрено**	[ískreno]
sincere (adj)	**искрен**	[ískren]
sincerity	**искреност** (ж)	[ískrenost]
open (person)	**открит**	[otkrít]
calm (adj)	**тих**	[tih]
frank (sincere)	**откровен**	[otkrovén]
naïve (adj)	**наивен**	[naíven]
absent-minded (adj)	**разсеян**	[rasséjan]
funny (odd)	**смешен**	[sméʃen]
greed, stinginess	**алчност** (ж)	[áltʃnost]
greedy, stingy (adj)	**алчен**	[áltʃen]
stingy (adj)	**стиснат**	[stísnat]
evil (adj)	**зъл**	[zəl]
stubborn (adj)	**инат**	[inát]
unpleasant (adj)	**неприятен**	[neprijáten]
selfish person (masc.)	**егоист** (м)	[egoíst]
selfish (adj)	**егоистичен**	[egoistítʃen]
coward	**страхливец** (м)	[strahlívets]
cowardly (adj)	**страхлив**	[strahlíf]

63. Sleep. Dreams

to sleep (vi)	**спя**	[sp^ja]
sleep, sleeping	**сън** (м)	[sən]
dream	**сън** (м)	[sən]
to dream (in sleep)	**сънувам**	[sənúvam]
sleepy (adj)	**сънен**	[sénen]
bed	**легло** (с)	[legló]
mattress	**дюшек** (м)	[d^juʃék]
blanket (eiderdown)	**одеяло** (с)	[odejálo]
pillow	**възглавница** (ж)	[vəzglávnitsa]
sheet	**чаршаф** (м)	[tʃarʃáf]
insomnia	**безсъние** (с)	[bessénie]
sleepless (adj)	**безсънен**	[bessénen]
sleeping pill	**приспивателно** (с)	[prispivátelno]
to take a sleeping pill	**взимам приспивателно**	[vzímam prispivátelno]
to feel sleepy	**искам да спя**	[ískam da sp^ja]

to yawn (vi)	**прозявам се**	[prozʲávam se]
to go to bed	**отивам да спя**	[otívam da spʲa]
to make up the bed	**оправям легло**	[oprávʲam legló]
to fall asleep	**заспивам**	[zaspívam]
nightmare	**кошмар** (м)	[koʃmár]
snore, snoring	**хъркане** (с)	[hə́rkane]
to snore (vi)	**хъркам**	[hə́rkam]
alarm clock	**будилник** (м)	[budílnik]
to wake (vt)	**събудя**	[səbúdʲa]
to wake up	**събуждам се**	[səbúʒdam se]
to get up (vi)	**ставам**	[stávam]
to have a wash	**измивам се**	[izmívam se]

64. Humour. Laughter. Gladness

humour (wit, fun)	**хумор** (м)	[húmor]
sense of humour	**чувство** (ж) **за хумор**	[ʧústvo za húmor]
to enjoy oneself	**веселя се**	[veselʲá se]
cheerful (merry)	**весел**	[vésel]
merriment (gaiety)	**веселба** (ж)	[veselbá]
smile	**усмивка** (ж)	[usmífka]
to smile (vi)	**усмихвам се**	[usmíhvam se]
to start laughing	**засмея се**	[zasméja se]
to laugh (vi)	**смея се**	[sméja se]
laugh, laughter	**смях** (м)	[smʲah]
anecdote	**виц** (м)	[vits]
funny (anecdote, etc.)	**смешен**	[sméʃen]
funny (odd)	**смешен**	[sméʃen]
to joke (vi)	**шегувам се**	[ʃegúvam se]
joke (verbal)	**шега** (ж)	[ʃegá]
joy (emotion)	**радост** (ж)	[rádost]
to rejoice (vi)	**радвам се**	[rádvam se]
joyful (adj)	**радостен**	[rádosten]

65. Discussion, conversation. Part 1

communication	**общуване** (с)	[obʃtúvane]
to communicate	**общувам**	[obʃtúvam]
conversation	**разговор** (м)	[rázgovor]
dialogue	**диалог** (м)	[dialók]
discussion (discourse)	**дискусия** (ж)	[diskúsija]
dispute (debate)	**спор** (м)	[spor]
to dispute, to debate	**споря**	[spórʲa]
interlocutor	**събеседник** (м)	[səbesédnik]
topic (theme)	**тема** (ж)	[téma]

point of view	**гледна точка** (ж)	[glédna tótʃka]
opinion (point of view)	**мнение** (с)	[mnénie]
speech (talk)	**слово** (с)	[slóvo]
discussion (of a report, etc.)	**обсъждане** (с)	[obsə́ʒdane]
to discuss (vt)	**обсъждам**	[obsə́ʒdam]
talk (conversation)	**беседа** (ж)	[beséda]
to talk (to chat)	**беседвам**	[besédvam]
meeting (encounter)	**среща** (ж)	[sréʃta]
to meet (vi, vt)	**срещам се**	[sréʃtam se]
proverb	**пословица** (ж)	[poslóvitsa]
saying	**поговорка** (ж)	[pogovórka]
riddle (poser)	**гатанка** (ж)	[gátanka]
to pose a riddle	**задавам гатанка**	[zadávam gátanka]
password	**парола** (ж)	[paróla]
secret	**секрет** (м)	[sekrét]
oath (vow)	**клетва** (ж)	[klétva]
to swear (an oath)	**заклевам се**	[zaklévam se]
promise	**обещание** (с)	[obeʃtánie]
to promise (vt)	**обещавам**	[obeʃtávam]
advice (counsel)	**съвет** (м)	[səvét]
to advise (vt)	**съветвам**	[səvétvam]
to follow one's advice	**слушам**	[slúʃam]
news	**новина** (ж)	[noviná]
sensation (news)	**сензация** (ж)	[senzátsija]
information (report)	**сведения** (с мн)	[svédenija]
conclusion (decision)	**извод** (м)	[ízvot]
voice	**глас** (м)	[glas]
compliment	**комплимент** (м)	[kompliment]
kind (nice)	**любезен**	[lʲubézen]
word	**дума** (ж)	[dúma]
phrase	**фраза** (ж)	[fráza]
answer	**отговор** (м)	[ótgovor]
truth	**истина** (ж)	[ístina]
lie	**лъжа** (ж)	[ləʒá]
thought	**мисъл** (ж)	[mísəl]
idea (inspiration)	**идея** (ж)	[idéja]
fantasy	**измислица** (ж)	[izmíslitsa]

66. Discussion, conversation. Part 2

respected (adj)	**уважаем**	[uvaʒáem]
to respect (vt)	**уважавам**	[uvaʒávam]
respect	**уважение** (с)	[uvaʒénie]
Dear … (letter)	**Уважаем …**	[uvaʒáem]
to introduce (sb to sb)	**запозная**	[zapoznája]
to make acquaintance	**запознавам се**	[zapoznávam se]

intention	**намерение** (с)	[namerénie]
to intend (have in mind)	**каня се**	[kánʲa se]
wish	**пожелание** (с)	[poʒelánie]
to wish (~ good luck)	**пожелая**	[poʒelája]
surprise (astonishment)	**учудване** (с)	[utʃúdvane]
to surprise (amaze)	**удивлявам**	[udivlʲávam]
to be surprised	**удивлявам се**	[udivlʲávam se]
to give (vt)	**дам**	[dam]
to take (get hold of)	**взема**	[vzéma]
to give back	**върна**	[vərna]
to return (give back)	**върна**	[vərna]
to apologize (vi)	**извинявам се**	[izvinʲávam se]
apology	**извинение** (с)	[izvinénie]
to forgive (vt)	**прощавам**	[proʃtávam]
to talk (speak)	**разговарям**	[razgovárʲam]
to listen (vi)	**слушам**	[slúʃam]
to hear out	**изслушам**	[isslúʃam]
to understand (vt)	**разбера**	[razberá]
to show (to display)	**покажа**	[pokáʒa]
to look at ...	**гледам**	[glédam]
to call (yell for sb)	**повикам**	[povíkam]
to distract (disturb)	**отвличам**	[otvlítʃam]
to disturb (vt)	**преча**	[prétʃa]
to pass (to hand sth)	**предам**	[predám]
demand (request)	**молба** (ж)	[molbá]
to request (ask)	**моля**	[mólʲa]
demand (firm request)	**изискване** (с)	[izískvane]
to demand (request firmly)	**изисквам**	[izískvam]
to tease (call names)	**дразня**	[dráznʲa]
to mock (make fun of)	**присмивам се**	[prismívam se]
mockery, derision	**подигравка** (ж)	[podigráfka]
nickname	**прякор** (м)	[prʲákor]
insinuation	**намек** (м)	[námek]
to insinuate (imply)	**намеквам**	[namékvam]
to mean (vt)	**подразбирам**	[podrazbíram]
description	**описание** (с)	[opisánie]
to describe (vt)	**опиша**	[opíʃa]
praise (compliments)	**похвала** (ж)	[pohvála]
to praise (vt)	**похваля**	[pohválʲa]
disappointment	**разочарование** (с)	[razotʃarovánie]
to disappoint (vt)	**разочаровам**	[razotʃaróvam]
to be disappointed	**разочаровам се**	[razotʃaróvam se]
supposition	**предположение** (с)	[predpoloʒénie]
to suppose (assume)	**предполагам**	[pretpolágam]
warning (caution)	**предпазване** (с)	[predpázvane]
to warn (vt)	**предпазя**	[pretpázʲa]

67. Discussion, conversation. Part 3

to talk into (convince)	**уговоря**	[ugovórʲa]
to calm down (vt)	**успокоявам**	[uspokojávam]
silence (~ is golden)	**мълчание** (с)	[məltʃánie]
to be silent (not speaking)	**мълча**	[məltʃá]
to whisper (vi, vt)	**шепна**	[ʃépna]
whisper	**шепот** (м)	[ʃépot]
frankly, sincerely (adv)	**откровено**	[otkrovéno]
in my opinion ...	**според мен ...**	[spóret men]
detail (of the story)	**подробност** (ж)	[podróbnost]
detailed (adj)	**подробен**	[podróben]
in detail (adv)	**подробно**	[podróbno]
hint, clue	**подсказка** (ж)	[potskáska]
to give a hint	**подскажа**	[potskáʒa]
look (glance)	**поглед** (м)	[póglet]
to have a look	**погледна**	[poglédna]
fixed (look)	**неподвижен**	[nepodvíʒen]
to blink (vi)	**мигам**	[mígam]
to wink (vi)	**мигна**	[mígna]
to nod (in assent)	**кимна**	[kímna]
sigh	**въздишка** (ж)	[vəzdíʃka]
to sigh (vi)	**въздъхна**	[vəzdə́hna]
to shudder (vi)	**стряскам се**	[strʲáskam se]
gesture	**жест** (м)	[ʒest]
to touch (one's arm, etc.)	**докосна се**	[dokósna se]
to seize (e.g., ~ by the arm)	**хващам**	[hváʃtam]
to tap (on the shoulder)	**тупам**	[túpam]
Look out!	**Внимавай!**	[vnimávaj]
Really?	**Нима?**	[nimá]
Good luck!	**Късмет!**	[kəsmét]
I see!	**Ясно!**	[jásno]
What a pity!	**Жалко!**	[ʒálko]

68. Agreement. Refusal

consent	**съгласие** (с)	[səglásie]
to consent (vi)	**съгласявам се**	[səglasʲávam se]
approval	**одобрение** (с)	[odobrénie]
to approve (vt)	**одобря**	[odobrʲá]
refusal	**отказ** (м)	[ótkaz]
to refuse (vi, vt)	**отказвам се**	[otkázvam se]
Great!	**Отлично!**	[otlítʃno]
All right!	**Добре!**	[dobré]
Okay! (I agree)	**Дадено!**	[dádeno]

forbidden (adj)	**забранен**	[zabranén]
it's forbidden	**забранено**	[zabranéno]
incorrect (adj)	**грешен**	[gréʃen]
to reject (~ a demand)	**отклоня**	[otklonʲá]
to support (cause, idea)	**подкрепям**	[potkrepʲám]
to accept (~ an apology)	**приема**	[priéma]
to confirm (vt)	**потвърдя**	[potvərdʲá]
confirmation	**потвърждение** (с)	[potvərʒdénie]
permission	**разрешение** (с)	[razreʃénie]
to permit (vt)	**разреша**	[razreʃá]
decision	**решение** (с)	[reʃénie]
to say nothing (hold one's tongue)	**премълча**	[preməltʃá]
condition (term)	**условие** (с)	[uslóvie]
excuse (pretext)	**привидна причина** (ж)	[privídna pritʃína]
praise (compliments)	**похвала** (ж)	[pohvála]
to praise (vt)	**похваля**	[pohválʲa]

69. Success. Good luck. Failure

success	**успех** (м)	[uspéh]
successfully (adv)	**успешно**	[uspéʃno]
successful (adj)	**успешен**	[uspéʃen]
luck (good luck)	**сполука** (ж)	[spolúka]
Good luck!	**Късмет!**	[kəsmét]
lucky (e.g. ~ day)	**сполучлив**	[spolutʃlíf]
lucky (fortunate)	**успешен**	[uspéʃen]
failure	**несполука** (ж)	[nespolúka]
misfortune	**несполука** (ж)	[nespolúka]
bad luck	**нещастие** (с)	[neʃtástie]
unsuccessful (adj)	**несполучлив**	[nespolutʃlív]
catastrophe	**катастрофа** (ж)	[katastrófa]
pride	**гордост** (ж)	[górdost]
proud (adj)	**горд**	[gort]
to be proud	**гордея се**	[gordéja se]
winner	**победител** (м)	[pobedítel]
to win (vi)	**победя**	[pobedʲá]
to lose (not win)	**загубя**	[zagúbʲa]
try	**опит** (м)	[ópit]
to try (vi)	**опитвам се**	[opítvam se]
chance (opportunity)	**шанс** (м)	[ʃans]

70. Quarrels. Negative emotions

shout (scream)	**вик** (м)	[vik]
to shout (vi)	**викам**	[víkam]

to start to cry out	**закрещя**	[zakreʃtʲá]
quarrel	**караница** (ж)	[káranitsa]
to quarrel (vi)	**карам се**	[káram se]
fight (squabble)	**скандал** (м)	[skandál]
to make a scene	**правя скандали**	[právʲa skandáli]
conflict	**конфликт** (м)	[konflíkt]
misunderstanding	**недоразумение** (с)	[nedorazuménie]
insult	**оскърбление** (с)	[oskərblénie]
to insult (vt)	**оскърбявам**	[oskərbʲávam]
insulted (adj)	**оскърбен**	[oskərbén]
resentment	**обида** (ж)	[obída]
to offend (vt)	**обидя**	[obídʲa]
to take offence	**обидя се**	[obídʲa se]
indignation	**възмущение** (с)	[vəzmuʃténie]
to be indignant	**възмущавам се**	[vəzmuʃtávam se]
complaint	**оплакване** (с)	[oplákvane]
to complain (vi, vt)	**оплаквам се**	[oplákvam se]
apology	**извинение** (с)	[izvinénie]
to apologize (vi)	**извинявам се**	[izvinʲávam se]
to beg pardon	**моля за прошка**	[mólʲa za próʃka]
criticism	**критика** (ж)	[krítika]
to criticize (vt)	**критикувам**	[kritikúvam]
accusation (charge)	**обвинение** (с)	[obvinénie]
to accuse (vt)	**обвинявам**	[obvinʲávam]
revenge	**отмъщение** (с)	[otməʃténie]
to avenge (get revenge)	**отмъщавам**	[otməʃtávam]
to pay back	**отплатя**	[otplatʲá]
disdain	**презрение** (с)	[prezrénie]
to despise (vt)	**презирам**	[prezíram]
hatred, hate	**омраза** (ж)	[omráza]
to hate (vt)	**мразя**	[mrázʲa]
nervous (adj)	**нервен**	[nérven]
to be nervous	**нервирам се**	[nervíram se]
angry (mad)	**сърдит**	[sərdít]
to make angry	**разсърдя**	[rassérdʲa]
humiliation	**унижение** (с)	[uniʒénie]
to humiliate (vt)	**унижавам**	[uniʒávam]
to humiliate oneself	**унижавам се**	[uniʒávam se]
shock	**шок** (м)	[ʃok]
to shock (vt)	**шокирам**	[ʃokíram]
trouble (e.g. serious ~)	**неприятност** (ж)	[neprijátnost]
unpleasant (adj)	**неприятен**	[neprijáten]
fear (dread)	**страх** (м)	[strah]
terrible (storm, heat)	**силен**	[sílen]
scary (e.g. ~ story)	**страшен**	[stráʃen]

horror	**ужас** (м)	[úʒas]
awful (crime, news)	**ужасен**	[uʒásen]
to begin to tremble	**затреперя**	[zatrepérʲa]
to cry (weep)	**плача**	[plátʃa]
to start crying	**заплача**	[zaplátʃa]
tear	**сълза** (ж)	[səlzá]
fault	**вина** (ж)	[viná]
guilt (feeling)	**вина** (ж)	[viná]
dishonor (disgrace)	**позор** (м)	[pozór]
protest	**протест** (м)	[protést]
stress	**стрес** (м)	[stres]
to disturb (vt)	**безпокоя**	[bespokojá]
to be furious	**ядосвам се**	[jadósvam se]
angry (adj)	**зъл**	[zəl]
to end (~ a relationship)	**прекъсвам**	[prekə́svam]
to swear (at sb)	**карам се**	[káram se]
to scare (become afraid)	**плаша се**	[pláʃa se]
to hit (strike with hand)	**ударя**	[udárʲa]
to fight (street fight, etc.)	**бия се**	[bíja se]
to settle (a conflict)	**урегулирам**	[uregulíram]
discontented (adj)	**недоволен**	[nedovólen]
furious (adj)	**яростен**	[járosten]
It's not good!	**Това не е хубаво!**	[tová ne e húbavo]
It's bad!	**Това е лошо!**	[tová e lóʃo]

Medicine

71. Diseases

illness	**болест** (ж)	[bólest]
to be ill	**боледувам**	[boledúvam]
health	**здраве** (с)	[zdráve]
runny nose (coryza)	**хрема** (ж)	[hréma]
tonsillitis	**ангина** (ж)	[angína]
cold (illness)	**настинка** (ж)	[nastínka]
to catch a cold	**настина**	[nastína]
bronchitis	**бронхит** (м)	[bronhít]
pneumonia	**пневмония** (ж)	[pnevmoníja]
flu, influenza	**грип** (м)	[grip]
shortsighted (adj)	**късоглед**	[kəsoglét]
longsighted (adj)	**далекоглед**	[dalekoglét]
strabismus (crossed eyes)	**кривогледство** (с)	[krivoglétstvo]
squint-eyed (adj)	**кривоглед**	[krivoglét]
cataract	**катаракта** (ж)	[katarákta]
glaucoma	**глаукома** (ж)	[glaukóma]
stroke	**инсулт** (м)	[insúlt]
heart attack	**инфаркт** (м)	[infárkt]
myocardial infarction	**инфаркт** (м) **на миокарда**	[infárkt na miokárda]
paralysis	**парализа** (ж)	[paráliza]
to paralyse (vt)	**парализирам**	[paralizíram]
allergy	**алергия** (ж)	[alérgija]
asthma	**астма** (ж)	[ástma]
diabetes	**диабет** (м)	[diabét]
toothache	**зъбобол** (м)	[zəboból]
caries	**кариес** (м)	[káries]
diarrhoea	**диария** (ж)	[diárija]
constipation	**запек** (м)	[zápek]
stomach upset	**разстройство** (с) **на стомаха**	[rastrójstvo na stomáha]
food poisoning	**отравяне** (с)	[otrávʲane]
to get food poisoning	**отровя се**	[otróvʲa se]
arthritis	**артрит** (м)	[artrít]
rickets	**рахит** (м)	[rahít]
rheumatism	**ревматизъм** (м)	[revmatízəm]
atherosclerosis	**атеросклероза** (ж)	[ateroskleróza]
gastritis	**гастрит** (м)	[gastrít]
appendicitis	**апандисит** (м)	[apandisít]

cholecystitis	**холецистит** (м)	[holetsistít]
ulcer	**язва** (ж)	[jázva]
measles	**дребна шарка** (ж)	[drébna ʃárka]
rubella (German measles)	**шарка** (ж)	[ʃárka]
jaundice	**жълтеница** (ж)	[ʒəltenítsa]
hepatitis	**хепатит** (м)	[hepatít]
schizophrenia	**шизофрения** (ж)	[ʃizofreníja]
rabies (hydrophobia)	**бяс** (м)	[bʲas]
neurosis	**невроза** (ж)	[nevróza]
concussion	**сътресение** (с) **на мозъка**	[sətresénie na mózəka]
cancer	**рак** (м)	[rak]
sclerosis	**склероза** (ж)	[skleróza]
multiple sclerosis	**множествена склероза** (ж)	[mnóʒestvena skleróza]
alcoholism	**алкохолизъм** (м)	[alkoholízəm]
alcoholic (n)	**алкохолик** (м)	[alkoholík]
syphilis	**сифилис** (м)	[sífilis]
AIDS	**СПИН** (м)	[spin]
tumour	**тумор** (м)	[túmor]
malignant (adj)	**злокачествен**	[zlokátʃestven]
benign (adj)	**доброкачествен**	[dobrokátʃestven]
fever	**треска** (ж)	[tréska]
malaria	**малария** (ж)	[malárija]
gangrene	**гангрена** (ж)	[gangréna]
seasickness	**морска болест** (ж)	[mórska bólest]
epilepsy	**епилепсия** (ж)	[epilépsija]
epidemic	**епидемия** (ж)	[epidémija]
typhus	**тиф** (м)	[tif]
tuberculosis	**туберкулоза** (ж)	[tuberkulóza]
cholera	**холера** (ж)	[holéra]
plague (bubonic ~)	**чума** (ж)	[tʃúma]

72. Symptoms. Treatments. Part 1

symptom	**симптом** (м)	[simptóm]
temperature	**температура** (ж)	[temperatúra]
high temperature (fever)	**висока температура** (ж)	[visóka temperatúra]
pulse (heartbeat)	**пулс** (м)	[puls]
dizziness (vertigo)	**световъртеж** (м)	[svetovərtéʃ]
hot (adj)	**горещ**	[goréʃt]
shivering	**тръпки** (ж мн)	[trə́pki]
pale (e.g. ~ face)	**бледен**	[bléden]
cough	**кашлица** (ж)	[káʃlitsa]
to cough (vi)	**кашлям**	[káʃʲam]
to sneeze (vi)	**кихам**	[kíham]
faint	**припадък** (м)	[pripádək]

to faint (vi)	**припадна**	[pripádna]
bruise (hématome)	**синина** (ж)	[sininá]
bump (lump)	**подутина** (ж)	[podutiná]
to bang (bump)	**ударя се**	[udárʲa se]
contusion (bruise)	**натъртване** (с)	[natértvane]
to get a bruise	**ударя се**	[udárʲa se]
to limp (vi)	**куцам**	[kútsam]
dislocation	**изкълчване** (с)	[iskéltʃvane]
to dislocate (vt)	**навехна**	[navéhna]
fracture	**фрактура** (ж)	[fraktúra]
to have a fracture	**счупя**	[stʃúpʲa]
cut (e.g. paper ~)	**порязване** (с)	[porʲázvane]
to cut oneself	**порежа се**	[poréʒa se]
bleeding	**кръвотечение** (с)	[krəvotetʃénie]
burn (injury)	**изгаряне** (с)	[izgárʲane]
to get burned	**опаря се**	[opárʲa se]
to prick (vt)	**бодна**	[bódna]
to prick oneself	**убода се**	[ubodá se]
to injure (vt)	**нараня**	[naranʲá]
injury	**рана** (ж)	[rána]
wound	**рана** (ж)	[rána]
trauma	**травма** (ж)	[trávma]
to be delirious	**бълнувам**	[bəlnúvam]
to stutter (vi)	**заеквам**	[zaékvam]
sunstroke	**слънчев удар** (м)	[slɘ́ntʃev údar]

73. Symptoms. Treatments. Part 2

pain, ache	**болка** (ж)	[bólka]
splinter (in foot, etc.)	**трънче** (с)	[trɘ́ntʃe]
sweat (perspiration)	**пот** (ж)	[pot]
to sweat (perspire)	**потя се**	[potʲá se]
vomiting	**повръщане** (с)	[povrɘ́ʃtane]
convulsions	**гърчове** (м мн)	[gɘ́rtʃove]
pregnant (adj)	**бременна**	[brémenna]
to be born	**родя се**	[rodʲá se]
delivery, labour	**раждане** (с)	[ráʒdane]
to deliver (~ a baby)	**раждам**	[ráʒdam]
abortion	**аборт** (м)	[abórt]
breathing, respiration	**дишане** (с)	[díʃane]
in-breath (inhalation)	**вдишване** (с)	[vdíʃvane]
out-breath (exhalation)	**издишване** (с)	[izdíʃvane]
to exhale (breathe out)	**издишам**	[izdíʃam]
to inhale (vi)	**направя вдишване**	[naprávʲa vdíʃvane]
disabled person	**инвалид** (м)	[invalít]
cripple	**сакат човек** (м)	[sakát tʃovék]

drug addict	**наркоман** (м)	[narkomán]
deaf (adj)	**глух**	[gluh]
mute (adj)	**ням**	[nʲam]
deaf mute (adj)	**глухоням**	[gluhonʲám]
mad, insane (adj)	**луд**	[lut]
madman (demented person)	**луд** (м)	[lut]
madwoman	**луда** (ж)	[lúda]
to go insane	**полудея**	[poludéja]
gene	**ген** (м)	[gen]
immunity	**имунитет** (м)	[imunitét]
hereditary (adj)	**наследствен**	[naslétstven]
congenital (adj)	**вроден**	[vrodén]
virus	**вирус** (м)	[vírus]
microbe	**микроб** (м)	[mikróp]
bacterium	**бактерия** (ж)	[baktérija]
infection	**инфекция** (ж)	[inféktsija]

74. Symptoms. Treatments. Part 3

hospital	**болница** (ж)	[bólnitsa]
patient	**пациент** (м)	[patsiént]
diagnosis	**диагноза** (ж)	[diagnóza]
cure	**лекуване** (с)	[lekúvane]
medical treatment	**лекуване** (с)	[lekúvane]
to get treatment	**лекувам се**	[lekúvam se]
to treat (~ a patient)	**лекувам**	[lekúvam]
to nurse (look after)	**грижа се**	[gríʒa se]
care (nursing ~)	**грижа** (ж)	[gríʒa]
operation, surgery	**операция** (ж)	[operátsija]
to bandage (head, limb)	**превържа**	[prevérʒa]
bandaging	**превързване** (с)	[prevérzvane]
vaccination	**ваксиниране** (с)	[vaksinírane]
to vaccinate (vt)	**ваксинирам**	[vaksiníram]
injection	**инжекция** (ж)	[inʒéktsija]
to give an injection	**инжектирам**	[inʒektíram]
attack	**пристъп, припáдък** (м)	[prístəp], [pripadək]
amputation	**ампутация** (ж)	[amputátsija]
to amputate (vt)	**ампутирам**	[amputíram]
coma	**кома** (ж)	[kóma]
to be in a coma	**намирам се в кома**	[namíram se v kóma]
intensive care	**реанимация** (ж)	[reanimátsija]
to recover (~ from flu)	**оздравявам**	[ozdravʲávam]
condition (patient's ~)	**състояние** (с)	[səstojánie]
consciousness	**съзнание** (с)	[səznánie]
memory (faculty)	**памет** (ж)	[pámet]

to pull out (tooth)	**вадя**	[vádʲa]
filling	**пломба** (ж)	[plómba]
to fill (a tooth)	**пломбирам**	[plombíram]
hypnosis	**хипноза** (ж)	[hipnóza]
to hypnotize (vt)	**хипнотизирам**	[hipnotizíram]

75. Doctors

doctor	**лекар** (м)	[lékar]
nurse	**медицинска сестра** (ж)	[meditsínska sestrá]
personal doctor	**личен лекар** (м)	[lítʃen lékar]
dentist	**зъболекар** (м)	[zəbolékar]
optician	**очен лекар** (м)	[ótʃen lékar]
general practitioner	**терапевт** (м)	[terapéft]
surgeon	**хирург** (м)	[hirúrk]
psychiatrist	**психиатър** (м)	[psihiátər]
paediatrician	**педиатър** (м)	[pediátər]
psychologist	**психолог** (м)	[psiholók]
gynaecologist	**гинеколог** (м)	[ginekolók]
cardiologist	**кардиолог** (м)	[kardiolók]

76. Medicine. Drugs. Accessories

medicine, drug	**лекарство** (с)	[lekárstvo]
remedy	**средство** (с)	[srétstvo]
to prescribe (vt)	**предпиша**	[pretpíʃa]
prescription	**рецепта** (ж)	[retsépta]
tablet, pill	**таблетка** (ж)	[tablétka]
ointment	**мехлем** (м)	[mehlém]
ampoule	**ампула** (ж)	[ampúla]
mixture, solution	**микстура** (ж)	[mikstúra]
syrup	**сироп** (м)	[ɕiróp]
capsule	**хапче** (с)	[háptʃe]
powder	**прах** (м)	[prah]
gauze bandage	**бинт** (м)	[bint]
cotton wool	**памук** (м)	[pamúk]
iodine	**йод** (м)	[jot]
plaster	**пластир** (м)	[plastír]
eyedropper	**капкомер** (м)	[kapkomér]
thermometer	**термометър** (м)	[termométər]
syringe	**спринцовка** (ж)	[sprintsófka]
wheelchair	**инвалидна количка** (ж)	[invalídna kolítʃka]
crutches	**патерици** (ж мн)	[páteritsi]
painkiller	**обезболяващо средство** (с)	[obezbolʲávaʃto srétstvo]

laxative	**очистително** (с)	[otʃistítelno]
spirits (ethanol)	**спирт** (м)	[spirt]
medicinal herbs	**билка** (ж)	[bílka]
herbal (~ tea)	**билков**	[bílkov]

77. Smoking. Tobacco products

tobacco	**тютюн** (м)	[tʲutʲún]
cigarette	**цигара** (ж)	[tsigára]
cigar	**пура** (ж)	[púra]
pipe	**лула** (ж)	[lulá]
packet (of cigarettes)	**кутия** (ж)	[kutíja]
matches	**кибрит** (м)	[kibrít]
matchbox	**кибритена кутийка** (ж)	[kibrítena kutíjka]
lighter	**запалка** (ж)	[zapálka]
ashtray	**пепелник** (м)	[pepelník]
cigarette case	**табакера** (ж)	[tabakéra]
cigarette holder	**мундщук** (м)	[mundʃtúk]
filter (cigarette tip)	**филтър** (м)	[fíltər]
to smoke (vi, vt)	**пуша**	[púʃa]
to light a cigarette	**запаля**	[zapálʲa]
smoking	**пушене** (с)	[púʃene]
smoker	**пушач** (м)	[puʃátʃ]
cigarette end	**фас** (м)	[fas]
smoke, fumes	**пушек** (м)	[púʃek]
ash	**пепел** (ж)	[pépel]

HUMAN HABITAT

City

78. City. Life in the city

city, town	**град** (м)	[grat]
capital city	**столица** (ж)	[stólitsa]
village	**село** (с)	[sélo]
city map	**план** (м) **на града**	[plan na gradá]
city centre	**център** (м) **на града**	[tséntər na gradá]
suburb	**предградие** (с)	[predgrádie]
suburban (adj)	**крайградски**	[krajgrátski]
outskirts	**покрайнина** (ж)	[pokrajniná]
environs (suburbs)	**околности** (мн)	[okólnosti]
city block	**квартал** (м)	[kvartál]
residential block (area)	**жилищен квартал** (м)	[ʒíliʃten kvartál]
traffic	**движение** (с)	[dviʒénie]
traffic lights	**светофар** (м)	[svetofár]
public transport	**градски транспорт** (м)	[grátski transpórt]
crossroads	**кръстовище** (с)	[krəstóviʃte]
zebra crossing	**зебра** (ж)	[zébra]
pedestrian subway	**подлез** (м)	[pódlez]
to cross (~ the street)	**пресичам**	[presítʃam]
pedestrian	**пешеходец** (м)	[peʃehódets]
pavement	**тротоар** (м)	[trotoár]
bridge	**мост** (м)	[most]
embankment (river walk)	**кей** (м)	[kej]
fountain	**фонтан** (м)	[fontán]
allée (garden walkway)	**алея** (ж)	[aléja]
park	**парк** (м)	[park]
boulevard	**булевард** (м)	[bulevárt]
square	**площад** (м)	[ploʃtát]
avenue (wide street)	**авеню** (с)	[avenʲú]
street	**улица** (ж)	[úlitsa]
side street	**пресечка** (ж)	[presétʃka]
dead end	**задънена улица** (ж)	[zadənena úlitsa]
house	**къща** (ж)	[kəʃta]
building	**сграда** (ж)	[zgráda]
skyscraper	**небостъргач** (м)	[nebostərgátʃ]
facade	**фасада** (ж)	[fasáda]
roof	**покрив** (м)	[pókriv]

window	**прозорец** (м)	[prozórets]
arch	**арка** (ж)	[árka]
column	**колона** (ж)	[kolóna]
corner	**ъгъл** (м)	[ə́gəl]
shop window	**витрина** (ж)	[vitrína]
signboard (store sign, etc.)	**табела** (ж)	[tabéla]
poster (e.g., playbill)	**афиш** (м)	[afíʃ]
advertising poster	**постер** (м)	[póster]
hoarding	**билборд** (м)	[bilbórt]
rubbish	**боклук** (м)	[boklúk]
rubbish bin	**кошче** (с)	[kóʃʧe]
to litter (vi)	**правя боклук**	[práv[j]a boklúk]
rubbish dump	**сметище** (с)	[smétiʃte]
telephone box	**телефонна будка** (ж)	[telefónna bútka]
lamppost	**стълб** (м) **с фенер**	[stəlp s fenér]
bench (park ~)	**пейка** (ж)	[péjka]
police officer	**полицай** (м)	[politsáj]
police	**полиция** (ж)	[polítsija]
beggar	**сиромах** (м)	[siromáh]
homeless (n)	**бездомник** (м)	[bezdómnik]

79. Urban institutions

shop	**магазин** (м)	[magazín]
chemist, pharmacy	**аптека** (ж)	[aptéka]
optician (spectacles shop)	**оптика** (ж)	[óptika]
shopping centre	**търговски център** (м)	[tərgófski tséntər]
supermarket	**супермаркет** (м)	[supermárket]
bakery	**хлебарница** (ж)	[hlebárnitsa]
baker	**фурнаджия** (ж)	[furnadʒíja]
cake shop	**сладкарница** (ж)	[slatkárnitsa]
grocery shop	**бакалия** (ж)	[bakalíja]
butcher shop	**месарница** (ж)	[mesárnitsa]
greengrocer	**магазин** (м) **за плодове и зеленчуци**	[magazín za plodové i zelenʧútsi]
market	**пазар** (м)	[pazár]
coffee bar	**кафене** (с)	[kafené]
restaurant	**ресторант** (м)	[restoránt]
pub, bar	**бирария** (ж)	[birárija]
pizzeria	**пицария** (ж)	[pitsaríja]
hairdresser	**фризьорски салон** (м)	[friz[j]órski salón]
post office	**поща** (ж)	[póʃta]
dry cleaners	**химическо чистене** (с)	[himíʧesko ʧístene]
photo studio	**фотостудио** (с)	[fotostúdio]
shoe shop	**магазин** (м) **за обувки**	[magazín za obúfki]
bookshop	**книжарница** (ж)	[kniʒárnitsa]

sports shop	**магазин** (м) **за спортни стоки**	[magazín za spórtni stóki]
clothes repair shop	**поправка** (ж) **на дрехи**	[popráfka na dréhi]
formal wear hire	**дрехи** (ж мн) **под наем**	[dréhi pot náem]
video rental shop	**филми** (м мн) **под наем**	[fílmi pot náem]
circus	**цирк** (м)	[tsirk]
zoo	**зоологическа градина** (ж)	[zoologítʃeska gradína]
cinema	**кино** (с)	[kíno]
museum	**музей** (м)	[muzéj]
library	**библиотека** (ж)	[bibliotéka]
theatre	**театър** (м)	[teátər]
opera (opera house)	**опера** (ж)	[ópera]
nightclub	**нощен клуб** (м)	[nóʃten klup]
casino	**казино** (с)	[kazíno]
mosque	**джамия** (ж)	[dʒamíja]
synagogue	**синагога** (ж)	[sinagóga]
cathedral	**катедрала** (ж)	[katedrála]
temple	**храм** (м)	[hram]
church	**църква** (ж)	[tsérkva]
college	**институт** (м)	[institút]
university	**университет** (м)	[universitét]
school	**училище** (с)	[utʃíliʃte]
prefecture	**префектура** (ж)	[prefektúra]
town hall	**кметство** (с)	[kmétstvo]
hotel	**хотел** (м)	[hotél]
bank	**банка** (ж)	[bánka]
embassy	**посолство** (с)	[posólstvo]
travel agency	**туристическа агенция** (ж)	[turistítʃeska agéntsija]
information office	**справки** (м мн)	[spráfki]
currency exchange	**обменно бюро** (с)	[obménno bʲúro]
underground, tube	**метро** (с)	[metró]
hospital	**болница** (ж)	[bólnitsa]
petrol station	**бензиностанция** (ж)	[benzino·stántsija]
car park	**паркинг** (м)	[párking]

80. Signs

signboard (store sign, etc.)	**табела** (ж)	[tabéla]
notice (door sign, etc.)	**надпис** (м)	[nádpis]
poster	**постер** (м)	[póster]
direction sign	**указател** (м)	[ukazátel]
arrow (sign)	**стрелка** (ж)	[strelká]
caution	**предпазване** (с)	[predpázvane]
warning sign	**предупреждение** (с)	[predupreʒdénie]
to warn (vt)	**предупредя**	[predupredʲá]

rest day (weekly ~)	**почивен ден** (м)	[poʧíven dén]
timetable (schedule)	**разписание** (с)	[raspisánie]
opening hours	**работно време** (с)	[rabótno vréme]
WELCOME!	**ДОБРЕ ДОШЛИ!**	[dobré doʃlí]
ENTRANCE	**ВХОД**	[vhot]
WAY OUT	**ИЗХОД**	[íshot]
PUSH	**БУТНИ**	[butní]
PULL	**ДРЪПНИ**	[drəpní]
OPEN	**ОТВОРЕНО**	[otvóreno]
CLOSED	**ЗАТВОРЕНО**	[zatvóreno]
WOMEN	**ЖЕНИ**	[ʒení]
MEN	**МЪЖЕ**	[məʒé]
DISCOUNTS	**НАМАЛЕНИЕ**	[namalénie]
SALE	**РАЗПРОДАЖБА**	[rasprodáʒba]
NEW!	**НОВА СТОКА**	[nóva stóka]
FREE	**БЕЗПЛАТНО**	[besplátno]
ATTENTION!	**ВНИМАНИЕ!**	[vnimánie]
NO VACANCIES	**НЯМА СВОБОДНИ МЕСТА**	[nʲáma svobódni mestá]
RESERVED	**РЕЗЕРВИРАНО**	[rezervírano]
ADMINISTRATION	**АДМИНИСТРАЦИЯ**	[administrátsija]
STAFF ONLY	**ЗАБРАНЕНО ЗА ВЪНШНИ ЛИЦА**	[zabráneno za venʃni lítsa]
BEWARE OF THE DOG!	**ЗЛО КУЧЕ**	[zlo kúʧe]
NO SMOKING	**ПУШЕНЕТО ЗАБРАНЕНО!**	[puʃenéto zabráneno]
DO NOT TOUCH!	**НЕ ПИПАЙ!**	[ne pípaj]
DANGEROUS	**ОПАСНО**	[opásno]
DANGER	**ОПАСНОСТ**	[opásnost]
HIGH VOLTAGE	**ВИСОКО НАПРЕЖЕНИЕ**	[visóko napreʒénie]
NO SWIMMING!	**КЪПАНЕТО ЗАБРАНЕНО**	[kəpaneto zabranéno]
OUT OF ORDER	**НЕ РАБОТИ**	[ne rabóti]
FLAMMABLE	**ОГНЕОПАСНО**	[ogneopásno]
FORBIDDEN	**ЗАБРАНЕНО**	[zabranéno]
NO TRESPASSING!	**МИНАВАНЕТО ЗАБРАНЕНО**	[minávaneto zabranéno]
WET PAINT	**ПАЗИ СЕ ОТ БОЯТА**	[pazi se ot bojáta]

81. Urban transport

bus, coach	**автобус** (м)	[aftobús]
tram	**трамвай** (м)	[tramváj]
trolleybus	**тролей** (м)	[troléj]
route (bus ~)	**маршрут** (м)	[marʃrút]
number (e.g. bus ~)	**номер** (м)	[nómer]
to go by ...	**пътувам с ...**	[pətúvam s]
to get on (~ the bus)	**качвам се в ...**	[káʧvam se v]

to get off ...	**сляза от ...**	[slʲáza ot]
stop (e.g. bus ~)	**спирка** (ж)	[spírka]
next stop	**следваща спирка** (ж)	[slédvaʃta spírka]
terminus	**последна спирка** (ж)	[poslédna spírka]
timetable	**разписание** (с)	[raspisánie]
to wait (vt)	**чакам**	[ʧákam]
ticket	**билет** (м)	[bilét]
fare	**цена** (ж) **на билета**	[tsená na biléta]
cashier (ticket seller)	**касиер** (м)	[kasiér]
ticket inspection	**контрола** (ж)	[kontróla]
ticket inspector	**контрольор** (м)	[kontrolʲór]
to be late (for ...)	**закъснявам**	[zakəsnʲávam]
to miss (~ the train, etc.)	**закъснея за ...**	[zakəsnéja za]
to be in a hurry	**бързам**	[bə́rzam]
taxi, cab	**такси** (с)	[taksí]
taxi driver	**таксиметров шофьор** (м)	[taksimétrof ʃofʲór]
by taxi	**с такси**	[s taksí]
taxi rank	**пиаца** (ж) **на такси**	[piátsa na taksí]
to call a taxi	**извикам такси**	[izvíkam taksí]
to take a taxi	**взема такси**	[vzéma taksí]
traffic	**улично движение** (с)	[úliʧno dviʒénie]
traffic jam	**задръстване** (с)	[zadrə́stvane]
rush hour	**час пик** (м)	[ʧas pík]
to park (vi)	**паркирам се**	[parkíram se]
to park (vt)	**паркирам**	[párkiram]
car park	**паркинг** (м)	[párking]
underground, tube	**метро** (с)	[metró]
station	**станция** (ж)	[stántsija]
to take the tube	**пътувам с метро**	[pətúvam s metró]
train	**влак** (м)	[vlak]
train station	**гара** (ж)	[gára]

82. Sightseeing

monument	**паметник** (м)	[pámetnik]
fortress	**крепост** (ж)	[krépost]
palace	**дворец** (м)	[dvoréts]
castle	**замък** (м)	[záməк]
tower	**кула** (ж)	[kúla]
mausoleum	**мавзолей** (м)	[mavzoléj]
architecture	**архитектура** (ж)	[arhitektúra]
medieval (adj)	**средновековен**	[srednovekóven]
ancient (adj)	**старинен**	[starínen]
national (adj)	**национален**	[natsionálen]
famous (monument, etc.)	**известен**	[izvésten]
tourist	**турист** (м)	[turíst]
guide (person)	**гид** (м)	[git]

excursion, sightseeing tour	**екскурзия** (ж)	[ekskúrzija]
to show (vt)	**показвам**	[pokázvam]
to tell (vt)	**разказвам**	[raskázvam]
to find (vt)	**намеря**	[namérʲa]
to get lost (lose one's way)	**загубя се**	[zagúbʲa se]
map (e.g. underground ~)	**схема** (ж)	[shéma]
map (e.g. city ~)	**план** (м)	[plan]
souvenir, gift	**сувенир** (м)	[suvenír]
gift shop	**сувенирен магазин** (м)	[suveníren magazín]
to take pictures	**снимам**	[snímam]
to have one's picture taken	**снимам се**	[snímam se]

83. Shopping

to buy (purchase)	**купувам**	[kupúvam]
shopping	**покупка** (ж)	[pokúpka]
to go shopping	**пазарувам**	[pazarúvam]
shopping	**пазаруване** (с)	[pazarúvane]
to be open (ab. shop)	**работя**	[rabótʲa]
to be closed	**затваря се**	[zatvárʲa se]
footwear, shoes	**обувки** (ж мн)	[obúfki]
clothes, clothing	**облекло** (с)	[oblekló]
cosmetics	**козметика** (ж)	[kozmétika]
food products	**продукти** (м мн)	[prodúkti]
gift, present	**подарък** (м)	[podárək]
shop assistant (masc.)	**продавач** (м)	[prodaváʧ]
shop assistant (fem.)	**продавачка** (ж)	[prodaváʧka]
cash desk	**каса** (ж)	[kása]
mirror	**огледало** (с)	[ogledálo]
counter (shop ~)	**щанд** (м)	[ʃtant]
fitting room	**пробна** (ж)	[próbna]
to try on	**пробвам**	[próbvam]
to fit (ab. dress, etc.)	**подхождам**	[podhóʒdam]
to fancy (vt)	**харесвам**	[harésvam]
price	**цена** (ж)	[tsená]
price tag	**етикет** (м)	[etikét]
to cost (vt)	**струвам**	[strúvam]
How much?	**Колко?**	[kólko]
discount	**намаление** (с)	[namalénie]
inexpensive (adj)	**нескъп**	[neskəp]
cheap (adj)	**евтин**	[éftin]
expensive (adj)	**скъп**	[skəp]
It's expensive	**Това е скъпо**	[tová e sképo]
hire (n)	**под наем** (м)	[pot náem]
to hire (~ a dinner jacket)	**взимам под наем**	[vzímam pot náem]

credit (trade credit)	**кредит** (м)	[krédit]
on credit (adv)	**на кредит**	[na krédit]

84. Money

money	**пари** (мн)	[parí]
currency exchange	**обмяна** (ж)	[obmʲána]
exchange rate	**курс** (м)	[kurs]
cashpoint	**банкомат** (м)	[bankomát]
coin	**монета** (ж)	[monéta]
dollar	**долар** (м)	[dólar]
euro	**евро** (с)	[évro]
lira	**лира** (ж)	[líra]
Deutschmark	**марка** (ж)	[márka]
franc	**франк** (м)	[frank]
pound sterling	**британска лира** (ж)	[británska líra]
yen	**йена** (ж)	[jéna]
debt	**дълг** (м)	[dəlk]
debtor	**длъжник** (м)	[dləʒník]
to lend (money)	**давам на заем**	[dávam na záem]
to borrow (vi, vt)	**взема на заем**	[vzéma na záem]
bank	**банка** (ж)	[bánka]
account	**сметка** (ж)	[smétka]
to deposit (vt)	**депозирам**	[depozíram]
to deposit into the account	**внеса в сметка**	[vnesá v smétka]
to withdraw (vt)	**тегля от сметката**	[téglʲa ot smétkata]
credit card	**кредитна карта** (ж)	[kréditna kárta]
cash	**налични пари** (мн)	[nalítʃni parí]
cheque	**чек** (м)	[tʃek]
to write a cheque	**подпиша чек**	[potpíʃa tʃek]
chequebook	**чекова книжка** (ж)	[tʃékova kníʃka]
wallet	**портфейл** (м)	[portféjl]
purse	**портмоне** (с)	[portmoné]
safe	**сейф** (м)	[sejf]
heir	**наследник** (м)	[naslédnik]
inheritance	**наследство** (с)	[naslétstvo]
fortune (wealth)	**състояние** (с)	[səstojánie]
lease	**наем** (м)	[náem]
rent (money)	**наем** (м)	[náem]
to rent (sth from sb)	**наемам**	[naémam]
price	**цена** (ж)	[tsená]
cost	**стойност** (ж)	[stójnost]
sum	**сума** (ж)	[súma]
to spend (vt)	**харча**	[hártʃa]
expenses	**разходи** (м мн)	[ráshodi]

to economize (vi, vt)	**пестя**	[pestʲá]
economical	**пестелив**	[pestelíf]
to pay (vi, vt)	**плащам**	[pláʃtam]
payment	**плащане** (c)	[pláʃtane]
change (give the ~)	**ресто** (c)	[résto]
tax	**данък** (м)	[dánək]
fine	**глоба** (ж)	[glóba]
to fine (vt)	**глобявам**	[globʲávam]

85. Post. Postal service

post office	**поща** (ж)	[póʃta]
post (letters, etc.)	**поща** (ж)	[póʃta]
postman	**пощальон** (м)	[poʃtalʲón]
opening hours	**работно време** (c)	[rabótno vréme]
letter	**писмо** (c)	[pismó]
registered letter	**препоръчано писмо** (c)	[preporə́tʃano pismó]
postcard	**картичка** (ж)	[kártitʃka]
telegram	**телеграма** (ж)	[telegráma]
parcel	**колет** (м)	[kolét]
money transfer	**паричен превод** (м)	[parítʃen prévot]
to receive (vt)	**получа**	[polútʃa]
to send (vt)	**изпратя**	[isprátʲa]
sending	**изпращане** (c)	[ispráʃtane]
address	**адрес** (м)	[adrés]
postcode	**пощенски код** (м)	[póʃtenski kot]
sender	**подател** (м)	[podátel]
receiver	**получател** (м)	[polutʃátel]
name (first name)	**име** (c)	[íme]
surname (last name)	**фамилия** (ж)	[famílija]
postage rate	**тарифа** (ж)	[tarífa]
standard (adj)	**обикновен**	[obiknovén]
economical (adj)	**икономичен**	[ikonomítʃen]
weight	**тегло** (c)	[tegló]
to weigh (~ letters)	**претеглям**	[pretéglʲam]
envelope	**плик** (м)	[plik]
postage stamp	**марка** (ж)	[márka]

Dwelling. House. Home

86. House. Dwelling

house	**къща** (ж)	[kǝʃta]
at home (adv)	**вкъщи**	[fkǝʃti]
yard	**двор** (м)	[dvor]
fence (iron ~)	**ограда** (ж)	[ográda]
brick (n)	**тухла** (ж)	[túhla]
brick (as adj)	**тухлен**	[túhlen]
stone (n)	**камък** (м)	[kámǝk]
stone (as adj)	**каменен**	[kámenen]
concrete (n)	**бетон** (м)	[betón]
concrete (as adj)	**бетонен**	[betónen]
new (new-built)	**нов**	[nov]
old (adj)	**стар**	[star]
decrepit (house)	**вехт**	[veht]
modern (adj)	**съвременен**	[sǝvrémenen]
multistorey (adj)	**многоетажен**	[mnogoetáʒen]
tall (~ building)	**висок**	[visók]
floor, storey	**етаж** (м)	[etáʃ]
single-storey (adj)	**едноетажен**	[ednoetáʒen]
ground floor	**долен етаж** (м)	[dólen etáʃ]
top floor	**горен етаж** (м)	[góren etáʃ]
roof	**покрив** (м)	[pókriv]
chimney	**тръба** (ж)	[trǝbá]
roof tiles	**керемида** (ж)	[keremída]
tiled (adj)	**керемиден**	[keremíden]
loft (attic)	**таван** (м)	[taván]
window	**прозорец** (м)	[prozórets]
glass	**стъкло** (с)	[stǝkló]
window ledge	**перваз** (м) **за прозорец**	[pervás za prozórets]
shutters	**капаци** (м мн)	[kapátsi]
wall	**стена** (ж)	[stená]
balcony	**балкон** (м)	[balkón]
downpipe	**улук** (м)	[ulúk]
upstairs (to be ~)	**горе**	[góre]
to go upstairs	**качвам се**	[kátʃvam se]
to come down (the stairs)	**слизам**	[slízam]
to move (to new premises)	**премествам се**	[preméstvam se]

87. House. Entrance. Lift

entrance	**вход** (м)	[vhot]
stairs (stairway)	**стълба** (ж)	[stə́lba]
steps	**стъпала** (с мн)	[stəpála]
banisters	**парапет** (м)	[parapét]
lobby (hotel ~)	**хол** (м)	[hol]
postbox	**пощенска кутия** (ж)	[póʃtenska kutíja]
waste bin	**контейнер** (м) **за отпадъци**	[kontéjner za otpádətsi]
refuse chute	**шахта** (ж) **за боклук**	[ʃáhta za boklúk]
lift	**асансьор** (м)	[asansʲór]
goods lift	**товарен асансьор** (м)	[továren asansʲór]
lift cage	**кабина** (ж)	[kabína]
to take the lift	**возя се в асансьора**	[vózʲa se v asansʲóra]
flat	**апартамент** (м)	[apartamént]
residents (~ of a building)	**живущи** (м мн)	[ʒivúʃti]
neighbour (masc.)	**съсед** (м)	[səsét]
neighbour (fem.)	**съседка** (ж)	[səsétka]
neighbours	**съседи** (м мн)	[səsédi]

88. House. Electricity

electricity	**електричество** (с)	[elektrítʃestvo]
light bulb	**крушка** (ж)	[krúʃka]
switch	**изключвател** (м)	[izklʲutʃvátel]
fuse (plug fuse)	**бушон** (м)	[buʃón]
cable, wire (electric ~)	**кабел** (м)	[kábel]
wiring	**инсталация** (ж)	[instalátsija]
electricity meter	**електромер** (м)	[elektromér]
readings	**показание** (с)	[pokazánie]

89. House. Doors. Locks

door	**врата** (ж)	[vratá]
gate (vehicle ~)	**порта** (ж)	[pórta]
handle, doorknob	**дръжка** (ж)	[drə́ʃka]
to unlock (unbolt)	**отключа**	[otklʲútʃa]
to open (vt)	**отварям**	[otvárʲam]
to close (vt)	**затварям**	[zatvárʲam]
key	**ключ** (м)	[klʲutʃ]
bunch (of keys)	**връзка** (ж)	[vrə́ska]
to creak (door, etc.)	**скърцам**	[skə́rtsam]
creak	**скърцане** (с)	[skə́rtsane]
hinge (door ~)	**панта** (ж)	[pánta]
doormat	**килимче** (с)	[kilímtʃe]
door lock	**брава** (ж)	[bráva]

keyhole	**ключалка** (ж)	[klʲutʃálka]
crossbar (sliding bar)	**резе** (с)	[rezé]
door latch	**резе** (с)	[rezé]
padlock	**катинар** (м)	[katinár]
to ring (~ the door bell)	**звъня**	[zvənʲá]
ringing (sound)	**звънец** (м)	[zvənéts]
doorbell	**звънец** (м)	[zvənéts]
doorbell button	**бутон** (м)	[butón]
knock (at the door)	**чукане** (с)	[tʃúkane]
to knock (vi)	**чукам**	[tʃúkam]
code	**код** (м)	[kot]
combination lock	**брава** (ж) **с код**	[bráva s kot]
intercom	**домофон** (м)	[domofón]
number (on the door)	**номер** (м)	[nómer]
doorplate	**табелка** (ж)	[tabélka]
peephole	**шпионка** (ж)	[ʃpiónka]

90. Country house

village	**село** (с)	[sélo]
vegetable garden	**зеленчукова градина** (ж)	[zelentʃúkova gradína]
fence	**ограда** (ж)	[ográda]
picket fence	**плет** (м)	[plet]
wicket gate	**вратичка** (ж) **на ограда**	[vratítʃka na ográda]
granary	**хамбар** (м)	[hambár]
cellar	**мазе** (с)	[mazé]
shed (garden ~)	**плевня** (ж)	[plévnʲa]
water well	**кладенец** (м)	[kládenets]
stove (wood-fired ~)	**печка** (ж)	[pétʃka]
to stoke the stove	**паля**	[pálʲa]
firewood	**дърва** (мн)	[dərvá]
log (firewood)	**цепеница** (ж)	[tsépenitsa]
veranda	**веранда** (ж)	[veránda]
deck (terrace)	**тераса** (ж)	[terása]
stoop (front steps)	**стъпала** (с мн)	[stəpála]
swing (hanging seat)	**люлка** (ж)	[lʲúlka]

91. Villa. Mansion

country house	**извънградска къща** (ж)	[izvəngrátska kə́ʃta]
country-villa	**вила** (ж)	[víla]
wing (~ of a building)	**крило** (с)	[kriló]
garden	**градина** (ж)	[gradína]
park	**парк** (м)	[park]
conservatory (greenhouse)	**оранжерия** (ж)	[oranʒérija]
to look after (garden, etc.)	**грижа се**	[gríʒa se]

swimming pool	**басейн** (м)	[baséjn]
gym (home gym)	**спортна зала** (ж)	[spórtna zála]
tennis court	**тенис корт** (м)	[ténis kort]
home theater (room)	**кинотеатър** (м)	[kinoteátər]
garage	**гараж** (м)	[garáʒ]
private property	**частна собственост** (ж)	[ʧásna sópstvenost]
private land	**частни владения** (с мн)	[ʧásni vladénija]
warning (caution)	**предупреждение** (с)	[predupreʒdénie]
warning sign	**предупредителен надпис** (м)	[predupredítelen nátpis]
security	**охрана** (ж)	[ohrána]
security guard	**охранител** (м)	[ohranítel]
burglar alarm	**сигнализация** (ж)	[signalizátsija]

92. Castle. Palace

castle	**замък** (м)	[zámək]
palace	**дворец** (м)	[dvoréts]
fortress	**крепост** (ж)	[krépost]
wall (round castle)	**стена** (ж)	[stená]
tower	**кула** (ж)	[kúla]
keep, donjon	**главна кула** (ж)	[glávna kúla]
portcullis	**подемна врата** (ж)	[podémna vratá]
subterranean passage	**подземен проход** (м)	[podzémen próhot]
moat	**ров** (м)	[rov]
chain	**верига** (ж)	[veríga]
arrow loop	**бойница** (ж)	[bojnítsa]
magnificent (adj)	**великолепен**	[velikolépen]
majestic (adj)	**величествен**	[velíʧestven]
impregnable (adj)	**непристъпен**	[nepristəpen]
medieval (adj)	**средновековен**	[srednovekóven]

93. Flat

flat	**апартамент** (м)	[apartamént]
room	**стая** (ж)	[stája]
bedroom	**спалня** (ж)	[spálnʲa]
dining room	**столова** (ж)	[stolová]
living room	**гостна** (ж)	[góstna]
study (home office)	**кабинет** (м)	[kabinét]
entry room	**антре** (с)	[antré]
bathroom	**баня** (ж)	[bánʲa]
water closet	**тоалетна** (ж)	[toalétna]
ceiling	**таван** (м)	[taván]
floor	**под** (м)	[pot]
corner	**ъгъл** (м)	[ə́gəl]

94. Flat. Cleaning

to clean (vi, vt)	**подреждам**	[podréʒdam]
dust	**прах** (м)	[prah]
dusty (adj)	**прашен**	[práʃen]
to dust (vt)	**изтривам прах**	[istrívam prah]
vacuum cleaner	**прахосмукачка** (ж)	[praho·smukátʃka]
to vacuum (vt)	**почиствам с прахосмукачка**	[potʃístvam s praho·smukátʃka]
to sweep (vi, vt)	**мета**	[metá]
sweepings	**боклук** (м)	[boklúk]
order	**ред** (м)	[ret]
disorder, mess	**безпорядък** (м)	[bespor'ádək]
mop	**четка** (ж) **за под**	[tʃétka za pot]
duster	**парцал** (м)	[partsál]
short broom	**метла** (ж)	[metlá]
dustpan	**лопатка** (ж) **за боклук**	[lopátka za boklúk]

95. Furniture. Interior

furniture	**мебели** (мн)	[mébeli]
table	**маса** (ж)	[mása]
chair	**стол** (м)	[stol]
bed	**легло** (с)	[legló]
sofa, settee	**диван** (м)	[diván]
armchair	**фотьойл** (м)	[fot'ójl]
bookcase	**книжен шкаф** (м)	[kníʒen ʃkaf]
shelf	**рафт** (м)	[raft]
wardrobe	**гардероб** (м)	[garderóp]
coat rack (wall-mounted ~)	**закачалка** (ж)	[zakatʃálka]
coat stand	**закачалка** (ж)	[zakatʃálka]
chest of drawers	**скрин** (м)	[skrin]
coffee table	**малка масичка** (ж)	[málka másitʃka]
mirror	**огледало** (с)	[ogledálo]
carpet	**килим** (м)	[kilím]
small carpet	**килимче** (с)	[kilímtʃe]
fireplace	**камина** (ж)	[kamína]
candle	**свещ** (м)	[sveʃt]
candlestick	**свещник** (м)	[svéʃtnik]
drapes	**пердета** (с мн)	[perdéta]
wallpaper	**тапети** (м мн)	[tapéti]
blinds (jalousie)	**щора** (ж)	[ʃtóra]
table lamp	**лампа** (ж) **за маса**	[lámpa za mása]
wall lamp (sconce)	**светилник** (м)	[svetílnik]

standard lamp	**лампион** (м)	[lampión]
chandelier	**полилей** (м)	[poliléj]
leg (of a chair, table)	**крак** (м)	[krak]
armrest	**подлакътник** (м)	[podlákətnik]
back (backrest)	**облегалка** (ж)	[oblegálka]
drawer	**чекмедже** (с)	[ʧekmedʒé]

96. Bedding

bedclothes	**спално бельо** (с)	[spálno belʲó]
pillow	**възглавница** (ж)	[vəzglávnitsa]
pillowslip	**калъфка** (ж)	[kaləfka]
duvet	**одеяло** (с)	[odejálo]
sheet	**чаршаф** (м)	[ʧarʃáf]
bedspread	**завивка** (ж)	[zavífka]

97. Kitchen

kitchen	**кухня** (ж)	[kúhnʲa]
gas	**газ** (м)	[gas]
gas cooker	**газова печка** (ж)	[gázova péʧka]
electric cooker	**електрическа печка** (ж)	[elektríʧeska péʧka]
oven	**фурна** (ж)	[fúrna]
microwave oven	**микровълнова печка** (ж)	[mikrovəlnova pəʧka]
refrigerator	**хладилник** (м)	[hladílnik]
freezer	**фризер** (м)	[frízer]
dishwasher	**съдомиялна машина** (ж)	[sədomijálna maʃína]
mincer	**месомелачка** (ж)	[meso·meláʧka]
juicer	**сокоизстисквачка** (ж)	[soko·isstiskváʧka]
toaster	**тостер** (м)	[tóster]
mixer	**миксер** (м)	[míkser]
coffee machine	**кафеварка** (ж)	[kafevárka]
coffee pot	**кафеник** (м)	[kafeník]
coffee grinder	**кафемелачка** (ж)	[kafe·meláʧka]
kettle	**чайник** (м)	[ʧájnik]
teapot	**чайник** (м)	[ʧájnik]
lid	**капачка** (ж)	[kapáʧka]
tea strainer	**цедка** (ж)	[tsétka]
spoon	**лъжица** (ж)	[ləʒítsa]
teaspoon	**чаена лъжица** (ж)	[ʧáena ləʒítsa]
soup spoon	**супена лъжица** (ж)	[súpena ləʒítsa]
fork	**вилица** (ж)	[vílitsa]
knife	**нож** (м)	[noʒ]
tableware (dishes)	**съдове** (м мн)	[sədove]
plate (dinner ~)	**чиния** (ж)	[ʧiníja]

saucer	**малка чинийка** (ж)	[málka ʧiníjka]
shot glass	**чашка** (ж)	[ʧáʃka]
glass (tumbler)	**чаша** (ж)	[ʧáʃa]
cup	**чаша** (ж)	[ʧáʃa]
sugar bowl	**захарница** (ж)	[zaharnítsa]
salt cellar	**солница** (ж)	[solnítsa]
pepper pot	**пиперница** (ж)	[pipérnitsa]
butter dish	**съд** (м) **за краве масло**	[sət za kráve masló]
stock pot (soup pot)	**тенджера** (ж)	[téndʒera]
frying pan (skillet)	**тиган** (м)	[tigán]
ladle	**черпак** (м)	[ʧerpák]
colander	**гевгир** (м)	[gevgír]
tray (serving ~)	**табла** (ж)	[tábla]
bottle	**бутилка** (ж)	[butílka]
jar (glass)	**буркан** (м)	[burkán]
tin (can)	**тенекия** (ж)	[tenekíja]
bottle opener	**отварачка** (ж)	[otvaráʧka]
tin opener	**отварачка** (ж)	[otvaráʧka]
corkscrew	**тирбушон** (м)	[tirbuʃón]
filter	**филтър** (м)	[fíltər]
to filter (vt)	**филтрирам**	[filtríram]
waste (food ~, etc.)	**боклук** (м)	[boklúk]
waste bin (kitchen ~)	**кофа** (ж) **за боклук**	[kófa za boklúk]

98. Bathroom

bathroom	**баня** (ж)	[bánʲa]
water	**вода** (ж)	[vodá]
tap	**смесител** (м)	[smesítel]
hot water	**топла вода** (ж)	[tópla vodá]
cold water	**студена вода** (ж)	[studéna vodá]
toothpaste	**паста** (ж) **за зъби**	[pásta za zəbi]
to clean one's teeth	**мия си зъбите**	[míja si zəbite]
toothbrush	**четка** (ж) **за зъби**	[ʧətka za zəbi]
to shave (vi)	**бръсна се**	[brəsna se]
shaving foam	**пяна** (ж) **за бръснене**	[pʲána za brəsnene]
razor	**бръснач** (м)	[brəsnáʧ]
to wash (one's hands, etc.)	**мия**	[míja]
to have a bath	**мия се**	[míja se]
shower	**душ** (м)	[duʃ]
to have a shower	**вземам душ**	[vzémam duʃ]
bath	**вана** (ж)	[vána]
toilet (toilet bowl)	**тоалетна чиния** (ж)	[toalétna ʧiníja]
sink (washbasin)	**мивка** (ж)	[mífka]
soap	**сапун** (м)	[sapún]

soap dish	**сапуниерка** (ж)	[sapuniérka]
sponge	**гъба** (ж)	[gə́ba]
shampoo	**шампоан** (м)	[ʃampoán]
towel	**кърпа** (ж)	[kə́rpa]
bathrobe	**хавлиен халат** (м)	[havlíen halát]
laundry (laundering)	**пране** (с)	[prané]
washing machine	**перална машина** (ж)	[perálna maʃína]
to do the laundry	**пера**	[perá]
washing powder	**прах** (м) **за пране**	[prah za prané]

99. Household appliances

TV, telly	**телевизор** (м)	[televízor]
tape recorder	**касетофон** (м)	[kasetofón]
video	**видео** (с)	[vídeo]
radio	**радиоприемник** (м)	[radio·priémnik]
player (CD, MP3, etc.)	**плейър** (м)	[pléər]
video projector	**прожекционен апарат** (м)	[proʒektsiónen aparát]
home cinema	**домашно кино** (с)	[domáʃno kíno]
DVD player	**DVD плейър** (м)	[dividí pléər]
amplifier	**усилвател** (м)	[usilvátel]
video game console	**игрова приставка** (ж)	[igrová pristáfka]
video camera	**видеокамера** (ж)	[video·kámera]
camera (photo)	**фотоапарат** (м)	[fotoaparát]
digital camera	**цифров фотоапарат** (м)	[tsífrov fotoaparát]
vacuum cleaner	**прахосмукачка** (ж)	[praho·smukátʃka]
iron (e.g. steam ~)	**ютия** (ж)	[jutíja]
ironing board	**дъска** (ж) **за гладене**	[dəská za gládene]
telephone	**телефон** (м)	[telefón]
mobile phone	**мобилен телефон** (м)	[mobílen telefón]
typewriter	**пишеща машинка** (ж)	[píʃeʃta maʃínka]
sewing machine	**шевна машина** (ж)	[ʃévna maʃína]
microphone	**микрофон** (м)	[mikrofón]
headphones	**слушалки** (ж мн)	[sluʃálki]
remote control (TV)	**пулт** (м)	[pult]
CD, compact disc	**CD диск** (м)	[sidí disk]
cassette, tape	**касета** (ж)	[kaséta]
vinyl record	**плоча** (ж)	[plótʃa]

100. Repairs. Renovation

renovations	**ремонт** (м)	[remónt]
to renovate (vt)	**правя ремонт**	[právʲa remónt]
to repair, to fix (vt)	**ремонтирам**	[remontíram]
to put in order	**подреждам**	[podréʒdam]

to redo (do again)	**преправям**	[prepráv^jam]
paint	**боя** (ж)	[bojá]
to paint (~ a wall)	**боядисвам**	[bojadísvam]
house painter	**бояджия** (м)	[bojadʒíja]
paintbrush	**четка** (ж)	[ʧétka]
whitewash	**вар** (ж)	[var]
to whitewash (vt)	**варосвам**	[varósvam]
wallpaper	**тапети** (м мн)	[tapéti]
to wallpaper (vt)	**слагам тапети**	[slágam tapéti]
varnish	**лак** (м)	[lak]
to varnish (vt)	**лакирам**	[lakíram]

101. Plumbing

water	**вода** (ж)	[vodá]
hot water	**топла вода** (ж)	[tópla vodá]
cold water	**студена вода** (ж)	[studéna vodá]
tap	**смесител** (м)	[smesítel]
drop (of water)	**капка** (ж)	[kápka]
to drip (vi)	**капя**	[káp^ja]
to leak (ab. pipe)	**тека**	[teká]
leak (pipe ~)	**теч** (ж)	[teʧ]
puddle	**локва** (ж)	[lókva]
pipe	**тръба** (ж)	[trəbá]
valve (e.g., ball ~)	**вентил** (м)	[véntil]
to be clogged up	**запуша се**	[zapúʃa se]
tools	**инструменти** (м мн)	[instruménti]
adjustable spanner	**раздвижен ключ** (м)	[razdvíʒen kl^juʧ]
to unscrew (lid, filter, etc.)	**отвъртам**	[otvə́rtam]
to screw (tighten)	**завъртам**	[zavə́rtam]
to unclog (vt)	**отпушвам**	[otpúʃvam]
plumber	**водопроводчик** (м)	[vodoprovótʧik]
basement	**мазе** (с)	[mazé]
sewerage (system)	**канализация** (ж)	[kanalizátsija]

102. Fire. Conflagration

fire (accident)	**огън** (м)	[ógən]
flame	**пламък** (м)	[plámək]
spark	**искра** (ж)	[iskrá]
smoke (from fire)	**пушек** (м)	[púʃek]
torch (flaming stick)	**факел** (м)	[fákel]
campfire	**клада** (ж)	[kláda]
petrol	**бензин** (м)	[benzín]
paraffin	**газ** (м)	[gas]

flammable (adj)	**горивен**	[goríven]
explosive (adj)	**взривоопасен**	[vzrivoopásen]
NO SMOKING	**ПУШЕНЕТО ЗАБРАНЕНО!**	[puʃenéto zabráneno]
safety	**безопасност** (ж)	[bezopásnost]
danger	**опасност** (ж)	[opásnost]
dangerous (adj)	**опасен**	[opásen]
to catch fire	**запаля се**	[zapálʲa se]
explosion	**експлозия** (ж)	[eksplózija]
to set fire	**подпаля**	[podpálʲa]
arsonist	**подпалвач** (м)	[podpalvátʃ]
arson	**подпалване** (с)	[podpálvane]
to blaze (vi)	**пламтя**	[plamtʲá]
to burn (be on fire)	**горя**	[gorʲá]
to burn down	**изгоря**	[izgorʲá]
firefighter, fireman	**пожарникар** (м)	[poʒarnikár]
fire engine	**пожарна кола** (ж)	[poʒárna kolá]
fire brigade	**пожарен екип** (м)	[poʒáren ekíp]
fire engine ladder	**пожарна стълба** (ж)	[poʒárna stəlba]
fire hose	**маркуч** (м)	[markútʃ]
fire extinguisher	**пожарогасител** (м)	[poʒarogasítel]
helmet	**каска** (ж)	[káska]
siren	**сирена** (ж)	[siréna]
to cry (for help)	**викам**	[víkam]
to call for help	**викам за помощ**	[víkam za pómoʃt]
rescuer	**спасител** (м)	[spasítel]
to rescue (vt)	**спасявам**	[spasʲávam]
to arrive (vi)	**пристигна**	[pristígna]
to extinguish (vt)	**загасявам**	[zagasʲávam]
water	**вода** (ж)	[vodá]
sand	**пясък** (м)	[pʲásək]
ruins (destruction)	**руини** (мн)	[ruiní]
to collapse (building, etc.)	**рухна**	[rúhna]
to fall down (vi)	**срутя се**	[srútʲa se]
to cave in (ceiling, floor)	**съборя се**	[səbórʲa se]
piece of debris	**отломка** (ж)	[otlómka]
ash	**пепел** (ж)	[pépel]
to suffocate (die)	**задуша се**	[zaduʃá se]
to be killed (perish)	**загина**	[zagína]

HUMAN ACTIVITIES

Job. Business. Part 1

103. Office. Working in the office

office (company ~)	**офис** (м)	[ófis]
office (director's ~)	**кабинет** (м)	[kabinét]
reception desk	**рецепция** (ж)	[retséptsija]
secretary	**секретар** (м)	[sekretár]
director	**директор** (м)	[diréktor]
manager	**мениджър** (м)	[ménidʒər]
accountant	**счетоводител** (м)	[stʃetovodítel]
employee	**сътрудник** (м)	[sətrúdnik]
furniture	**мебели** (мн)	[mébeli]
desk	**маса** (ж)	[mása]
desk chair	**фотьойл** (м)	[fotʲójl]
drawer unit	**шкафче** (с)	[ʃkáftʃe]
coat stand	**закачалка** (ж)	[zakatʃálka]
computer	**компютър** (м)	[kompʲútər]
printer	**принтер** (м)	[prínter]
fax machine	**факс** (м)	[faks]
photocopier	**ксерокс** (м)	[kséroks]
paper	**хартия** (ж)	[hartíja]
office supplies	**канцеларски материали** (ж мн)	[kantselárski materiáli]
mouse mat	**подложка** (ж) **за мишка**	[podlóʃka za míʃka]
sheet of paper	**лист** (м)	[list]
catalogue	**каталог** (м)	[katalók]
phone directory	**справочник** (м)	[spravótʃnik]
documentation	**документация** (ж)	[dokumentátsija]
brochure (e.g. 12 pages ~)	**брошура** (ж)	[broʃúra]
leaflet (promotional ~)	**листовка** (ж)	[listófka]
sample	**образец** (м)	[obrazéts]
training meeting	**тренинг** (м)	[tréning]
meeting (of managers)	**съвещание** (с)	[səveʃtánie]
lunch time	**обедна почивка** (ж)	[óbedna potʃífka]
to make a copy	**ксерокопирам**	[kserokopíram]
to make multiple copies	**размножа**	[razmnoʒá]
to receive a fax	**получавам факс**	[polutʃávam faks]
to send a fax	**изпращам факс**	[ispráʃtam faks]
to call (by phone)	**обаждам се**	[obáʒdam se]

to answer (vt)	**отговоря**	[otgovórʲa]
to put through	**свържа**	[svérʒa]
to arrange, to set up	**назначавам**	[naznaʧávam]
to demonstrate (vt)	**демонстрирам**	[demonstríram]
to be absent	**отсъствам**	[otséstvam]
absence	**отсъствие** (с)	[otséstvie]

104. Business processes. Part 1

business	**дело** (с), **бизнес** (м)	[délo], [bíznes]
firm	**фирма** (ж)	[fírma]
company	**компания** (ж)	[kompánija]
corporation	**корпорация** (ж)	[korporátsija]
enterprise	**предприятие** (с)	[predprijátie]
agency	**агенция** (ж)	[agéntsija]
agreement (contract)	**договор** (м)	[dógovor]
contract	**контракт** (м)	[kontrákt]
deal	**сделка** (ж)	[sdélka]
order (to place an ~)	**поръчка** (ж)	[poréʧka]
terms (of the contract)	**условие** (с)	[uslóvie]
wholesale (adv)	**на едро**	[na édro]
wholesale (adj)	**на едро**	[na édro]
wholesale (n)	**продажба** (ж) **на едро**	[prodáʒba na édro]
retail (adj)	**на дребно**	[na drébno]
retail (n)	**продажба** (ж) **на дребно**	[prodáʒba na drébno]
competitor	**конкурент** (м)	[konkurént]
competition	**конкуренция** (ж)	[konkuréntsija]
to compete (vi)	**конкурирам**	[konkuríram]
partner (associate)	**партньор** (м)	[partnʲór]
partnership	**партньорство** (с)	[partnʲórstvo]
crisis	**криза** (ж)	[kríza]
bankruptcy	**фалит** (м)	[falít]
to go bankrupt	**фалирам**	[falíram]
difficulty	**трудност** (ж)	[trúdnost]
problem	**проблем** (м)	[problém]
catastrophe	**катастрофа** (ж)	[katastrófa]
economy	**икономика** (ж)	[ikonómika]
economic (~ growth)	**икономически**	[ikonomíʧeski]
economic recession	**икономически спад** (м)	[ikonomíʧeski spat]
goal (aim)	**цел** (ж)	[tsel]
task	**задача** (ж)	[zadáʧa]
to trade (vi)	**търгувам**	[tərgúvam]
network (distribution ~)	**мрежа** (ж)	[mréʒa]
inventory (stock)	**склад** (м)	[sklat]
range (assortment)	**асортимент** (м)	[asortimént]

leader (leading company)	**лидер** (м)	[líder]
large (~ company)	**голям**	[golʲám]
monopoly	**монопол** (м)	[monopól]
theory	**теория** (ж)	[teórija]
practice	**практика** (ж)	[práktika]
experience (in my ~)	**опит** (м)	[ópit]
trend (tendency)	**тенденция** (ж)	[tendéntsija]
development	**развитие** (с)	[razvítie]

105. Business processes. Part 2

profit (foregone ~)	**изгода** (ж)	[izgóda]
profitable (~ deal)	**изгоден**	[izgóden]
delegation (group)	**делегация** (ж)	[delegátsija]
salary	**работна заплата** (ж)	[rabótna zapláta]
to correct (an error)	**поправям**	[poprávʲam]
business trip	**командировка** (ж)	[komandirófka]
commission	**комисия** (ж)	[komísija]
to control (vt)	**контролирам**	[kontrolíram]
conference	**конференция** (ж)	[konferéntsija]
licence	**лиценз** (м)	[litsénz]
reliable (~ partner)	**надежден**	[nadéʒden]
initiative (undertaking)	**начинание** (с)	[natʃinánie]
norm (standard)	**норма** (ж)	[nórma]
circumstance	**обстоятелство** (с)	[obstojátelstvo]
duty (of an employee)	**задължение** (с)	[zadəlʒénie]
organization (company)	**организация** (ж)	[organizátsija]
organization (process)	**организиране** (с)	[organizíranz]
organized (adj)	**организиран**	[organizíran]
cancellation	**отмяна** (ж)	[otmʲána]
to cancel (call off)	**отменя**	[otmenʲá]
report (official ~)	**отчет** (м)	[ottʃét]
patent	**патент** (м)	[patént]
to patent (obtain patent)	**патентовам**	[patentóvam]
to plan (vt)	**планирам**	[planíram]
bonus (money)	**премия** (ж)	[prémija]
professional (adj)	**професионален**	[profesionálen]
procedure	**процедура** (ж)	[protsedúra]
to examine (contract, etc.)	**разгледам**	[razglédam]
calculation	**изчисляване** (с)	[istʃislʲávane]
reputation	**репутация** (ж)	[reputátsija]
risk	**риск** (м)	[risk]
to manage, to run	**ръководя**	[rəkovódʲa]
information (report)	**сведения** (с мн)	[svédenija]
property	**собственост** (ж)	[sóbstvenost]

union	**съюз** (м)	[səjúz]
life insurance	**застраховка** (ж) **живот**	[zastrahófka ʒivót]
to insure (vt)	**застраховам**	[zastrahóvam]
insurance	**застраховка** (ж)	[zastrahófka]
auction (~ sale)	**търгове** (с)	[térgove]
to notify (inform)	**уведомявам**	[uvedomʲávam]
management (process)	**управление** (с)	[upravlénie]
service (~ industry)	**услуга** (ж)	[uslúga]
forum	**форум** (м)	[fórum]
to function (vi)	**функционирам**	[funktsioníram]
stage (phase)	**етап** (м)	[etáp]
legal (~ services)	**юридически**	[juridítʃeski]
lawyer (legal advisor)	**юрист** (м)	[juríst]

106. Production. Works

plant	**завод** (м)	[zavót]
factory	**фабрика** (ж)	[fábrika]
workshop	**цех** (м)	[tseh]
works, production site	**производство** (с)	[proizvótstvo]
industry (manufacturing)	**промишленост** (ж)	[promíʃlenost]
industrial (adj)	**промишлен**	[promíʃlen]
heavy industry	**тежка промишленост** (ж)	[téʃka promíʃlenost]
light industry	**лека промишленост** (ж)	[léka promíʃlenost]
products	**продукция** (ж)	[prodúktsija]
to produce (vt)	**произвеждам**	[proizvéʒdam]
raw materials	**суровини** (ж мн)	[suroviní]
foreman (construction ~)	**бригадир** (м)	[brigadír]
workers team (crew)	**бригада** (ж)	[brigáda]
worker	**работник** (м)	[rabótnik]
working day	**работен ден** (м)	[rabóten den]
pause (rest break)	**почивка** (ж)	[potʃífka]
meeting	**събрание** (с)	[səbránie]
to discuss (vt)	**обсъждам**	[obsə́ʒdam]
plan	**план** (м)	[plan]
to fulfil the plan	**изпълнявам план**	[ispəlnʲávam plan]
rate of output	**норма** (ж)	[nórma]
quality	**качество** (с)	[kátʃestvo]
control (checking)	**контрола** (ж)	[kontróla]
quality control	**контрол** (м) **за качество**	[kontról za kátʃestvo]
workplace safety	**безопасност** (ж) **на труда**	[bezopásnost na trudá]
discipline	**дисциплина** (ж)	[distsiplína]
violation (of safety rules, etc.)	**нарушение** (с)	[naruʃénie]
to violate (rules)	**нарушавам**	[naruʃávam]
strike	**стачка** (ж)	[státʃka]
striker	**стачник** (м)	[státʃnik]

to be on strike	**стачкувам**	[statʃkúvam]
trade union	**профсъюз** (м)	[profsəjúz]
to invent (machine, etc.)	**изобретявам**	[izobretʲávam]
invention	**изобретение** (с)	[izobreténie]
research	**изследване** (с)	[isslédvane]
to improve (make better)	**подобрявам**	[podobrʲávam]
technology	**технология** (ж)	[tehnológija]
technical drawing	**чертеж** (м)	[tʃertéʒ]
load, cargo	**товар** (м)	[továr]
loader (person)	**хамалин** (м)	[hamálin]
to load (vehicle, etc.)	**натоварвам**	[natovárvam]
loading (process)	**товарене** (с)	[továrene]
to unload (vi, vt)	**разтоварвам**	[raztovárvam]
unloading	**разтоварване** (с)	[raztovárvane]
transport	**транспорт** (м)	[transpórt]
transport company	**транспортна компания** (ж)	[transpórtna kompánija]
to transport (vt)	**транспортирам**	[transportíram]
wagon	**вагон** (м)	[vagón]
tank (e.g., oil ~)	**цистерна** (ж)	[tsistérna]
lorry	**камион** (м)	[kamión]
machine tool	**машина** (ж)	[maʃína]
mechanism	**механизъм** (м)	[mehanízəm]
industrial waste	**отпадъци** (мн)	[otpádətsi]
packing (process)	**опаковане** (ж)	[opakóvane]
to pack (vt)	**опаковам**	[opakóvam]

107. Contract. Agreement

contract	**контракт** (м)	[kontrákt]
agreement	**съглашение** (с)	[səglaʃénie]
addendum	**приложение** (с)	[priloʒénie]
to sign a contract	**сключа договор**	[sklʲútʃa dógovor]
signature	**подпис** (м)	[pótpis]
to sign (vt)	**подпиша**	[potpíʃa]
seal (stamp)	**печат** (м)	[petʃát]
subject of the contract	**предмет** (м) **на договор**	[predmét na dógovor]
clause	**точка** (ж)	[tótʃka]
parties (in contract)	**страни** (ж мн)	[straní]
legal address	**юридически адрес** (м)	[juridítʃeski adrés]
to violate the contract	**наруша договор**	[naruʃá dógovor]
commitment (obligation)	**задължение** (с)	[zadəlʒénie]
responsibility	**отговорност** (с)	[otgovórnost]
force majeure	**форсмажор** (м)	[fors·maʒór]
dispute	**спор** (м)	[spor]
penalties	**глоба** (ж)	[glóba]

108. Import & Export

import	**внос** (м)	[vnos]
importer	**вносител** (м)	[vnosítel]
to import (vt)	**внасям**	[vnás'am]
import (as adj.)	**вносен**	[vnósen]
export (exportation)	**експорт** (м)	[ekspórt]
exporter	**износител** (м)	[iznosítel]
to export (vt)	**изнасям**	[iznás'am]
export (as adj.)	**експортен**	[ekspórten]
goods (merchandise)	**стока** (ж)	[stóka]
consignment, lot	**партида** (ж)	[partída]
weight	**тегло** (с)	[tegló]
volume	**обем** (м)	[obém]
cubic metre	**кубически метър** (м)	[kubítʃeski métər]
manufacturer	**производител** (м)	[proizvodítel]
transport company	**транспортна компания** (ж)	[transpórtna kompánija]
container	**контейнер** (м)	[kontéjner]
border	**граница** (ж)	[gránitsa]
customs	**митница** (ж)	[mítnitsa]
customs duty	**мито** (с)	[mitó]
customs officer	**митничар** (м)	[mitnitʃár]
smuggling	**контрабанда** (ж)	[kontrabánda]
contraband (smuggled goods)	**контрабанда** (ж)	[kontrabánda]

109. Finances

share, stock	**акция** (ж)	[áktsija]
bond (certificate)	**облигация** (ж)	[obligátsija]
promissory note	**полица** (ж)	[pólitsa]
stock exchange	**борса** (ж)	[bórsa]
stock price	**курс** (м) **на акции**	[kurs na áktsii]
to go down (become cheaper)	**поевтинея**	[poeftinéja]
to go up (become more expensive)	**поскъпнея**	[poskəpnéja]
share	**дял** (м)	[d'al]
controlling interest	**контролен пакет** (м)	[kontrólen pakét]
investment	**инвестиции** (ж мн)	[investítsii]
to invest (vt)	**инвестирам**	[investíram]
percent	**лихвен процент** (м)	[líhven protsént]
interest (on investment)	**проценти** (м мн)	[protsénti]
profit	**печалба** (ж)	[petʃálba]

profitable (adj)	**печеливш**	[petʃelívʃ]
tax	**данък** (м)	[dánək]
currency (foreign ~)	**валута** (ж)	[valúta]
national (adj)	**национален**	[natsionálen]
exchange (currency ~)	**обмяна** (ж)	[obmʲána]
accountant	**счетоводител** (м)	[stʃetovodítel]
accounting	**счетоводство** (с)	[stʃetovótstvo]
bankruptcy	**фалит** (м)	[falít]
collapse, ruin	**фалит** (м)	[falít]
ruin	**фалиране** (с)	[falírane]
to be ruined (financially)	**фалирам**	[falíram]
inflation	**инфлация** (ж)	[inflátsija]
devaluation	**девалвация** (ж)	[devalvátsija]
capital	**капитал** (м)	[kapitál]
income	**доход** (м)	[dóhot]
turnover	**оборот** (м)	[oborót]
resources	**ресурси** (мн)	[resúrsi]
monetary resources	**парични средства** (с мн)	[parítʃni srétstva]

110. Marketing

marketing	**маркетинг** (м)	[markéting]
market	**пазар** (м)	[pazár]
market segment	**пазарен сегмент** (м)	[pazáren segmént]
product	**продукт** (м)	[produkt]
goods (merchandise)	**стока** (ж)	[stóka]
trademark	**търговска марка** (ж)	[təгgófska márka]
logotype	**фирмена марка** (ж)	[fírmena márka]
logo	**лого** (с)	[lógo]
demand	**търсене** (с)	[társene]
supply	**предложение** (с)	[predloʒénie]
need	**нужда** (ж)	[núʒda]
consumer	**потребител** (м)	[potrebítel]
analysis	**анализ** (м)	[análiz]
to analyse (vt)	**анализирам**	[analizíram]
positioning	**позициониране** (с)	[pozitsionírane]
to position (vt)	**позиционирам**	[pozitsioníram]
price	**цена** (ж)	[tsená]
pricing policy	**ценова политика** (ж)	[tsenová politíka]
price formation	**ценообразуване** (с)	[tseno·obrazúvane]

111. Advertising

advertising	**реклама** (ж)	[reklámа]
to advertise (vt)	**рекламирам**	[reklamíram]

budget	**бюджет** (м)	[bʲudʒét]
ad, advertisement	**реклама** (ж)	[rekláma]
TV advertising	**телевизионна реклама** (ж)	[televiziónna rekláma]
radio advertising	**радио реклама** (ж)	[rádio rekláma]
outdoor advertising	**външна реклама** (ж)	[vǝnʃna rekláma]
mass medias	**масмедия** (ж)	[masmédija]
periodical (n)	**периодично издание** (с)	[periodítʃno izdánie]
image (public appearance)	**имидж** (м)	[ímidʒ]
slogan	**лозунг** (м)	[lózung]
motto (maxim)	**девиз** (м)	[devíz]
campaign	**кампания** (ж)	[kampánija]
advertising campaign	**рекламна кампания** (ж)	[reklámna kampánija]
target group	**целева аудитория** (ж)	[tselevá auditórija]
business card	**визитка** (ж)	[vizítka]
leaflet (promotional ~)	**листовка** (ж)	[listófka]
brochure (e.g. 12 pages ~)	**брошура** (ж)	[broʃúra]
pamphlet	**диплянка** (ж)	[diplʲánka]
newsletter	**бюлетин** (с)	[bʲuletín]
signboard (store sign, etc.)	**табела** (ж)	[tabéla]
poster	**постер** (м)	[póster]
hoarding	**билборд** (м)	[bilbórt]

112. Banking

bank	**банка** (ж)	[bánka]
branch (of a bank)	**клон** (м)	[klon]
consultant	**консултант** (м)	[konsultánt]
manager (director)	**управител** (м)	[uprávitel]
bank account	**сметка** (ж)	[smétka]
account number	**номер** (м) **на сметка**	[nómer na smétka]
current account	**текуща сметка** (ж)	[tekúʃta smétka]
deposit account	**спестовна сметка** (ж)	[spestóvna smétka]
to open an account	**откривам сметка**	[otkrívam smétka]
to close the account	**закривам сметка**	[zakrívam smétka]
to deposit into the account	**депозирам в сметка**	[depozíram f smétka]
to withdraw (vt)	**тегля от сметката**	[téglʲa ot smétkata]
deposit	**влог** (м)	[vlok]
to make a deposit	**направя влог**	[napràvʲa vlok]
wire transfer	**превод** (м)	[prévot]
to wire, to transfer	**направя превод**	[napràvʲa prévot]
sum	**сума** (ж)	[súma]
How much?	**Колко?**	[kólko]
signature	**подпис** (м)	[pótpis]
to sign (vt)	**подпиша**	[potpíʃa]

credit card	**кредитна карта** (ж)	[kréditna kárta]
code (PIN code)	**код** (м)	[kot]
credit card number	**номер на кредитна карта** (м)	[nómer na kréditna kárta]
cashpoint	**банкомат** (м)	[bankomát]
cheque	**чек** (м)	[ʧek]
to write a cheque	**подпиша чек**	[potpíʃa ʧek]
chequebook	**чекова книжка** (ж)	[ʧékova kníʃka]
loan (bank ~)	**кредит** (м)	[krédit]
to apply for a loan	**кандидатствам за кредит**	[kandidátstvam za krédit]
to get a loan	**взимам кредит**	[vzímam krédit]
to give a loan	**предоставям кредит**	[predostávʲam krédit]
guarantee	**гаранция** (ж)	[garántsija]

113. Telephone. Phone conversation

telephone	**телефон** (м)	[telefón]
mobile phone	**мобилен телефон** (м)	[mobílen telefón]
answerphone	**телефонен секретар** (м)	[telefónen sekretár]
to call (by phone)	**обаждам се**	[obáʒdam se]
call, ring	**обаждане** (с)	[obáʒdane]
to dial a number	**набирам номер**	[nabíram nómer]
Hello!	**Ало!**	[álo]
to ask (vt)	**питам**	[pítam]
to answer (vi, vt)	**отговарям**	[otgovárʲam]
to hear (vt)	**чувам**	[ʧúvam]
well (adv)	**добре**	[dobré]
not well (adv)	**лошо**	[lóʃo]
noises (interference)	**шумове** (м мн)	[ʃúmove]
receiver	**слушалка** (ж)	[sluʃálka]
to pick up (~ the phone)	**вдигам слушалката**	[vdígam sluʃálkata]
to hang up (~ the phone)	**затварям телефона**	[zatvárʲam telefóna]
busy (engaged)	**заета**	[zaéta]
to ring (ab. phone)	**звъня**	[zvənʲá]
telephone book	**телефонен справочник** (м)	[telefónen spravóʧnik]
local (adj)	**селищен**	[séliʃten]
local call	**селищен разговор** (м)	[séliʃten rázgovor]
trunk (e.g. ~ call)	**междуградски**	[meʒdugrátski]
trunk call	**междуградски разговор** (м)	[meʒdugrátski rázgovor]
international (adj)	**международен**	[meʒdunaróden]
international call	**международен разговор** (м)	[meʒdunaróden rázgovor]

114. Mobile telephone

mobile phone	**мобилен телефон** (м)	[mobílen telefón]
display	**дисплей** (м)	[dispIéj]
button	**бутон** (м)	[butón]
SIM card	**SIM-карта** (ж)	[sim-kárta]
battery	**батерия** (ж)	[batérija]
to be flat (battery)	**изтощавам**	[iztoʃtávam]
charger	**зареждащо устройство** (с)	[zaréʒdaʃto ustrójstvo]
menu	**меню** (с)	[men'ú]
settings	**настройки** (ж мн)	[nastrójki]
tune (melody)	**мелодия** (ж)	[melódija]
to select (vt)	**избера**	[izberá]
calculator	**калкулатор** (м)	[kalkulátor]
voice mail	**телефонен секретар** (м)	[telefónen sekretár]
alarm clock	**будилник** (м)	[budílnik]
contacts	**телефонен справочник** (м)	[telefónen spravótʃnik]
SMS (text message)	**SMS съобщение** (с)	[esemés səobʃténie]
subscriber	**абонат** (м)	[abonát]

115. Stationery

ballpoint pen	**химикалка** (ж)	[himikálka]
fountain pen	**перодръжка** (ж)	[perodrə́ʒka]
pencil	**молив** (м)	[móliv]
highlighter	**маркер** (м)	[márker]
felt-tip pen	**флумастер** (м)	[flumáster]
notepad	**тефтер** (м)	[teftér]
diary	**ежедневник** (м)	[eʒednévnik]
ruler	**линийка** (ж)	[línijka]
calculator	**калкулатор** (м)	[kalkulátor]
rubber	**гума** (ж)	[gúma]
drawing pin	**кабърче** (с)	[kábərtʃe]
paper clip	**кламер** (м)	[klámer]
glue	**лепило** (с)	[lepílo]
stapler	**телбод** (м)	[telbót]
hole punch	**перфоратор** (м)	[perforátor]
pencil sharpener	**острилка** (ж)	[ostrílka]

116. Various kinds of documents

account (report)	**отчет** (м)	[ottʃét]
agreement	**съглашение** (с)	[səglaʃénie]

application form	**заявка** (ж)	[zajáfka]
authentic (adj)	**оригинален**	[originálen]
badge (identity tag)	**бадж** (м)	[badʒ]
business card	**визитка** (ж)	[vizítka]
certificate (~ of quality)	**сертификат** (м)	[sertifikát]
cheque (e.g. draw a ~)	**чек** (м)	[ʧek]
bill (in restaurant)	**сметка** (ж)	[smétka]
constitution	**конституция** (ж)	[konstitútsija]
contract (agreement)	**договор** (м)	[dógovor]
copy	**копие** (с)	[kópie]
copy (of a contract, etc.)	**екземпляр** (м)	[ekzempl^jár]
customs declaration	**декларация** (ж)	[deklarátsija]
document	**документ** (м)	[dokumént]
driving licence	**шофьорска книжка** (ж)	[ʃof^jórska kníʃka]
addendum	**приложение** (с)	[priloʒénie]
form	**анкета** (ж)	[ankéta]
ID card (e.g., warrant card)	**удостоверение** (с)	[udostoverénie]
inquiry (request)	**запитване** (с)	[zapítvane]
invitation card	**покана** (ж)	[pokána]
invoice	**сметка** (ж)	[smétka]
law	**закон** (м)	[zakón]
letter (mail)	**писмо** (с)	[pismó]
letterhead	**бланка** (ж)	[blánka]
list (of names, etc.)	**списък** (м)	[spísək]
manuscript	**ръкопис** (м)	[rəkopís]
newsletter	**бюлетина** (ж)	[b^juletína]
note (short letter)	**записка** (ж)	[zápiska]
pass (for worker, visitor)	**пропуск** (м)	[própusk]
passport	**паспорт** (м)	[paspórt]
permit	**разрешение** (с)	[razreʃénie]
curriculum vitae, CV	**резюме** (с)	[rez^jumé]
debt note, IOU	**разписка** (ж)	[ráspiska]
receipt (for purchase)	**квитанция** (ж)	[kvitántsija]
till receipt	**бележка** (ж)	[beléʃka]
report (mil.)	**рапорт** (м)	[ráport]
to show (ID, etc.)	**предявявам**	[pred^jav^jávam]
to sign (vt)	**подпиша**	[potpíʃa]
signature	**подпис** (м)	[pótpis]
seal (stamp)	**печат** (м)	[peʧát]
text	**текст** (м)	[tekst]
ticket (for entry)	**билет** (м)	[bilét]
to cross out	**задраскам**	[zadráskam]
to fill in (~ a form)	**попълня**	[popéln^ja]
waybill (shipping invoice)	**фактура** (ж)	[faktúra]
will (testament)	**завещание** (с)	[zaveʃtánie]

117. Kinds of business

accounting services — **счетоводни услуги** (ж мн) [stʃetovódni uslúgi]
advertising — **реклама** (ж) [reklláma]
advertising agency — **рекламна агенция** (ж) [reklámna agéntsija]
air-conditioners — **климатици** (м мн) [klimatítsi]
airline — **авиокомпания** (ж) [aviokompánija]

alcoholic beverages — **алкохолни напитки** (ж мн) [alkohólni napítki]
antiques (antique dealers) — **антиквариат** (м) [antikvariát]
art gallery (contemporary ~) — **галерия** (ж) [galérija]
audit services — **одиторски услуги** (ж мн) [odítorski uslúgi]

banking industry — **банков бизнес** (м) [bánkov bíznes]
beauty salon — **козметичен салон** (м) [kozmetítʃen salón]
bookshop — **книжарница** (ж) [kniʒárnitsa]
brewery — **пивоварна** (ж) [pivovárna]
business centre — **бизнес-център** (м) [bíznes-tséntər]
business school — **бизнес-училище** (с) [bíznes-utʃíliʃte]

casino — **казино** (с) [kazíno]
chemist, pharmacy — **аптека** (ж) [aptéka]
cinema — **кинотеатър** (м) [kinoteátər]
construction — **строителство** (с) [stroítelstvo]
consulting — **консултиране** (с) [konsultírane]

dental clinic — **стоматология** (ж) [stomatológija]
design — **дизайн** (м) [dizájn]
dry cleaners — **химическо чистене** (с) [himítʃesko tʃístene]

employment agency — **агенция** (ж) **за подбор на персонал** [agéntsija za podbór na personál]

financial services — **финансови услуги** (ж мн) [finánsovi uslúgi]
food products — **хранителни стоки** (ж мн) [hranítelni stóki]
furniture (e.g. house ~) — **мебели** (мн) [mébeli]
clothing, garment — **облекло** (с) [oblekló]
hotel — **хотел** (м) [hotél]

ice-cream — **сладолед** (м) [sladolét]
industry (manufacturing) — **промишленост** (ж) [promíʃlenost]
insurance — **застраховане** (с) [zastrahóvane]
Internet — **интернет** (м) [internét]
investments (finance) — **инвестиции** (ж мн) [investítsii]
jeweller — **златар** (м) [zlatár]
jewellery — **златарски изделия** (с мн) [zlatárski izdélija]

laundry (shop) — **пералня** (ж) [perálnʲa]
legal adviser — **юридически услуги** (ж мн) [juridítʃeski uslúgi]
light industry — **лека промишленост** (ж) [léka promíʃlenost]
magazine — **списание** (с) [spisánie]
mail order selling — **каталожна търговия** (ж) [katalóʒna tərgovíja]
medicine — **медицина** (ж) [meditsína]
museum — **музей** (м) [muzéj]
news agency — **информационна агенция** (ж) [informatsiónna agéntsija]

newspaper	**вестник** (м)	[vésnik]
nightclub	**нощен клуб** (м)	[nóʃten klup]
oil (petroleum)	**нефт** (м)	[neft]
courier services	**куриерска служба** (ж)	[kuriérska slúʒba]
pharmaceutics	**фармацевтика** (ж)	[farmatséftika]
printing (industry)	**полиграфия** (ж)	[poligrafíja]
pub	**бар** (м)	[bar]
publishing house	**издателство** (с)	[izdátelstvo]
radio (~ station)	**радио** (с)	[rádio]
real estate	**недвижими имоти** (мн)	[nedvíʒimi imóti]
restaurant	**ресторант** (м)	[restoránt]
security company	**охранителна агенция** (ж)	[ohranítelna agéntsija]
shop	**магазин** (м)	[magazín]
sport	**спорт** (м)	[sport]
stock exchange	**борса** (ж)	[bórsa]
supermarket	**супермаркет** (м)	[supermárket]
swimming pool (public ~)	**басейн** (м)	[baséjn]
tailor shop	**ателие** (с)	[atelié]
television	**телевизия** (ж)	[televízija]
theatre	**театър** (м)	[teátər]
trade (commerce)	**търговия** (ж)	[tərgovíja]
transport companies	**превоз** (м)	[prévos]
travel	**туризъм** (м)	[turízəm]
undertakers	**погребални услуги** (мн)	[pogrebálni uslúgi]
veterinary surgeon	**ветеринар** (м)	[veterinár]
warehouse	**склад** (м)	[sklat]
waste collection	**извозване** (с) **на боклук**	[izvózvane na boklúk]

Job. Business. Part 2

118. Show. Exhibition

exhibition, show	**изложба** (ж)	[izlóʒba]
trade show	**търговска изложба** (ж)	[tərgófska izlóʒba]
participation	**участие** (с)	[uʧástie]
to participate (vi)	**участвам**	[uʧástvam]
participant (exhibitor)	**участник** (м)	[uʧásnik]
director	**директор** (м)	[diréktor]
organizers' office	**дирекция** (ж)	[diréktsija]
organizer	**организатор** (м)	[organizátor]
to organize (vt)	**организирам**	[organizíram]
participation form	**заявка** (ж) **за участие**	[zajáfka za uʧástie]
to fill in (vt)	**попълня**	[popəlnʲa]
details	**детайли** (м мн)	[detájli]
information	**информация** (ж)	[informátsija]
price (cost, rate)	**цена** (ж)	[tsená]
including	**включително**	[fklʲuʧítelno]
to include (vt)	**включвам**	[fklʲúʧvam]
to pay (vi, vt)	**плащам**	[pláʃtam]
registration fee	**регистрационна такса** (ж)	[registratsiónna táksa]
entrance	**вход** (м)	[vhot]
pavilion, hall	**павилион** (м)	[pavilión]
to register (vt)	**регистрирам**	[registríram]
badge (identity tag)	**бадж** (м)	[badʒ]
stand	**щанд** (м)	[ʃtant]
to reserve, to book	**резервирам**	[rezervíram]
display case	**витрина** (ж)	[vitrína]
spotlight	**светилник** (м)	[svetílnik]
design	**дизайн** (м)	[dizájn]
to place (put, set)	**нареждам**	[naréʒdam]
distributor	**дистрибутор** (м)	[distribútor]
supplier	**доставчик** (м)	[dostávʧik]
country	**страна** (ж)	[straná]
foreign (adj)	**чуждестранен**	[ʧuʒdestránen]
product	**продукт** (м)	[prodúkt]
association	**асоциация** (ж)	[asotsiátsija]
conference hall	**конферентна зала** (ж)	[konferéntna zála]
congress	**конгрес** (м)	[kongrés]

contest (competition)	**конкурс** (м)	[konkúrs]
visitor (attendee)	**посетител** (м)	[posetítel]
to visit (attend)	**посещавам**	[poseʃtávam]
customer	**клиент** (м)	[kliént]

119. Mass Media

newspaper	**вестник** (м)	[vésnik]
magazine	**списание** (с)	[spisánie]
press (printed media)	**преса** (ж)	[présa]
radio	**радио** (с)	[rádio]
radio station	**радиостанция** (ж)	[radiostántsija]
television	**телевизия** (ж)	[televízija]
presenter, host	**водещ** (м)	[vódeʃt]
newsreader	**диктор** (м)	[díktor]
commentator	**коментатор** (м)	[komentátor]
journalist	**журналист** (м)	[ʒurnalíst]
correspondent (reporter)	**кореспондент** (м)	[korespondént]
press photographer	**фотокореспондент** (м)	[foto·korespondént]
reporter	**репортер** (м)	[reportér]
editor	**редактор** (м)	[redáktor]
editor-in-chief	**главен редактор** (м)	[gláven redáktor]
to subscribe (to ...)	**абонирам се**	[aboníram se]
subscription	**абониране** (с)	[abonírane]
subscriber	**абонат** (м)	[abonát]
to read (vi, vt)	**чета**	[tʃeta]
reader	**читател** (м)	[tʃitátel]
circulation (of a newspaper)	**тираж** (м)	[tiráʒ]
monthly (adj)	**месечен**	[mésetʃen]
weekly (adj)	**седмичен**	[sédmitʃen]
issue (edition)	**брой** (м)	[broj]
new (~ issue)	**последен**	[posléden]
headline	**заглавие** (с)	[zaglávie]
short article	**кратка статия** (ж)	[krátka státija]
column (regular article)	**рубрика** (ж)	[rúbrika]
article	**статия** (ж)	[státija]
page	**страница** (ж)	[stránitsa]
reportage, report	**репортаж** (м)	[reportáʒ]
event (happening)	**събитие** (с)	[səbítie]
sensation (news)	**сензация** (ж)	[senzátsija]
scandal	**скандал** (м)	[skandál]
scandalous (adj)	**скандален**	[skandálen]
great (~ scandal)	**голям (скандал)**	[golʲám skandál]
programme (e.g. cooking ~)	**предаване** (с)	[predávane]
interview	**интервю** (с)	[intervʲú]
live broadcast	**пряко предаване** (с)	[prʲáko predávane]
channel	**канал** (м)	[kanál]

120. Agriculture

agriculture	**селско стопанство** (с)	[sélsko stopánstvo]
peasant (masc.)	**селянин** (м)	[sél^janin]
peasant (fem.)	**селянка** (ж)	[sél^janka]
farmer	**фермер** (м)	[férmer]
tractor	**трактор** (м)	[tráktor]
combine, harvester	**комбайн** (м)	[kombájn]
plough	**плуг** (м)	[pluk]
to plough (vi, vt)	**ора**	[orá]
ploughland	**разорана нива** (ж)	[razorána níva]
furrow (in field)	**бразда** (ж)	[brazdá]
to sow (vi, vt)	**сея**	[séja]
seeder	**сеялка** (ж)	[sejálka]
sowing (process)	**сеитба** (ж)	[seídba]
scythe	**коса** (ж)	[kosá]
to mow, to scythe	**кося**	[kos^já]
spade (tool)	**лопата** (ж)	[lopáta]
to till (vt)	**копая**	[kopája]
hoe	**мотика** (ж)	[motíka]
to hoe, to weed	**плевя**	[plev^já]
weed (plant)	**плевел** (м)	[plével]
watering can	**лейка** (ж)	[léjka]
to water (plants)	**поливам**	[polívam]
watering (act)	**поливане** (с)	[polívane]
pitchfork	**вила** (ж)	[víla]
rake	**гребло** (с)	[grebló]
fertiliser	**тор** (м)	[tor]
to fertilise (vt)	**наторявам**	[nator^jávam]
manure (fertiliser)	**оборски тор** (м)	[obórski tor]
field	**поле** (с)	[polé]
meadow	**ливада** (ж)	[liváda]
vegetable garden	**зеленчукова градина** (ж)	[zelentʃúkova gradína]
orchard (e.g. apple ~)	**градина** (ж)	[gradína]
to graze (vt)	**паса**	[pasá]
herdsman	**пастир** (м)	[pastír]
pasture	**пасище** (с)	[pásiʃte]
cattle breeding	**животновъдство** (с)	[ʒivotnovátstvo]
sheep farming	**овцевъдство** (с)	[ovtsevátstvo]
plantation	**плантация** (ж)	[plantátsija]
row (garden bed ~s)	**леха** (ж)	[lehá]
hothouse	**парник** (м)	[párnik]

drought (lack of rain)	**суша** (ж)	[súʃa]
dry (~ summer)	**сушав**	[súʃav]
cereal crops	**зърнени култури** (мн)	[zə́rneni kultúri]
to harvest, to gather	**събирам**	[səbíram]
miller (person)	**воденичар** (с)	[vodenitʃár]
mill (e.g. gristmill)	**воденица** (ж)	[vodenítsa]
to grind (grain)	**меля зърно**	[mélʲa zə́rno]
flour	**брашно** (с)	[braʃnó]
straw	**слама** (ж)	[sláma]

121. Building. Building process

building site	**строеж** (м)	[stroéʃ]
to build (vt)	**строя**	[strojá]
building worker	**строител** (м)	[stroítel]
project	**проект** (м)	[proékt]
architect	**архитект** (м)	[arhitékt]
worker	**работник** (м)	[rabótnik]
foundations (of a building)	**фундамент** (м)	[fundamént]
roof	**покрив** (м)	[pókriv]
foundation pile	**пилот** (м)	[pilót]
wall	**стена** (ж)	[stená]
reinforcing bars	**арматура** (ж)	[armatúra]
scaffolding	**скеле** (с)	[skéle]
concrete	**бетон** (м)	[betón]
granite	**гранит** (м)	[granít]
stone	**камък** (м)	[kámək]
brick	**тухла** (ж)	[túhla]
sand	**пясък** (м)	[pʲásək]
cement	**цимент** (м)	[tsimént]
plaster (for walls)	**мазилка** (ж)	[mazílka]
to plaster (vt)	**слагам мазилка**	[slágam mazílka]
paint	**боя** (ж)	[bojá]
to paint (~ a wall)	**боядисвам**	[bojadísvam]
barrel	**бъчва** (ж)	[bə́tʃva]
crane	**кран** (м)	[kran]
to lift, to hoist (vt)	**вдигам**	[vdígam]
to lower (vt)	**спускам**	[spúskam]
bulldozer	**булдозер** (м)	[buldózer]
excavator	**екскаватор** (м)	[ekskavátor]
scoop, bucket	**кофа** (ж)	[kófa]
to dig (excavate)	**копая**	[kopája]
hard hat	**каска** (ж)	[káska]

122. Science. Research. Scientists

science	**наука** (ж)	[naúka]
scientific (adj)	**научен**	[naútʃen]
scientist	**учен** (м)	[útʃen]
theory	**теория** (ж)	[teórija]
axiom	**аксиома** (ж)	[aksióma]
analysis	**анализ** (м)	[análiz]
to analyse (vt)	**анализирам**	[analizíram]
argument (strong ~)	**аргумент** (м)	[argumént]
substance (matter)	**вещество** (с)	[veʃtestvó]
hypothesis	**хипотеза** (ж)	[hipotéza]
dilemma	**дилема** (ж)	[diléma]
dissertation	**дисертация** (ж)	[disertátsija]
dogma	**догма** (ж)	[dógma]
doctrine	**доктрина** (ж)	[doktrína]
research	**изследване** (с)	[isslédvane]
to research (vt)	**изследвам**	[isslédvam]
tests (laboratory ~)	**контрола** (ж)	[kontróla]
laboratory	**лаборатория** (ж)	[laboratórija]
method	**метод** (м)	[métot]
molecule	**молекула** (ж)	[molekúla]
monitoring	**мониторинг** (м)	[monitóring]
discovery (act, event)	**откритие** (с)	[otkrítie]
postulate	**постулат** (м)	[postulát]
principle	**принцип** (м)	[príntsip]
forecast	**прогноза** (ж)	[prognóza]
to forecast (vt)	**прогнозирам**	[prognozíram]
synthesis	**синтеза** (ж)	[sintéza]
trend (tendency)	**тенденция** (ж)	[tendéntsija]
theorem	**теорема** (ж)	[teoréma]
teachings	**учение** (с)	[utʃénie]
fact	**факт** (м)	[fakt]
expedition	**експедиция** (ж)	[ekspedítsija]
experiment	**експеримент** (м)	[eksperimént]
academician	**академик** (м)	[akademík]
bachelor (e.g. ~ of Arts)	**бакалавър** (м)	[bakalávər]
doctor (PhD)	**доктор** (м)	[dóktor]
Associate Professor	**доцент** (м)	[dotsént]
Master (e.g. ~ of Arts)	**магистър** (м)	[magístər]
professor	**професор** (м)	[profésor]

Professions and occupations

123. Job search. Dismissal

job	**работа** (ж)	[rábota]
staff (work force)	**щат** (м)	[ʃtat]
career	**кариера** (ж)	[kariéra]
prospects (chances)	**перспектива** (ж)	[perspektíva]
skills (mastery)	**майсторство** (с)	[májstorstvo]
selection (screening)	**подбиране** (с)	[podbírane]
employment agency	**агенция** (ж) **за подбор на персонал**	[agéntsija za podbór na personál]
curriculum vitae, CV	**резюме** (с)	[rezʲumé]
job interview	**интервю** (с)	[intervʲú]
vacancy	**вакантно място** (с)	[vakántno mʲásto]
salary, pay	**работна заплата** (ж)	[rabótna zapláta]
pay, compensation	**плащане** (с)	[pláʃtane]
position (job)	**длъжност** (ж)	[dléʒnost]
duty (of an employee)	**задължение** (с)	[zadəlʒénie]
range of duties	**кръг** (м)	[krək]
busy (I'm ~)	**зает**	[zaét]
to fire (dismiss)	**уволня**	[uvolnʲá]
dismissal	**уволнение** (с)	[uvolnénie]
unemployment	**безработица** (ж)	[bezrabótitsa]
unemployed (n)	**безработен човек** (м)	[bezrabóten tʃovék]
retirement	**пенсия** (ж)	[pénsija]
to retire (from job)	**пенсионирам се**	[pensioníram se]

124. Business people

director	**директор** (м)	[diréktor]
manager (director)	**управител** (м)	[uprávitel]
boss	**ръководител** (м)	[rəkovodítel]
superior	**началник** (м)	[natʃálnik]
superiors	**началство** (с)	[natʃálstvo]
president	**президент** (м)	[prezidént]
chairman	**председател** (м)	[pretsedátel]
deputy (substitute)	**заместник** (м)	[zamésnik]
assistant	**помощник** (м)	[pomóʃtnik]
secretary	**секретар** (м)	[sekretár]

personal assistant	**личен секретар** (м)	[lítʃen sekretár]
businessman	**бизнесмен** (м)	[biznesmén]
entrepreneur	**предприемач** (м)	[predpriemátʃ]
founder	**основател** (м)	[osnovátel]
to found (vt)	**основа**	[osnová]
founding member	**учредител** (м)	[utʃredítel]
partner	**партньор** (м)	[partnʲór]
shareholder	**акционер** (м)	[aktsionér]
millionaire	**милионер** (м)	[milionér]
billionaire	**милиардер** (м)	[miliardér]
owner, proprietor	**собственик** (м)	[sóbstvenik]
landowner	**земевладелец** (м)	[zemevladélets]
client	**клиент** (м)	[kliént]
regular client	**постоянен клиент** (м)	[postojánen kliént]
buyer (customer)	**купувач** (м)	[kupuvátʃ]
visitor	**посетител** (м)	[posetítel]
professional (n)	**професионалист** (м)	[profesionalíst]
expert	**експерт** (м)	[ekspért]
specialist	**специалист** (м)	[spetsialíst]
banker	**банкер** (м)	[bankér]
broker	**брокер** (м)	[bróker]
cashier	**касиер** (м)	[kasiér]
accountant	**счетоводител** (м)	[stʃetovodítel]
security guard	**охранител** (м)	[ohranítel]
investor	**инвеститор** (м)	[investítor]
debtor	**длъжник** (м)	[dləʒník]
creditor	**кредитор** (м)	[kredítor]
borrower	**заемател** (м)	[zaemátel]
importer	**вносител** (м)	[vnosítel]
exporter	**износител** (м)	[iznosítel]
manufacturer	**производител** (м)	[proizvodítel]
distributor	**дистрибутор** (м)	[distribútor]
middleman	**посредник** (м)	[posrédnik]
consultant	**консултант** (м)	[konsultánt]
sales representative	**представител** (м)	[pretstávitel]
agent	**агент** (м)	[agént]
insurance agent	**застрахователен агент** (м)	[zastrahovátelen agent]

125. Service professions

cook	**готвач** (м)	[gotvátʃ]
chef (kitchen chef)	**главен готвач** (м)	[gláven gotvátʃ]
baker	**фурнаджия** (ж)	[furnadʒíja]
barman	**барман** (м)	[bárman]

waiter	**сервитьор** (м)	[servit'ór]
waitress	**сервитьорка** (ж)	[servit'órka]
lawyer, barrister	**адвокат** (м)	[advokát]
lawyer (legal expert)	**юрист** (м)	[juríst]
notary public	**нотариус** (м)	[notárius]
electrician	**монтьор** (м)	[mont'ór]
plumber	**водопроводчик** (м)	[vodoprovóttʃik]
carpenter	**дърводелец** (м)	[dərvodélets]
masseur	**масажист** (м)	[masaʒíst]
masseuse	**масажистка** (ж)	[masaʒístka]
doctor	**лекар** (м)	[lékar]
taxi driver	**таксиметров шофьор** (м)	[taksimétrof ʃof'ór]
driver	**шофьор** (м)	[ʃof'ór]
delivery man	**куриер** (м)	[kuriér]
chambermaid	**камериерка** (ж)	[kameriérka]
security guard	**охранител** (м)	[ohranítel]
flight attendant (fem.)	**стюардеса** (ж)	[st'uardésa]
schoolteacher	**учител** (м)	[utʃítel]
librarian	**библиотекар** (м)	[bibliotekár]
translator	**преводач** (м)	[prevodátʃ]
interpreter	**преводач** (м)	[prevodátʃ]
guide	**гид** (м)	[git]
hairdresser	**фризьор** (м)	[friz'ór]
postman	**пощальон** (м)	[poʃtal'ón]
salesman (store staff)	**продавач** (м)	[prodavátʃ]
gardener	**градинар** (м)	[gradinár]
domestic servant	**слуга** (м)	[slugá]
maid (female servant)	**слугиня** (ж)	[slugín'a]
cleaner (cleaning lady)	**чистачка** (ж)	[tʃistátʃka]

126 Military professions and ranks

private	**редник** (м)	[rédnik]
sergeant	**сержант** (м)	[serʒánt]
lieutenant	**лейтенант** (м)	[lejtenánt]
captain	**капитан** (м)	[kapitán]
major	**майор** (м)	[majór]
colonel	**полковник** (м)	[polkóvnik]
general	**генерал** (м)	[generál]
marshal	**маршал** (м)	[márʃal]
admiral	**адмирал** (м)	[admirál]
military (n)	**военен** (м)	[voénen]
soldier	**войник** (м)	[vojník]
officer	**офицер** (м)	[ofitsér]

commander	**командир** (м)	[komandír]
border guard	**митничар** (м)	[mitnitʃár]
radio operator	**радист** (м)	[radíst]
scout (searcher)	**разузнавач** (м)	[razuznavátʃ]
pioneer (sapper)	**сапьор** (м)	[sapʲór]
marksman	**стрелец** (м)	[streléts]
navigator	**щурман** (м)	[ʃtúrman]

127. Officials. Priests

king	**крал** (м)	[kral]
queen	**кралица** (ж)	[kralítsa]
prince	**принц** (м)	[prints]
princess	**принцеса** (ж)	[printsésa]
czar	**цар** (м)	[tsar]
czarina	**царица** (ж)	[tsarítsa]
president	**президент** (м)	[prezidént]
Secretary (minister)	**министър** (м)	[minístər]
prime minister	**министър-председател** (м)	[minístər-pretsedátel]
senator	**сенатор** (м)	[senátor]
diplomat	**дипломат** (м)	[diplomát]
consul	**консул** (м)	[kónsul]
ambassador	**посланик** (м)	[poslánik]
counselor (diplomatic officer)	**съветник** (м)	[səvétnik]
official, functionary (civil servant)	**чиновник** (м)	[tʃinóvnik]
prefect	**префект** (м)	[prefékt]
mayor	**кмет** (м)	[kmet]
judge	**съдия** (м)	[sədijá]
prosecutor	**прокурор** (м)	[prokurór]
missionary	**мисионер** (м)	[misionér]
monk	**монах** (м)	[monáh]
abbot	**абат** (м)	[abát]
rabbi	**равин** (м)	[ravín]
vizier	**везир** (м)	[vezír]
shah	**шах** (м)	[ʃah]
sheikh	**шейх** (м)	[ʃejh]

128. Agricultural professions

beekeeper	**пчеловъд** (м)	[ptʃelovət]
shepherd	**пастир** (м)	[pastír]
agronomist	**агроном** (м)	[agronóm]
cattle breeder	**животновъд** (м)	[ʒivotnovət]

veterinary surgeon	**ветеринар** (м)	[veterinár]
farmer	**фермер** (м)	[férmer]
winemaker	**винар** (м)	[vinár]
zoologist	**зоолог** (м)	[zoolók]
cowboy	**каубой** (м)	[káuboj]

129. Art professions

actor	**актьор** (м)	[aktjór]
actress	**актриса** (ж)	[aktrísa]
singer (masc.)	**певец** (м)	[pevéts]
singer (fem.)	**певица** (ж)	[pevítsa]
dancer (masc.)	**танцьор** (м)	[tantsʲór]
dancer (fem.)	**танцьорка** (ж)	[tantsʲórka]
performer (masc.)	**артист** (м)	[artíst]
performer (fem.)	**артистка** (ж)	[artístka]
musician	**музикант** (м)	[muzikánt]
pianist	**пианист** (м)	[pianíst]
guitar player	**китарист** (м)	[kitaríst]
conductor (orchestra ~)	**диригент** (м)	[dirigént]
composer	**композитор** (м)	[kompozítor]
impresario	**импресарио** (м)	[impresário]
film director	**режисьор** (м)	[reʒisʲór]
producer	**продуцент** (м)	[produtsént]
scriptwriter	**сценарист** (м)	[stsenaríst]
critic	**критик** (м)	[kritík]
writer	**писател** (м)	[pisátel]
poet	**поет** (м)	[poét]
sculptor	**скулптор** (м)	[skúlptor]
artist (painter)	**художник** (м)	[hudóʒnik]
juggler	**жонгльор** (м)	[ʒonglʲór]
clown	**клоун** (м)	[klóun]
acrobat	**акробат** (м)	[akrobát]
magician	**фокусник** (м)	[fókusnik]

130. Various professions

doctor	**лекар** (м)	[lékar]
nurse	**медицинска сестра** (ж)	[meditsínska sestrá]
psychiatrist	**психиатър** (м)	[psihiátər]
dentist	**стоматолог** (м)	[stomatolók]
surgeon	**хирург** (м)	[hirúrk]
astronaut	**астронавт** (м)	[astronáft]
astronomer	**астроном** (м)	[astronóm]

driver (of a taxi, etc.)	**шофьор** (м)	[ʃofʲór]
train driver	**машинист** (м)	[maʃiníst]
mechanic	**механик** (м)	[mehánik]
miner	**миньор** (м)	[minʲór]
worker	**работник** (м)	[rabótnik]
locksmith	**шлосер** (м)	[ʃlóser]
joiner (carpenter)	**дърводелец** (м)	[dərvodélets]
turner (lathe operator)	**стругар** (м)	[strugár]
building worker	**строител** (м)	[stroítel]
welder	**заварчик** (м)	[zavártʃik]
professor (title)	**професор** (м)	[profésor]
architect	**архитект** (м)	[arhitékt]
historian	**историк** (м)	[istorík]
scientist	**учен** (м)	[útʃen]
physicist	**физик** (м)	[fizík]
chemist (scientist)	**химик** (м)	[himík]
archaeologist	**археолог** (м)	[arheolók]
geologist	**геолог** (м)	[geolók]
researcher (scientist)	**изследовател** (м)	[issledovátel]
babysitter	**детегледачка** (ж)	[detegledátʃka]
teacher, educator	**учител, педагог** (м)	[utʃítel], [pedagók]
editor	**редактор** (м)	[redáktor]
editor-in-chief	**главен редактор** (м)	[gláven redáktor]
correspondent	**кореспондент** (м)	[korespondént]
typist (fem.)	**машинописка** (ж)	[maʃinopíska]
designer	**дизайнер** (м)	[dizájner]
computer expert	**компютърен специалист** (м)	[kompʲútəren spetsialíst]
programmer	**програмист** (м)	[programíst]
engineer (designer)	**инженер** (м)	[inʒenér]
sailor	**моряк** (м)	[morʲák]
seaman	**матрос** (м)	[matrós]
rescuer	**спасител** (м)	[spasítel]
firefighter	**пожарникар** (м)	[poʒarnikár]
police officer	**полицай** (м)	[politsáj]
watchman	**пазач** (м)	[pazátʃ]
detective	**детектив** (м)	[detektíf]
customs officer	**митничар** (м)	[mitnitʃár]
bodyguard	**телохранител** (с)	[telohranítel]
prison officer	**надзирател** (м)	[nadzirátel]
inspector	**инспектор** (м)	[inspéktor]
sportsman	**спортист** (м)	[sportíst]
trainer, coach	**треньор** (м)	[trenʲór]
butcher	**месар** (м)	[mesár]
cobbler (shoe repairer)	**обущар** (м)	[obuʃtár]
merchant	**търговец** (м)	[tərgóvets]

loader (person)	**хамалин** (м)	[hamálin]
fashion designer	**моделиер** (м)	[modeliér]
model (fem.)	**модел** (м)	[modél]

131. Occupations. Social status

schoolboy	**ученик** (м)	[utʃeník]
student (college ~)	**студент** (м)	[studént]
philosopher	**философ** (м)	[filosóf]
economist	**икономист** (м)	[ikonomíst]
inventor	**изобретател** (м)	[izobretátel]
unemployed (n)	**безработен човек** (м)	[bezrabóten tʃovék]
retiree, pensioner	**пенсионер** (м)	[pensionér]
spy, secret agent	**шпионин** (м)	[ʃpiónin]
prisoner	**затворник** (м)	[zatvórnik]
striker	**стачник** (м)	[státʃnik]
bureaucrat	**бюрократ** (м)	[bʲurokrát]
traveller (globetrotter)	**пътешественик** (м)	[pəteʃéstvenik]
gay, homosexual (n)	**хомосексуалист** (м)	[homoseksualíst]
hacker	**хакер** (м)	[háker]
hippie	**хипи** (м)	[hípi]
bandit	**бандит** (м)	[bandít]
hit man, killer	**наемен убиец** (м)	[naémen ubíets]
drug addict	**наркоман** (м)	[narkomán]
drug dealer	**наркотрафикант** (м)	[narkotrafikánt]
prostitute (fem.)	**проститутка** (ж)	[prostitútka]
pimp	**сутеньор** (м)	[sutenʲór]
sorcerer	**магьосник** (м)	[magʲósnik]
sorceress (evil ~)	**магьосница** (ж)	[magʲósnitsa]
pirate	**пират** (м)	[pirát]
slave	**роб** (м)	[rop]
samurai	**самурай** (м)	[samuráj]
savage (primitive)	**дивак** (м)	[divák]

Sports

132. Kinds of sports. Sportspersons

sportsman	**спортист** (м)	[sportíst]
kind of sport	**вид** (м) **спорт**	[vit sport]
basketball	**баскетбол** (м)	[básketbol]
basketball player	**баскетболист** (м)	[basketbolíst]
baseball	**бейзбол** (м)	[bejzból]
baseball player	**бейзболист** (м)	[bejzbolíst]
football	**футбол** (м)	[fúdbol]
football player	**футболист** (м)	[fudbolíst]
goalkeeper	**вратар** (м)	[vratár]
ice hockey	**хокей** (м)	[hókej]
ice hockey player	**хокеист** (м)	[hokeíst]
volleyball	**волейбол** (м)	[vólejbol]
volleyball player	**волейболист** (м)	[volejbolíst]
boxing	**бокс** (м)	[boks]
boxer	**боксьор** (м)	[boks^jór]
wrestling	**борба** (ж)	[borbá]
wrestler	**борец** (м)	[boréts]
karate	**карате** (с)	[karáte]
karate fighter	**каратист** (м)	[karatíst]
judo	**джудо** (с)	[dʒúdo]
judo athlete	**джудист** (м)	[dʒudíst]
tennis	**тенис** (м)	[ténis]
tennis player	**тенисист** (м)	[tenisíst]
swimming	**плуване** (с)	[plúvane]
swimmer	**плувец** (м)	[pluvéts]
fencing	**фехтовка** (ж)	[fehtófka]
fencer	**фехтувач** (м)	[fehtuvátʃ]
chess	**шахмат** (м)	[ʃáhmát]
chess player	**шахматист** (м)	[ʃahmatíst]
alpinism	**алпинизъм** (м)	[alpinízəm]
alpinist	**алпинист** (м)	[alpiníst]
running	**бягане** (с)	[b^jágane]

runner	**бегач** (м)	[begátʃ]
athletics	**лека атлетика** (ж)	[léka atlétika]
athlete	**атлет** (м)	[atlét]
horse riding	**конен спорт** (м)	[kónen sport]
horse rider	**ездач** (м)	[ezdátʃ]
figure skating	**фигурно пързаляне** (с)	[fígurno pərzálʲane]
figure skater (masc.)	**фигурист** (м)	[figuríst]
figure skater (fem.)	**фигуристка** (ж)	[figurístka]
powerlifting	**тежка атлетика** (ж)	[téʃka atlétika]
powerlifter	**щангист** (м)	[ʃtangíst]
car racing	**автомобилни състезания** (с мн)	[aftomobílni səstezánija]
racer (driver)	**автомобилен състезател** (м)	[aftomobílen səstezátel]
cycling	**колоездене** (с)	[koloézdene]
cyclist	**колоездач** (м)	[koloezdátʃ]
long jump	**скок** (м) **на дължина**	[skok na dəlʒiná]
pole vaulting	**овчарски скок** (м)	[oftʃárski skok]
jumper	**скачач** (м)	[skatʃátʃ]

133. Kinds of sports. Miscellaneous

American football	**американски футбол** (м)	[amerikánski fúdbol]
badminton	**бадминтон** (м)	[bádminton]
biathlon	**биатлон** (м)	[biatlón]
billiards	**билярд** (м)	[bilʲárt]
bobsleigh	**бобслей** (м)	[bobsléj]
bodybuilding	**културизъм** (м)	[kulturízəm]
water polo	**водна топка** (ж)	[vódna tópka]
handball	**хандбал** (м)	[hándbal]
golf	**голф** (м)	[golf]
rowing	**гребане** (с)	[grébane]
scuba diving	**дайвинг** (м)	[dájving]
cross-country skiing	**ски бягане** (с мн)	[ski bʲágane]
table tennis (ping-pong)	**тенис** (м) **на маса**	[ténis na mása]
sailing	**спорт** (м) **с платноходки**	[sport s platnohótki]
rally	**рали** (с)	[ráli]
rugby	**ръгби** (с)	[rəgbi]
snowboarding	**сноуборд** (м)	[snóubort]

134. Gym

barbell	**щанга** (ж)	[ʃtánga]
dumbbells	**гири** (ж мн)	[gíri]

training machine	**тренажор** (м)	[trenaʒór]
exercise bicycle	**велоергометър** (м)	[veloergométər]
treadmill	**писта** (ж) **за бягане**	[písta za bʲágane]
horizontal bar	**лост** (м)	[lost]
parallel bars	**успоредка** (ж)	[úsporetka]
vault (vaulting horse)	**кон** (м)	[kon]
mat (exercise ~)	**дюшек** (м)	[dʲuʃék]
aerobics	**аеробика** (ж)	[aeróbika]
yoga	**йога** (ж)	[jóga]

135. Ice hockey

ice hockey	**хокей** (м)	[hókej]
ice hockey player	**хокеист** (м)	[hokeíst]
to play ice hockey	**играя хокей**	[igrája hókej]
ice	**лед** (м)	[let]
puck	**шайба** (ж)	[ʃájba]
ice hockey stick	**стик** (м)	[stik]
ice skates	**кънки** (мн)	[kənki]
board (ice hockey rink ~)	**мантинела** (ж)	[mantinéla]
shot	**удар** (м)	[údar]
goaltender	**вратар** (м)	[vratár]
goal (score)	**гол** (м)	[gol]
to score a goal	**вкарам гол**	[fkáram gol]
period	**третина** (ж)	[tretína]
substitutes bench	**резервна скамейка** (ж)	[rezérvna skaméjka]

136. Football

football	**футбол** (м)	[fúdbol]
football player	**футболист** (м)	[fudbolíst]
to play football	**играя футбол**	[igrája fúdbol]
major league	**висша лига** (ж)	[vísʃa líga]
football club	**футболен клуб** (м)	[fúdbolen klup]
coach	**треньор** (м)	[trenʲór]
owner, proprietor	**собственик** (м)	[sóbstvenik]
team	**отбор** (м)	[otbór]
team captain	**капитан** (м) **на отбора**	[kapitán na odbóra]
player	**играч** (м)	[igrátʃ]
substitute	**резервен играч** (м)	[rezérven igrátʃ]
forward	**нападател** (м)	[napadátel]
centre forward	**централен нападател** (м)	[tsentrálen napadátel]
scorer	**голмайстор** (м)	[golmájstor]

defender, back	**защитник** (м)	[zaʃtítnik]
midfielder, halfback	**полузащитник** (м)	[poluzaʃtítnik]
match	**мач** (м)	[matʃ]
to meet (vi, vt)	**срещам се**	[sréʃtam se]
final	**финал** (м)	[finál]
semi-final	**полуфинал** (м)	[polufinál]
championship	**шампионат** (м)	[ʃampionát]
period, half	**полувреме** (с)	[poluvréme]
first period	**първо полувреме** (с)	[pərvo poluvréme]
half-time	**почивка** (ж)	[potʃífka]
goal	**врата** (ж)	[vratá]
goalkeeper	**вратар** (м)	[vratár]
goalpost	**странична греда** (ж)	[straníʧna gredá]
crossbar	**напречна греда** (ж)	[napréʧna gredá]
net	**мрежа** (ж)	[mréʒa]
to concede a goal	**пропусна топка**	[propúsna tópka]
ball	**топка** (ж)	[tópka]
pass	**пас** (м)	[pas]
kick	**удар** (м)	[údar]
to kick (~ the ball)	**бия**	[bíja]
free kick (direct ~)	**наказателен удар** (м)	[nakazátelen údar]
corner kick	**ъглов удар** (м)	[əglov údar]
attack	**атака** (ж)	[atáka]
counterattack	**контраатака** (ж)	[kóntra·atáka]
combination	**комбинация** (ж)	[kombinátsija]
referee	**арбитър** (м)	[arbítər]
to blow the whistle	**свиря**	[svírʲa]
whistle (sound)	**свирка** (ж)	[svírka]
foul, misconduct	**нарушение** (с)	[naruʃénie]
to commit a foul	**наруша**	[naruʃá]
to send off	**отстраня**	[otstranʲá]
yellow card	**жълт картон** (м)	[ʒəlt kartón]
red card	**червен картон** (м)	[ʧervén kartón]
disqualification	**дисквалификация** (ж)	[diskvalifikátsija]
to disqualify (vt)	**дисквалифицирам**	[diskvalifitsíram]
penalty kick	**дузпа** (ж)	[dúspa]
wall	**стена** (ж)	[stená]
to score (vi, vt)	**вкарам**	[fkáram]
goal (score)	**гол** (м)	[gol]
to score a goal	**вкарам гол**	[fkáram gol]
substitution	**смяна** (ж)	[smʲána]
to replace (a player)	**сменя**	[smenʲá]
rules	**правила** (с мн)	[pravilá]
tactics	**тактика** (ж)	[táktika]
stadium	**стадион** (м)	[stadión]
terrace	**трибуна** (ж)	[tribúna]

fan, supporter	**запалянко** (м)	[zapalʲánko]
to shout (vi)	**викам**	[víkam]
scoreboard	**табло** (с)	[tabló]
score	**резултат** (м)	[rezultát]
defeat	**поражение** (с)	[poraʒénie]
to lose (not win)	**загубя**	[zagúbʲa]
draw	**наравно**	[narávno]
to draw (vi)	**завърша наравно**	[zavérʃa narávno]
victory	**победа** (ж)	[pobéda]
to win (vi, vt)	**победя**	[pobedʲá]
champion	**шампион** (м)	[ʃampíon]
best (adj)	**най-добър**	[naj-dobér]
to congratulate (vt)	**поздравявам**	[pozdravʲávam]
commentator	**коментатор** (м)	[komentátor]
to commentate (vt)	**коментирам**	[komentíram]
broadcast	**предаване** (с)	[predávane]

137. Alpine skiing

skis	**ски** (мн)	[ski]
to ski (vi)	**карам ски**	[káram ski]
mountain-ski resort	**планински курорт** (м)	[planínski kurórt]
ski lift	**лифт** (м)	[lift]
ski poles	**щеки** (ж мн)	[ʃtéki]
slope	**склон** (м)	[sklon]
slalom	**слалом** (м)	[slálom]

138. Tennis. Golf

golf	**голф** (м)	[golf]
golf club	**голф клуб** (м)	[golf klúp]
golfer	**играч** (м) **на голф**	[igrátʃ na golf]
hole	**дупка** (ж)	[dúpka]
club	**стик** (м)	[stik]
golf trolley	**количка** (ж) **за голф**	[kolítʃka za golf]
tennis	**тенис** (м)	[ténis]
tennis court	**корт** (м)	[kort]
serve	**сервис** (м)	[sérvis]
to serve (vt)	**сервирам**	[servíram]
racket	**ракета** (ж)	[rakéta]
net	**мрежа** (ж)	[mréʒa]
ball	**топка** (ж)	[tópka]

139. Chess

chess	**шахмат** (м)	[ʃáhmát]
chessmen	**шахматни фигури** (ж мн)	[ʃáhmátni fíguri]
chess player	**шахматист** (м)	[ʃahmatíst]
chessboard	**шахматна дъска** (ж)	[ʃáhmatna dəská]
chessman	**фигура** (ж)	[fígura]
White (white pieces)	**бели** (мн)	[béli]
Black (black pieces)	**черни** (мн)	[ʧérni]
pawn	**пионка** (ж)	[piónka]
bishop	**офицер** (м)	[ofitsér]
knight	**кон** (м)	[kon]
rook	**топ** (м)	[top]
queen	**царица** (ж)	[tsarítsa]
king	**цар** (м)	[tsar]
move	**ход** (м)	[hot]
to move (vi, vt)	**предвижвам**	[predvíʒvam]
to sacrifice (vt)	**жертвам**	[ʒértvam]
castling	**рокада** (ж)	[rokáda]
check	**шах** (м)	[ʃah]
checkmate	**мат** (м)	[mat]
chess tournament	**шахматен турнир** (м)	[ʃáhmaten turnír]
Grand Master	**гросмайстор** (м)	[grosmájstor]
combination	**комбинация** (ж)	[kombinátsija]
game (in chess)	**партия** (ж)	[pártija]
draughts	**шашки** (мн)	[ʃáʃki]

140. Boxing

boxing	**бокс** (м)	[boks]
fight (bout)	**бой** (м)	[boj]
boxing match	**двубой** (м)	[dvubój]
round (in boxing)	**рунд** (м)	[runt]
ring	**ринг** (м)	[rink]
gong	**гонг** (м)	[gonk]
punch	**удар** (м)	[údar]
knockdown	**нокдаун** (м)	[nokdáun]
knockout	**нокаут** (м)	[nokáut]
to knock out	**нокаутирам**	[nokautíram]
boxing glove	**боксьорска ръкавица** (ж)	[boksʲórska rəkavítsa]
referee	**рефер** (м)	[réfer]
lightweight	**лека категория** (ж)	[léka kategórija]
middleweight	**средна категория** (ж)	[srédna kategórija]
heavyweight	**тежка категория** (ж)	[téʃka kategórija]

141. Sports. Miscellaneous

Olympic Games	**олимпийски игри** (ж мн)	[olimpíjski igrí]
winner	**победител** (м)	[pobedítel]
to be winning	**побеждавам**	[pobeʒdávam]
to win (vi)	**спечеля**	[spetʃélʲa]
leader	**водач** (м)	[vodátʃ]
to lead (vi)	**водя**	[vódʲa]
first place	**първо място** (с)	[pərvo mʲásto]
second place	**второ място** (с)	[ftóro mʲásto]
third place	**трето място** (с)	[tréto mʲásto]
medal	**медал** (м)	[medál]
trophy	**трофей** (м)	[troféj]
prize cup (trophy)	**купа** (ж)	[kupá]
prize (in game)	**награда** (ж)	[nagráda]
main prize	**първа награда** (ж)	[pərva nagráda]
record	**рекорд** (м)	[rekórt]
to set a record	**поставям рекорд**	[postávʲam rekórt]
final	**финал** (м)	[finál]
final (adj)	**финален**	[finálen]
champion	**шампион** (м)	[ʃampíon]
championship	**шампионат** (м)	[ʃampionát]
stadium	**стадион** (м)	[stadión]
terrace	**трибуна** (ж)	[tribúna]
fan, supporter	**запалянко** (м)	[zapalʲánko]
opponent, rival	**съперник** (м)	[səpérnik]
start (start line)	**старт** (м)	[start]
finish line	**финиш** (м)	[fíniʃ]
defeat	**загуба** (ж)	[záguba]
to lose (not win)	**загубя**	[zagúbʲa]
referee	**съдия** (м)	[sədijá]
jury (judges)	**жури** (с)	[ʒúri]
score	**резултат** (м)	[rezultát]
draw	**наравно** (с)	[narávno]
to draw (vi)	**завърша наравно**	[zavərʃa narávno]
point	**точка** (ж)	[tótʃka]
result (final score)	**резултат** (м)	[rezultát]
half-time	**почивка** (ж)	[potʃífka]
doping	**допинг** (м)	[dóping]
to penalise (vt)	**наказвам**	[nakázvam]
to disqualify (vt)	**дисквалифицирам**	[diskvalifitsíram]
apparatus	**уред** (м)	[úret]
javelin	**копие** (с)	[kópie]

shot (metal ball)	**гюлле** (с)	[gʲulé]
ball (snooker, etc.)	**топка** (ж)	[tópka]
aim (target)	**цел** (ж)	[tsel]
target	**мишена** (ж)	[miʃéna]
to shoot (vi)	**стрелям**	[strélʲam]
accurate (~ shot)	**точен**	[tóʧen]
trainer, coach	**треньор** (м)	[trenʲór]
to train (sb)	**тренирам**	[treníram]
to train (vi)	**тренирам се**	[treníram se]
training	**тренировка** (ж)	[trenirófka]
gym	**спортна зала** (ж)	[spórtna zála]
exercise (physical)	**упражнение** (с)	[upraʒnénie]
warm-up (athlete ~)	**загряване** (с)	[zagrʲávane]

Education

142. School

school	**училище** (с)	[utʃíliʃte]
headmaster	**директор** (м) **на училище**	[diréktor na utʃíliʃte]
student (m)	**ученик** (м)	[utʃeník]
student (f)	**ученичка** (ж)	[utʃenítʃka]
schoolboy	**ученик** (м)	[utʃeník]
schoolgirl	**ученичка** (ж)	[utʃenítʃka]
to teach (sb)	**уча**	[útʃa]
to learn (language, etc.)	**уча**	[útʃa]
to learn by heart	**уча наизуст**	[útʃa naizúst]
to learn (~ to count, etc.)	**уча се**	[útʃa se]
to be at school	**ходя на училище**	[hódʲa na utʃíliʃte]
to go to school	**отивам на училище**	[otívam na utʃíliʃte]
alphabet	**алфавит** (м)	[alfavít]
subject (at school)	**предмет** (м)	[predmét]
classroom	**клас** (м)	[klas]
lesson	**час** (м)	[tʃas]
playtime, break	**междучасие** (с)	[meʒdutʃásie]
school bell	**звънец** (м)	[zvənéts]
school desk	**чин** (м)	[tʃin]
blackboard	**дъска** (ж)	[dəská]
mark	**бележка** (ж)	[beléʃka]
good mark	**добра оценка** (ж)	[dobrá otsénka]
bad mark	**лоша оценка** (ж)	[lóʃa otsénka]
to give a mark	**пиша оценка** (ж)	[píʃa otsénka]
mistake, error	**грешка** (ж)	[gréʃka]
to make mistakes	**правя грешки**	[právʲa gréʃki]
to correct (an error)	**поправям**	[poprávʲam]
crib	**пищов** (м)	[piʃtóv]
homework	**домашно** (с)	[domáʃno]
exercise (in education)	**упражнение** (с)	[upraʒnénie]
to be present	**присъствам**	[prisə́stvam]
to be absent	**отсъствам**	[otsə́stvam]
to punish (vt)	**наказвам**	[nakázvam]
punishment	**наказание** (с)	[nakazánie]
conduct (behaviour)	**поведение** (с)	[povedénie]
school report	**дневник** (м)	[dnévnik]

pencil	**молив** (м)	[móliv]
rubber	**гума** (ж)	[gúma]
chalk	**тебешир** (м)	[tebeʃír]
pencil case	**несесер** (м)	[nesesér]
schoolbag	**раница** (ж)	[ránitsa]
pen	**химикалка** (ж)	[himikálka]
exercise book	**тетрадка** (ж)	[tetrátka]
textbook	**учебник** (м)	[utʃóbnik]
compasses	**пергел** (м)	[pergél]
to make technical drawings	**чертая**	[tʃertája]
technical drawing	**чертеж** (м)	[tʃertéʒ]
poem	**стихотворение** (с)	[stihotvorénie]
by heart (adv)	**наизуст**	[naizúst]
to learn by heart	**уча наизуст**	[útʃa naizúst]
school holidays	**ваканция** (ж)	[vakántsija]
to be on holiday	**във ваканция съм**	[vəf vakántsija səm]
to spend holidays	**прекарвам ваканция**	[prekárvam vakántsija]
test (at school)	**контролна работа** (ж)	[kontrólna rábota]
essay (composition)	**съчинение** (с)	[sətʃinénie]
dictation	**диктовка** (ж)	[diktófka]
exam (examination)	**изпит** (м)	[íspit]
to do an exam	**полагам изпити**	[polágam íspiti]
experiment (e.g., chemistry ~)	**опит** (м)	[ópit]

143. College. University

academy	**академия** (ж)	[akadémija]
university	**университет** (м)	[universitét]
faculty (e.g., ~ of Medicine)	**факултет** (м)	[fakultét]
student (masc.)	**студент** (м)	[studént]
student (fem.)	**студентка** (ж)	[studéntka]
lecturer (teacher)	**преподавател** (м)	[prepodavátel]
lecture hall, room	**аудитория** (ж)	[auditórija]
graduate	**абсолвент** (м)	[absolvént]
diploma	**диплома** (ж)	[díploma]
dissertation	**дисертация** (ж)	[disertátsija]
study (report)	**изследване** (с)	[isslédvane]
laboratory	**лаборатория** (ж)	[laboratórija]
lecture	**лекция** (ж)	[léktsija]
coursemate	**състудент** (м)	[səstudént]
scholarship, bursary	**стипендия** (ж)	[stipéndija]
academic degree	**научна степен** (ж)	[naútʃna stépen]

144. Sciences. Disciplines

mathematics	**математика** (ж)	[matemátika]
algebra	**алгебра** (ж)	[álgebra]
geometry	**геометрия** (ж)	[geométrija]
astronomy	**астрономия** (ж)	[astronómija]
biology	**биология** (ж)	[biológija]
geography	**география** (ж)	[geográfija]
geology	**геология** (ж)	[geológija]
history	**история** (ж)	[istórija]
medicine	**медицина** (ж)	[meditsína]
pedagogy	**педагогика** (ж)	[pedagógika]
law	**право** (с)	[právo]
physics	**физика** (ж)	[fízika]
chemistry	**химия** (ж)	[hímija]
philosophy	**философия** (ж)	[filosófija]
psychology	**психология** (ж)	[psihológija]

145. Writing system. Orthography

grammar	**граматика** (ж)	[gramátika]
vocabulary	**лексика** (ж)	[léksika]
phonetics	**фонетика** (ж)	[fonétika]
noun	**съществително име** (с)	[səʃtestvítelno íme]
adjective	**прилагателно име** (с)	[prilagátelno íme]
verb	**глагол** (м)	[glagól]
adverb	**наречие** (с)	[narétʃie]
pronoun	**местоимение** (с)	[mestoiménie]
interjection	**междуметие** (с)	[meʒdumétie]
preposition	**предлог** (м)	[predlók]
root	**корен** (м) **на думата**	[kóren na dúmata]
ending	**окончание** (с)	[okontʃánie]
prefix	**представка** (ж)	[pretstáfka]
syllable	**сричка** (ж)	[srítʃka]
suffix	**наставка** (ж)	[nastáfka]
stress mark	**ударение** (с)	[udarénie]
apostrophe	**апостроф** (м)	[apostróf]
full stop	**точка** (ж)	[tótʃka]
comma	**запетая** (ж)	[zapetája]
semicolon	**точка** (ж) **и запетая**	[tótʃka i zapetája]
colon	**двоеточие** (с)	[dvoetótʃie]
ellipsis	**многоточие** (с)	[mnogotótʃie]
question mark	**въпросителен знак** (м)	[vəprosítelen znák]
exclamation mark	**удивителна** (ж)	[udivítelna]

inverted commas	**кавички** (мн)	[kavítʃki]
in inverted commas	**в кавички**	[v kavítʃki]
parenthesis	**скоби** (ж мн)	[skóbi]
in parenthesis	**в скоби**	[v skóbi]
hyphen	**дефис** (м)	[defís]
dash	**тире** (с)	[tiré]
space (between words)	**бяло поле** (с)	[bʲálo polé]
letter	**буква** (ж)	[búkva]
capital letter	**главна буква** (ж)	[glávna búkva]
vowel (n)	**гласен звук** (м)	[glásen zvuk]
consonant (n)	**съгласен звук** (м)	[səglásen zvuk]
sentence	**изречение** (с)	[izretʃénie]
subject	**подлог** (м)	[pódlok]
predicate	**сказуемо** (с)	[skazúemo]
line	**ред** (м)	[ret]
on a new line	**от нов ред**	[ot nóv ret]
paragraph	**абзац** (м)	[abzáts]
word	**дума** (ж)	[dúma]
group of words	**словосъчетание** (с)	[slovo·sətʃetánie]
expression	**израз** (м)	[ízraz]
synonym	**синоним** (м)	[sinoním]
antonym	**антоним** (м)	[antoním]
rule	**правило** (с)	[právilo]
exception	**изключение** (с)	[izklʲutʃénie]
correct (adj)	**верен**	[véren]
conjugation	**спрежение** (с)	[spreʒénie]
declension	**склонение** (с)	[sklonénie]
nominal case	**падеж** (м)	[padéʒ]
question	**въпрос** (м)	[vəprós]
to underline (vt)	**подчертая**	[podtʃertája]
dotted line	**пунктир** (м)	[punktír]

146. Foreign languages

language	**език** (м)	[ezík]
foreign (adj)	**чужд**	[tʃuʒd]
foreign language	**чужд език** (м)	[tʃuʒd ezík]
to study (vt)	**изучавам**	[izutʃávam]
to learn (language, etc.)	**уча**	[útʃa]
to read (vi, vt)	**чета**	[tʃeta]
to speak (vi, vt)	**говоря**	[govórʲa]
to understand (vt)	**разбирам**	[razbíram]
to write (vt)	**пиша**	[píʃa]
fast (adv)	**бързо**	[bérzo]
slowly (adv)	**бавно**	[bávno]

fluently (adv)	**свободно**	[svobódno]
rules	**правила** (с мн)	[pravilá]
grammar	**граматика** (ж)	[gramátika]
vocabulary	**лексика** (ж)	[léksika]
phonetics	**фонетика** (ж)	[fonétika]
textbook	**учебник** (м)	[utʃébnik]
dictionary	**речник** (м)	[rétʃnik]
teach-yourself book	**самоучител** (м)	[samoutʃítel]
phrasebook	**разговорник** (м)	[razgovórnik]
cassette, tape	**касета** (ж)	[kaséta]
videotape	**видеокасета** (ж)	[video·kaséta]
CD, compact disc	**CD диск** (м)	[sidí disk]
DVD	**DVD** (м)	[dividí]
alphabet	**алфавит** (м)	[alfavít]
to spell (vt)	**спелувам**	[spelúvam]
pronunciation	**произношение** (с)	[proiznoʃénie]
accent	**акцент** (м)	[aktsént]
with an accent	**с акцент**	[s aktsént]
without an accent	**без акцент**	[bez aktsént]
word	**дума** (ж)	[dúma]
meaning	**смисъл** (м)	[smísəl]
course (e.g. a French ~)	**курсове** (м мн)	[kúrsove]
to sign up	**запиша се**	[zapíʃa se]
teacher	**преподавател** (м)	[prepodavátel]
translation (process)	**превод** (м)	[prévot]
translation (text, etc.)	**превод** (м)	[prévot]
translator	**преводач** (м)	[prevodátʃ]
interpreter	**преводач** (м)	[prevodátʃ]
polyglot	**полиглот** (м)	[poliglót]
memory	**памет** (ж)	[pámet]

147. Fairy tale characters

Father Christmas	**Дядо Коледа**	[dʲádo kóleda]
mermaid	**русалка** (ж)	[rusálka]
magician, wizard	**вълшебник** (м)	[vəlʃébnik]
fairy	**вълшебница** (ж)	[vəlʃébnitsa]
magic (adj)	**вълшебен**	[vəlʃében]
magic wand	**вълшебна пръчица** (ж)	[vəlʃébna prətʃitsa]
fairy tale	**приказка** (ж)	[príkaska]
miracle	**чудо** (с)	[tʃúdo]
dwarf	**джудже** (с)	[dʒudʒé]
to turn into ...	**превърна се в ...**	[prevérna se v]
ghost	**привидение** (с)	[privídénie]

phantom	**призрак** (м)	[prízrak]
monster	**чудовище** (с)	[ʧudóviʃte]
dragon	**ламя** (ж)	[lamʲá]
giant	**великан** (м)	[velikán]

148. Zodiac Signs

Aries	**Овен** (м)	[ovén]
Taurus	**Телец** (м)	[teléts]
Gemini	**Близнаци** (м мн)	[bliznátsi]
Cancer	**Рак** (м)	[rak]
Leo	**Лъв** (м)	[ləv]
Virgo	**Дева** (ж)	[déva]
Libra	**Везни** (ж мн)	[vezní]
Scorpio	**Скорпион** (м)	[skorpión]
Sagittarius	**Стрелец** (м)	[streléts]
Capricorn	**Козирог** (м)	[kózirok]
Aquarius	**Водолей** (м)	[vodoléj]
Pisces	**Риби** (ж мн)	[ríbi]
character	**характер** (м)	[harákter]
character traits	**черти** (ж мн) **на характера**	[ʧertí na haráktera]
behaviour	**поведение** (с)	[povedénie]
to tell fortunes	**гледам**	[glédam]
fortune-teller	**гледачка** (ж)	[gledáʧka]
horoscope	**хороскоп** (м)	[horoskóp]

Arts

149. Theatre

theatre	**театър** (м)	[teátər]
opera	**опера** (ж)	[ópera]
operetta	**оперета** (ж)	[operéta]
ballet	**балет** (м)	[balét]
theatre poster	**афиш** (м)	[afíʃ]
theatre company	**трупа** (ж)	[trúpa]
tour	**гастроли** (м мн)	[gastróli]
to be on tour	**гастролирам**	[gastrolíram]
to rehearse (vi, vt)	**репетирам**	[repetíram]
rehearsal	**репетиция** (ж)	[repetítsija]
repertoire	**репертоар** (м)	[repertuár]
performance	**представление** (с)	[pretstavlénie]
theatrical show	**спектакъл** (м)	[spektákəl]
play	**пиеса** (ж)	[piésa]
ticket	**билет** (м)	[bilét]
booking office	**билетна каса** (ж)	[bilétna kása]
lobby, foyer	**хол** (м)	[hol]
coat check (cloakroom)	**гардероб** (м)	[garderóp]
cloakroom ticket	**номерче** (с)	[nómerʧe]
binoculars	**бинокъл** (м)	[binókəl]
usher	**контрольор** (м)	[kontrolʲór]
stalls (orchestra seats)	**партер** (м)	[párter]
balcony	**балкон** (м)	[balkón]
dress circle	**първи балкон** (м)	[pə́rvi balkón]
box	**ложа** (ж)	[lóʒa]
row	**ред** (м)	[ret]
seat	**място** (с)	[mʲásto]
audience	**публика** (ж)	[públika]
spectator	**зрител** (м)	[zrítel]
to clap (vi, vt)	**аплодирам**	[aplodíram]
applause	**аплодисменти** (м мн)	[aplodisménti]
ovation	**овации** (ж мн)	[ovátsii]
stage	**сцена** (ж)	[stséna]
curtain	**завеса** (ж)	[zavésa]
scenery	**декорация** (ж)	[dekorátsija]
backstage	**кулиси** (ж мн)	[kulísi]
scene (e.g. the last ~)	**сцена** (ж)	[stséna]
act	**действие** (с)	[déjstvie]
interval	**антракт** (м)	[antrákt]

150. Cinema

actor	**актьор** (м)	[aktjór]
actress	**актриса** (ж)	[aktrísa]
cinema (industry)	**кино** (с)	[kíno]
film	**филм** (м)	[film]
episode	**серия** (ж)	[sérija]
detective film	**детективски филм** (м)	[detektífski film]
action film	**екшън филм** (м)	[ékʃən film]
adventure film	**приключенски филм** (м)	[priklʲutʃénski film]
science fiction film	**фантастичен филм** (м)	[fantastítʃen film]
horror film	**филм** (м) **на ужаси**	[film na úʒasi]
comedy film	**кинокомедия** (ж)	[kinokomédija]
melodrama	**мелодрама** (ж)	[melodráma]
drama	**драма** (ж)	[dráma]
fictional film	**игрален филм** (м)	[igrálen film]
documentary	**документален филм** (м)	[dokumentálen film]
cartoon	**анимационен филм** (м)	[animatsiónen film]
silent films	**нямо кино** (с)	[nʲámo kíno]
role (part)	**роля** (ж)	[rólʲa]
leading role	**главна роля** (ж)	[glávna rólʲa]
to play (vi, vt)	**играя**	[igrája]
film star	**кинозвезда** (ж)	[kinozvezdá]
well-known (adj)	**известен**	[izvésten]
famous (adj)	**прочут**	[protʃút]
popular (adj)	**популярен**	[populʲáren]
script (screenplay)	**сценарий** (м)	[stsenárij]
scriptwriter	**сценарист** (м)	[stsenaríst]
film director	**режисьор** (м)	[reʒisʲór]
producer	**продуцент** (м)	[produtsént]
assistant	**асистент** (м)	[asistént]
cameraman	**оператор** (м)	[operátor]
stuntman	**каскадьор** (м)	[kaskadʲór]
to shoot a film	**снимам филм**	[snímam film]
audition, screen test	**проби** (ж мн)	[próbi]
shooting	**снимане** (с)	[snímane]
film crew	**снимачен екип** (м)	[snimátʃen ekíp]
film set	**снимачна площадка** (ж)	[snimátʃna ploʃtátka]
camera	**кинокамера** (ж)	[kinokámera]
cinema	**кинотеатър** (м)	[kinoteátər]
screen (e.g. big ~)	**екран** (м)	[ekrán]
to show a film	**прожектирам филм**	[proʒektíram film]
soundtrack	**звукова пътека** (ж)	[zvúkova pətéka]
special effects	**специални ефекти** (м мн)	[spetsiálni efékti]
subtitles	**субтитри** (мн)	[suptítri]

credits	**титри** (мн)	[títri]
translation	**превод** (м)	[prévot]

151. Painting

art	**изкуство** (с)	[izkústvo]
fine arts	**изящни изкуства** (с мн)	[izʲáʃtni iskústva]
art gallery	**галерия** (ж)	[galérija]
art exhibition	**изложба** (ж) **на картини**	[izlóʒba na kartíni]
painting (art)	**живопис** (м)	[ʒivopís]
graphic art	**графика** (ж)	[gráfika]
abstract art	**абстракционизъм** (м)	[abstraktsionízəm]
impressionism	**импресионизъм** (м)	[impresionízəm]
picture (painting)	**картина** (ж)	[kartína]
drawing	**рисунка** (ж)	[risúnka]
poster	**постер** (м)	[póster]
illustration (picture)	**илюстрация** (ж)	[ilʲustrátsija]
miniature	**миниатюра** (ж)	[miniatʲúra]
copy (of painting, etc.)	**копие** (с)	[kópie]
reproduction	**репродукция** (ж)	[reprodúktsija]
mosaic	**мозайка** (ж)	[mozájka]
stained glass window	**стъклопис** (м)	[stəklopís]
fresco	**фреска** (ж)	[fréska]
engraving	**гравюра** (ж)	[gravʲúra]
bust (sculpture)	**бюст** (м)	[bʲust]
sculpture	**скулптура** (ж)	[skulptúra]
statue	**статуя** (ж)	[státuja]
plaster of Paris	**гипс** (м)	[gips]
plaster (as adj)	**от гипс**	[ot gips]
portrait	**портрет** (м)	[portrét]
self-portrait	**автопортрет** (м)	[aftoportrét]
landscape painting	**пейзаж** (м)	[pejzáʒ]
still life	**натюрморт** (м)	[natʲurmórt]
caricature	**карикатура** (ж)	[karikatúra]
sketch	**скица** (ж)	[skítsa]
paint	**боя** (ж)	[bojá]
watercolor paint	**акварел** (м)	[akvarél]
oil (paint)	**маслени бои** (ж мн)	[másleni boí]
pencil	**молив** (м)	[móliv]
Indian ink	**туш** (м)	[tuʃ]
charcoal	**въглен** (м)	[vəglen]
to draw (vi, vt)	**рисувам**	[risúvam]
to paint (vi, vt)	**рисувам**	[risúvam]
to pose (vi)	**позирам**	[pozíram]
artist's model (masc.)	**модел** (м)	[modél]

artist's model (fem.)	**модел** (м)	[modél]
artist (painter)	**художник** (м)	[hudóʒnik]
work of art	**произведение** (с)	[proizvedénie]
masterpiece	**шедьовър** (м)	[ʃedʲóvər]
studio (artist's workroom)	**ателие** (с)	[atelié]
canvas (cloth)	**платно** (с)	[platnó]
easel	**статив** (м)	[statíf]
palette	**палитра** (ж)	[palítra]
frame (picture ~, etc.)	**рамка** (ж)	[rámka]
restoration	**реставрация** (ж)	[restavrátsija]
to restore (vt)	**реставрирам**	[restavríram]

152. Literature & Poetry

literature	**литература** (ж)	[literatúra]
author (writer)	**автор** (м)	[áftor]
pseudonym	**псевдоним** (м)	[psevdoním]
book	**книга** (ж)	[kníga]
volume	**том** (м)	[tom]
table of contents	**съдържание** (с)	[sədərʒánie]
page	**страница** (ж)	[stránitsa]
main character	**главен герой** (м)	[gláven gerój]
autograph	**автограф** (м)	[aftográf]
short story	**разказ** (м)	[rázkaz]
story (novella)	**повест** (ж)	[póvest]
novel	**роман** (м)	[román]
work (writing)	**съчинение** (с)	[sətʃinénie]
fable	**басня** (ж)	[básnʲa]
detective novel	**детективски роман** (м)	[detektífski román]
poem (verse)	**стихотворение** (с)	[stihotvorénie]
poetry	**поезия** (ж)	[poézija]
poem (epic, ballad)	**поема** (ж)	[poéma]
poet	**поет** (м)	[poét]
fiction	**белетристика** (ж)	[beletrístika]
science fiction	**научна фантастика** (ж)	[naútʃna fantástika]
adventures	**приключения** (с мн)	[priklʲutʃénija]
educational literature	**учебна литература** (ж)	[utʃébna literatúra]
children's literature	**детска литература** (ж)	[détska literatúra]

153. Circus

circus	**цирк** (м)	[tsirk]
programme	**програма** (ж)	[prográma]
performance	**представление** (с)	[pretstavlénie]
act (circus ~)	**номер** (м)	[nómer]
circus ring	**арена** (ж)	[aréna]

pantomime (act)	**пантомима** (ж)	[pantomíma]
clown	**клоун** (м)	[klóun]
acrobat	**акробат** (м)	[akrobát]
acrobatics	**акробатика** (ж)	[akrobátika]
gymnast	**гимнастик** (м)	[gimnastík]
acrobatic gymnastics	**гимнастика** (ж)	[gimnástika]
somersault	**салто** (с)	[sálto]
strongman	**атлет** (м)	[atlét]
tamer (e.g., lion ~)	**укротител** (м)	[ukrotítel]
rider (circus horse ~)	**ездач** (м)	[ezdátʃ]
assistant	**асистент** (м)	[asistént]
stunt	**трик** (м)	[trik]
magic trick	**фокус** (м)	[fókus]
conjurer, magician	**фокусник** (м)	[fókusnik]
juggler	**жонгльор** (м)	[ʒongl^jór]
to juggle (vi, vt)	**жонглирам**	[ʒonglíram]
animal trainer	**дресьор** (м)	[dres^jór]
animal training	**дресиране** (с)	[dresírane]
to train (animals)	**дресирам**	[dresíram]

154. Music. Pop music

music	**музика** (ж)	[múzika]
musician	**музикант** (м)	[muzikánt]
musical instrument	**музикален инструмент** (м)	[muzikálen instrumént]
to play ...	**свиря на ...**	[svír^ja na]
guitar	**китара** (ж)	[kitára]
violin	**цигулка** (ж)	[tsigúlka]
cello	**чело** (с)	[tʃélo]
double bass	**контрабас** (м)	[kontrabás]
harp	**арфа** (ж)	[árfa]
piano	**пиано** (с)	[piáno]
grand piano	**роял** (м)	[rojál]
organ	**орган** (м)	[orgán]
wind instruments	**духови инструменти** (м мн)	[dúhovi instruménti]
oboe	**обой** (м)	[obój]
saxophone	**саксофон** (м)	[saksofón]
clarinet	**кларнет** (м)	[klarnét]
flute	**флейта** (ж)	[fléjta]
trumpet	**тръба** (ж)	[trəbá]
accordion	**акордеон** (м)	[akordeón]
drum	**барабан** (м)	[barabán]
duo	**дует** (м)	[duét]
trio	**трио** (с)	[trío]
quartet	**квартет** (м)	[kvartét]

choir	**хор** (м)	[hor]
orchestra	**оркестър** (м)	[orkéstər]
pop music	**поп музика** (ж)	[pop múzika]
rock music	**рок музика** (ж)	[rok múzika]
rock group	**рок-група** (ж)	[rok-grúpa]
jazz	**джаз** (м)	[dʒaz]
idol	**кумир** (м)	[kumír]
admirer, fan	**почитател** (м)	[potʃitátel]
concert	**концерт** (м)	[kontsért]
symphony	**симфония** (ж)	[simfónija]
composition	**съчинение** (с)	[sətʃinénie]
to compose (write)	**съчинявам**	[sətʃinʲávam]
singing (n)	**пеене** (с)	[péene]
song	**песен** (ж)	[pésen]
tune (melody)	**мелодия** (ж)	[melódija]
rhythm	**ритъм** (м)	[rítəm]
blues	**блус** (м)	[blus]
sheet music	**ноти** (ж мн)	[nóti]
baton	**диригентска палка** (ж)	[dirigénska pálka]
bow	**лък** (м)	[lək]
string	**струна** (ж)	[strúna]
case (e.g. guitar ~)	**калъф** (м)	[kaléf]

Rest. Entertainment. Travel

155. Trip. Travel

tourism, travel	**туризъм** (м)	[turízəm]
tourist	**турист** (м)	[turíst]
trip, voyage	**пътешествие** (с)	[pəteʃéstvie]
adventure	**приключение** (с)	[prikl^jutʃénie]
trip, journey	**пътуване** (с)	[pətúvane]
holiday	**отпуска** (ж)	[ótpuska]
to be on holiday	**бъда в отпуска**	[bə́da v ótpuska]
rest	**почивка** (ж)	[potʃífka]
train	**влак** (м)	[vlak]
by train	**с влак**	[s vlak]
aeroplane	**самолет** (м)	[samolét]
by aeroplane	**със самолет**	[səs samolét]
by car	**с кола**	[s kolá]
by ship	**с кораб**	[s kórap]
luggage	**багаж** (м)	[bagáʃ]
suitcase	**куфар** (м)	[kúfar]
luggage trolley	**количка** (ж) **за багаж**	[kolítʃka za bagáʃ]
passport	**паспорт** (м)	[paspórt]
visa	**виза** (ж)	[víza]
ticket	**билет** (м)	[bilét]
air ticket	**самолетен билет** (м)	[samoléten bilét]
guidebook	**пътеводител** (м)	[pətevodítel]
map (tourist ~)	**карта** (ж)	[kárta]
area (rural ~)	**местност** (ж)	[méstnost]
place, site	**място** (с)	[m^jásto]
exotica (n)	**екзотика** (ж)	[ekzótika]
exotic (adj)	**екзотичен**	[ekzotítʃen]
amazing (adj)	**удивителен**	[udivítelen]
group	**група** (ж)	[grúpa]
excursion, sightseeing tour	**екскурзия** (ж)	[ekskúrzija]
guide (person)	**гид** (м)	[git]

156. Hotel

hotel	**хотел** (м)	[hotél]
motel	**мотел** (м)	[motél]
three-star (~ hotel)	**три звезди**	[tri zvezdí]

five-star	**пет звезди**	[pet zvezdí]
to stay (in a hotel, etc.)	**отсядам**	[ots^jádam]
room	**стая** (ж) **в хотел**	[stája f hotél]
single room	**еднинична стая** (ж)	[ediníʧna stája]
double room	**двойна стая** (ж)	[dvójna stája]
to book a room	**резервирам стая**	[rezervíram stája]
half board	**полупансион** (м)	[polupansión]
full board	**пълен пансион** (м)	[pəlen pansión]
with bath	**с баня**	[s bán^ja]
with shower	**с душ**	[s duʃ]
satellite television	**сателитна телевизия** (ж)	[satelítna televízija]
air-conditioner	**климатик** (м)	[klimatík]
towel	**кърпа** (ж)	[kərpa]
key	**ключ** (м)	[kl^juʧ]
administrator	**администратор** (м)	[administrátor]
chambermaid	**камериерка** (ж)	[kameriérka]
porter	**носач** (м)	[nosáʧ]
doorman	**портиер** (м)	[portiér]
restaurant	**ресторант** (м)	[restoránt]
pub, bar	**бар** (м)	[bar]
breakfast	**закуска** (ж)	[zakúska]
dinner	**вечеря** (ж)	[veʧér^ja]
buffet	**шведска маса** (ж)	[ʃvétska mása]
lobby	**вестибюл** (м)	[vestib^júl]
lift	**асансьор** (м)	[asans^jór]
DO NOT DISTURB	**НЕ МЕ БЕЗПОКОЙТЕ!**	[ne me bespokójte]
NO SMOKING	**ПУШЕНЕТО ЗАБРАНЕНО!**	[puʃenéto zabráneno]

157. Books. Reading

book	**книга** (ж)	[kníga]
author	**автор** (м)	[áftor]
writer	**писател** (м)	[pisátel]
to write (~ a book)	**напиша**	[napíʃa]
reader	**читател** (м)	[ʧitátel]
to read (vi, vt)	**чета**	[ʧeta]
reading (activity)	**четене** (с)	[ʧétene]
silently (to oneself)	**на ум**	[na úm]
aloud (adv)	**на глас**	[na glás]
to publish (vt)	**издавам**	[izdávam]
publishing (process)	**издание** (с)	[izdánie]
publisher	**издател** (м)	[izdátel]
publishing house	**издателство** (с)	[izdátelstvo]
to come out (be released)	**излизам**	[izlízam]

release (of a book)	**излизане** (с)	[izlízane]
print run	**тираж** (м)	[tiráʒ]
bookshop	**книжарница** (ж)	[kniʒárnitsa]
library	**библиотека** (ж)	[bibliotéka]
story (novella)	**повест** (ж)	[póvest]
short story	**разказ** (м)	[rázkaz]
novel	**роман** (м)	[román]
detective novel	**детективски роман** (м)	[detektífski román]
memoirs	**мемоари** (мн)	[memoári]
legend	**легенда** (ж)	[legénda]
myth	**мит** (м)	[mit]
poetry, poems	**стихове** (м мн)	[stihové]
autobiography	**автобиография** (ж)	[aftobiográfija]
selected works	**избрани съчинения**	[izbráni sətʃinénija]
science fiction	**фантастика** (ж)	[fantástika]
title	**название** (с)	[nazvánie]
introduction	**въведение** (с)	[vəvedénie]
title page	**заглавна страница** (ж)	[zaglávna stránitsa]
chapter	**глава** (ж)	[glavá]
extract	**откъс** (м)	[ótkəs]
episode	**епизод** (м)	[epizót]
plot (storyline)	**сюжет** (м)	[sʲuʒét]
contents	**съдържание** (с)	[sədərʒánie]
main character	**главен герой** (м)	[gláven gerój]
volume	**том** (м)	[tom]
cover	**корица** (ж)	[korítsa]
binding	**подвързия** (ж)	[podvərzíja]
bookmark	**маркер** (м)	[márker]
page	**страница** (ж)	[stránitsa]
to page through	**прелиствам**	[prelístvam]
margins	**полета** (с мн)	[poléta]
annotation (marginal note, etc.)	**бележка** (ж)	[beléʃka]
footnote	**забележка** (ж)	[zabeléʃka]
text	**текст** (м)	[tekst]
type, fount	**шрифт** (м)	[ʃrift]
misprint, typo	**печатна грешка** (ж)	[petʃátna gréʃka]
translation	**превод** (м)	[prévot]
to translate (vt)	**превеждам**	[prevéʒdam]
original (n)	**оригинал** (м)	[originál]
famous (adj)	**прочут**	[protʃút]
unknown (not famous)	**неизвестен**	[neizvésten]
interesting (adj)	**интересен**	[interésen]
bestseller	**бестселър** (м)	[bestsélər]

dictionary	**речник** (м)	[rétʃnik]
textbook	**учебник** (м)	[utʃébnik]
encyclopedia	**енциклопедия** (ж)	[entsiklopédija]

158. Hunting. Fishing

hunting	**лов** (м)	[lov]
to hunt (vi, vt)	**ловувам**	[lovúvam]
hunter	**ловец** (м)	[lovéts]
to shoot (vi)	**стрелям**	[strélʲam]
rifle	**пушка** (ж)	[púʃka]
bullet (shell)	**патрон** (м)	[patrón]
shot (lead balls)	**сачма** (ж)	[satʃmá]
steel trap	**капан** (м)	[kapán]
snare (for birds, etc.)	**примка** (ж)	[prímka]
to lay a steel trap	**залагам капан**	[zalágam kapán]
poacher	**бракониер** (м)	[brakoniér]
game (in hunting)	**дивеч** (ж)	[dívetʃ]
hound dog	**ловно куче** (с)	[lóvno kútʃe]
safari	**сафари** (с)	[safári]
mounted animal	**препарирано животно** (с)	[preparírano ʒivótno]
fisherman	**рибар** (м)	[ribár]
fishing (angling)	**риболов** (м)	[ribolóv]
to fish (vi)	**ловя риба**	[lovʲá ríba]
fishing rod	**въдица** (ж)	[vəditsa]
fishing line	**месина** (ж)	[mesína]
hook	**кука** (ж)	[kúka]
float	**плувка** (ж)	[plúfka]
bait	**стръв** (ж)	[strəv]
to cast a line	**хвърлям въдица**	[hvə́rlʲam vəditsa]
to bite (ab. fish)	**кълва**	[kəlvá]
catch (of fish)	**улов** (м)	[úlof]
ice-hole	**дупка** (ж) **в леда**	[dúpka v ledá]
fishing net	**мрежа** (ж)	[mréʒa]
boat	**лодка** (ж)	[lótka]
to net (to fish with a net)	**ловя с мрежа**	[lovʲá s mréʒa]
to cast[throw] the net	**хвърлям мрежа**	[hvə́rlʲam mréʒa]
to haul the net in	**изваждам мрежа**	[izváʒdam mréʒa]
whaler (person)	**китоловец** (м)	[kitolóvets]
whaleboat	**китоловен кораб** (м)	[kitolóven kórap]
harpoon	**харпун** (м)	[harpún]

159. Games. Billiards

billiards	**билярд** (м)	[bilʲárt]
billiard room, hall	**билярдна зала** (ж)	[bilʲárdna zála]

ball (snooker, etc.)	**билярдна топка** (ж)	[bilʲárdna tópka]
to pocket a ball	**вкарам топка**	[fkáram tópka]
cue	**щека** (ж)	[ʃtéka]
pocket	**дупка** (ж)	[dúpka]

160. Games. Playing cards

diamonds	**каро** (с)	[karó]
spades	**пики** (ж мн)	[píki]
hearts	**купи** (ж мн)	[kúpi]
clubs	**спатии** (ж мн)	[spatíi]
ace	**асо** (с)	[asó]
king	**поп** (м)	[pop]
queen	**дама** (ж)	[dáma]
jack, knave	**вале** (м)	[valé]
playing card	**карта** (ж)	[kárta]
cards	**карти** (ж мн)	[kárti]
trump	**коз** (м)	[kos]
pack of cards	**тесте** (с)	[testé]
to deal (vi, vt)	**раздавам**	[razdávam]
to shuffle (cards)	**размесвам**	[razmésvam]
lead, turn (n)	**ход** (м)	[hot]
cardsharp	**шмекер** (м)	[ʃméker]

161. Casino. Roulette

casino	**казино** (с)	[kazíno]
roulette (game)	**рулетка** (ж)	[rulétka]
bet	**залагане** (с)	[zalágane]
to place bets	**залагам**	[zalágam]
red	**червено** (с)	[ʧervéno]
black	**черно** (с)	[ʧérno]
to bet on red	**залагам на червено**	[zalágam na ʧervéno]
to bet on black	**залагам на черно**	[zalágam na ʧérno]
croupier (dealer)	**крупие** (с)	[krupié]
to spin the wheel	**въртя барабан**	[vərtʲá barabán]
rules (~ of the game)	**правила** (с мн) **на игра**	[pravilá na igrá]
chip	**пул** (м)	[pul]
to win (vi, vt)	**спечеля**	[speʧélʲa]
win (winnings)	**печалба** (ж)	[peʧálba]
to lose (~ 100 dollars)	**загубя**	[zagúbʲa]
loss (losses)	**загуба** (ж)	[záguba]
player	**играч** (м)	[igráʧ]
blackjack (card game)	**блекджек** (м)	[blekdʒék]

craps (dice game)	**игра** (ж) **на зарове**	[igrá na zárove]
fruit machine	**игрален автомат** (м)	[igrálen aftomát]

162. Rest. Games. Miscellaneous

to stroll (vi, vt)	**разхождам се**	[rashóʒdam se]
stroll (leisurely walk)	**разходка** (ж)	[rashótka]
car ride	**пътуване** (с)	[pətúvane]
adventure	**приключение** (с)	[prikl^jutʃénie]
picnic	**пикник** (м)	[píknik]
game (chess, etc.)	**игра** (ж)	[igrá]
player	**играч** (м)	[igrátʃ]
game (one ~ of chess)	**партия** (ж)	[pártija]
collector (e.g. philatelist)	**колекционер** (м)	[kolektsionér]
to collect (stamps, etc.)	**колекционирам**	[kolektsioníram]
collection	**колекция** (ж)	[koléktsija]
crossword puzzle	**кръстословица** (ж)	[krəstoslóvitsa]
racecourse (hippodrome)	**хиподрум** (м)	[hipodrúm]
disco (discotheque)	**дискотека** (ж)	[diskotéka]
sauna	**сауна** (ж)	[sáuna]
lottery	**лотария** (ж)	[lotárija]
camping trip	**поход** (м)	[póhot]
camp	**лагер** (м)	[láger]
tent (for camping)	**палатка** (ж)	[palátka]
compass	**компас** (м)	[kompás]
camper	**турист** (м)	[turíst]
to watch (film, etc.)	**гледам**	[glédam]
viewer	**телезрител** (м)	[telezrítel]
TV show (TV program)	**телевизионно предаване** (с)	[televiziónno predávane]

163. Photography

camera (photo)	**фотоапарат** (м)	[fotoaparát]
photo, picture	**снимка** (ж)	[snímka]
photographer	**фотограф** (м)	[fotográf]
photo studio	**фотостудио** (с)	[fotostúdio]
photo album	**фотоалбум** (м)	[fotoalbúm]
camera lens	**обектив** (м)	[obektív]
telephoto lens	**телеобектив** (м)	[teleobektíf]
filter	**филтър** (м)	[fíltər]
lens	**леща** (ж)	[léʃta]
optics (high-quality ~)	**оптика** (ж)	[óptika]
diaphragm (aperture)	**диафрагма** (ж)	[diafrágma]

exposure time (shutter speed)	**експозиция** (ж)	[ekspozítsija]
viewfinder	**визьор** (м)	[vizʲór]
digital camera	**цифрова камера** (ж)	[tsífrova kámera]
tripod	**статив** (м)	[statíf]
flash	**светкавица** (ж)	[svetkávitsa]
to photograph (vt)	**снимам**	[snímam]
to take pictures	**снимам**	[snímam]
to have one's picture taken	**снимам се**	[snímam se]
focus	**фокус** (м)	[fókus]
to focus	**нагласявам рязкост**	[naglasʲávam rʲáskost]
sharp, in focus (adj)	**рязък**	[rʲázək]
sharpness	**рязкост** (ж)	[rʲáskost]
contrast	**контраст** (м)	[kontrást]
contrast (as adj)	**контрастен**	[kontrásten]
picture (photo)	**снимка** (ж)	[snímka]
negative (n)	**негатив** (м)	[negatíf]
film (a roll of ~)	**фотолента** (ж)	[fotolénta]
frame (still)	**кадър** (м)	[kádər]
to print (photos)	**печатам**	[petʃátam]

164. Beach. Swimming

beach	**плаж** (м)	[plaʒ]
sand	**пясък** (м)	[pʲásək]
deserted (beach)	**пустинен**	[pustínen]
suntan	**тен** (м)	[ten]
to get a tan	**пека се**	[peká se]
tanned (adj)	**почернял**	[potʃernʲál]
sunscreen	**крем** (м) **за тен**	[krem za ten]
bikini	**бикини** (мн)	[bikíni]
swimsuit, bikini	**бански костюм** (м)	[bánski kostʲúm]
swim trunks	**плувки** (мн)	[plúfki]
swimming pool	**басейн** (м)	[baséjn]
to swim (vi)	**плувам**	[plúvam]
shower	**душ** (м)	[duʃ]
to change (one's clothes)	**преобличам се**	[preoblítʃam se]
towel	**кърпа** (ж)	[kə́rpa]
boat	**лодка** (ж)	[lótka]
motorboat	**катер** (м)	[káter]
water ski	**водни ски** (мн)	[vódni ski]
pedalo	**водно колело** (с)	[vódno koleló]
surfing	**сърфинг** (м)	[sə́rfing]
surfer	**сърфист** (м)	[sərfíst]

scuba set	**акваланг** (м)	[akvaláng]
flippers (swim fins)	**плавници** (ж мн)	[plávnitsi]
mask (diving ~)	**маска** (ж)	[máska]
diver	**гмуркач** (м)	[gmurkátʃ]
to dive (vi)	**гмуркам се**	[gmúrkam se]
underwater (adv)	**под вода**	[pot vodá]
beach umbrella	**чадър** (м)	[tʃadǝ́r]
beach chair (sun lounger)	**шезлонг** (м)	[ʃezlóng]
sunglasses	**очила** (мн)	[otʃilá]
air mattress	**плажен дюшек** (м)	[plaʒén dʲuʃék]
to play (amuse oneself)	**играя**	[igrája]
to go for a swim	**къпя се**	[kǝ́pʲa se]
beach ball	**топка** (ж)	[tópka]
to inflate (vt)	**надувам**	[nadúvam]
inflatable, air (adj)	**надуваем**	[naduváem]
wave	**вълна** (ж)	[vǝlná]
buoy (line of ~s)	**шамандура** (ж)	[ʃamandúra]
to drown (ab. person)	**давя се**	[dávʲa se]
to save, to rescue	**спасявам**	[spasʲávam]
life jacket	**спасителна жилетка** (ж)	[spasítelna ʒilétka]
to observe, to watch	**наблюдавам**	[nablʲudávam]
lifeguard	**спасител** (м)	[spasítel]

TECHNICAL EQUIPMENT. TRANSPORT

Technical equipment

165. Computer

computer	**компютър** (м)	[kompʲútər]
notebook, laptop	**лаптоп** (м)	[laptóp]
to turn on	**включа**	[fklʲútʃa]
to turn off	**изключа**	[isklʲútʃa]
keyboard	**клавиатура** (ж)	[klaviatúra]
key	**клавиш** (м)	[klavíʃ]
mouse	**мишка** (ж)	[míʃka]
mouse mat	**подложка** (ж) **за мишка**	[podlóʃka za míʃka]
button	**бутон** (м)	[butón]
cursor	**курсор** (м)	[kursór]
monitor	**монитор** (м)	[monítor]
screen	**екран** (м)	[ekrán]
hard disk	**твърд диск** (м)	[tvə́rd dísk]
hard disk capacity	**капацитет** (м) **на твърдия диск**	[kapatsitə́t na tvə́rdija disk]
memory	**памет** (ж)	[pámet]
random access memory	**операционна памет** (ж)	[operatsiónna pámet]
file	**файл** (м)	[fajl]
folder	**папка** (ж)	[pápka]
to open (vt)	**отворя**	[otvórʲa]
to close (vt)	**затворя**	[zatvórʲa]
to save (vt)	**съхраня**	[səhranʲá]
to delete (vt)	**изтрия**	[istríja]
to copy (vt)	**копирам**	[kopíram]
to sort (vt)	**сортирам**	[sortíram]
to transfer (copy)	**копира**	[kopíra]
programme	**програма** (ж)	[prográma]
software	**софтуер** (м)	[softuér]
programmer	**програмист** (м)	[programíst]
to program (vt)	**програмирам**	[programíram]
hacker	**хакер** (м)	[háker]
password	**парола** (ж)	[paróla]
virus	**вирус** (м)	[vírus]
to find, to detect	**намеря**	[namérʲa]

byte	**байт** (м)	[bajt]
megabyte	**мегабайт** (м)	[megabájt]
data	**данни** (мн)	[dánni]
database	**база** (ж) **данни**	[báza dánni]
cable (USB, etc.)	**кабел** (м)	[kábel]
to disconnect (vt)	**разединя**	[razedinʲá]
to connect (sth to sth)	**съединя**	[səedinʲá]

166. Internet. E-mail

Internet	**интернет** (м)	[internét]
browser	**браузър** (м)	[bráuzər]
search engine	**търсачка** (ж)	[tərsátʃka]
provider	**интернет доставчик** (м)	[ínternet dostáftʃik]
webmaster	**уеб майстор** (м)	[web májstor]
website	**уеб сайт** (м)	[web sajt]
web page	**уеб страница** (ж)	[web stránitsa]
address (e-mail ~)	**адрес** (м)	[adrés]
address book	**адресна книга** (ж)	[adrésna kníga]
postbox	**пощенска кутия** (ж)	[póʃtenska kutíja]
post	**поща** (ж)	[póʃta]
full (adj)	**препълнен**	[prepəlnen]
message	**съобщение** (с)	[səobʃténie]
incoming messages	**входящи съобщения** (с мн)	[fhodʲáʃti səobʃténija]
outgoing messages	**изходящи съобщения** (с мн)	[ishodʲáʃti səobʃténija]
sender	**подател** (м)	[podátel]
to send (vt)	**изпратя**	[isprátʲa]
sending (of mail)	**изпращане** (с)	[ispráʃtane]
receiver	**получател** (м)	[polutʃátel]
to receive (vt)	**получа**	[polútʃa]
correspondence	**кореспонденция** (ж)	[korespondéntsija]
to correspond (vi)	**кореспондирам**	[korespondíram]
file	**файл** (м)	[fajl]
to download (vt)	**свалям**	[sválʲam]
to create (vt)	**създам**	[səzdám]
to delete (vt)	**изтрия**	[istríja]
deleted (adj)	**изтрит**	[istrít]
connection (ADSL, etc.)	**връзка** (ж)	[vrəska]
speed	**скорост** (ж)	[skórost]
modem	**модем** (м)	[modém]
access	**достъп** (м)	[dóstəp]
port (e.g. input ~)	**порт** (м)	[port]
connection (make a ~)	**връзка** (ж)	[vrəska]
to connect to ... (vi)	**се свържа с ...**	[se svərʒa s]

to select (vt)	**избера**	[izberá]
to search (for ...)	**търся**	[tərsʲa]

167. Electricity

electricity	**електричество** (с)	[elektrítʃestvo]
electric, electrical (adj)	**електрически**	[elektrítʃeski]
electric power station	**електроцентрала** (ж)	[elektro·tsentrála]
energy	**енергия** (ж)	[enérgija]
electric power	**електроенергия** (ж)	[elektro·enérgija]
light bulb	**крушка** (ж)	[krúʃka]
torch	**фенер** (м)	[fenér]
street light	**фенер** (м)	[fenér]
light	**електричество** (с)	[elektrítʃestvo]
to turn on	**включвам**	[fklʲútʃvam]
to turn off	**изключвам**	[isklʲútʃvam]
to turn off the light	**изключвам ток**	[isklʲútʃvam tok]
to burn out (vi)	**прегоря**	[pregorʲá]
short circuit	**късо съединение** (с)	[késo səedinənie]
broken wire	**прекъсване** (с)	[prekésvane]
contact (electrical ~)	**контакт** (м)	[kontákt]
light switch	**изключвател** (м)	[izklʲutʃvátel]
socket outlet	**контакт** (м)	[kontákt]
plug	**щепсел** (м)	[ʃtépsel]
extension lead	**удължител** (м)	[udəʒítel]
fuse	**предпазител** (м)	[predpázitel]
cable, wire	**кабел** (м)	[kábel]
wiring	**инсталация** (ж)	[instalátsija]
ampere	**ампер** (м)	[ampér]
amperage	**сила** (ж) **на тока**	[síla na tóka]
volt	**волт** (м)	[volt]
voltage	**напрежение** (с)	[napreʒénie]
electrical device	**електроуред** (м)	[elektroúret]
indicator	**индикатор** (м)	[indikátor]
electrician	**електротехник** (м)	[elektrotehník]
to solder (vt)	**запоявам**	[zapojávam]
soldering iron	**поялник** (м)	[pojálnik]
electric current	**ток** (м)	[tok]

168. Tools

tool, instrument	**инструмент** (м)	[instrumént]
tools	**инструменти** (м мн)	[instruménti]
equipment (factory ~)	**оборудване** (с)	[oborúdvane]

hammer	**чук** (м)	[ʧuk]
screwdriver	**отвертка** (ж)	[otvértka]
axe	**брадва** (ж)	[brádva]
saw	**трион** (м)	[trión]
to saw (vt)	**режа с трион**	[réʒa s trión]
plane (tool)	**ренде** (с)	[rendé]
to plane (vt)	**рендосвам**	[rendósvam]
soldering iron	**поялник** (м)	[pojálnik]
to solder (vt)	**запоявам**	[zapojávam]
file (tool)	**пила** (ж)	[pilá]
carpenter pincers	**клещи** (мн)	[kléʃti]
combination pliers	**плоски клещи** (мн)	[plóski kléʃti]
chisel	**длето** (с)	[dletó]
drill bit	**свредел** (с)	[svredél]
electric drill	**дрелка** (ж)	[drélka]
to drill (vi, vt)	**пробивам с дрелка**	[probívam s drélka]
knife	**нож** (м)	[noʒ]
pocket knife	**сгъваем нож** (м)	[sgəváem noʒ]
blade	**острие** (с)	[ostrié]
sharp (blade, etc.)	**остър**	[óstər]
dull, blunt (adj)	**тъп**	[təp]
to get blunt (dull)	**затъпявам се**	[zatəpʲávam se]
to sharpen (vt)	**точа**	[tóʧa]
bolt	**болт** (м)	[bolt]
nut	**гайка** (ж)	[gájka]
thread (of a screw)	**резба** (ж)	[rezbá]
wood screw	**винт** (м)	[vint]
nail	**пирон** (м)	[pirón]
nailhead	**глава** (ж)	[glavá]
ruler (for measuring)	**линийка** (ж)	[línijka]
tape measure	**рулетка** (ж)	[rulétka]
spirit level	**нивелир** (с)	[nivelír]
magnifying glass	**лупа** (ж)	[lúpa]
measuring instrument	**измервателен уред** (м)	[izmervátelen úret]
to measure (vt)	**измервам**	[izmérvam]
scale (temperature ~, etc.)	**скала** (ж)	[skála]
readings	**показание** (с)	[pokazánie]
compressor	**компресор** (м)	[komprésor]
microscope	**микроскоп** (м)	[mikroskóp]
pump (e.g. water ~)	**помпа** (ж)	[pómpa]
robot	**робот** (м)	[robót]
laser	**лазер** (м)	[lázer]
spanner	**гаечен ключ** (м)	[gáeʧen klʲuʧ]
adhesive tape	**тиксо** (с)	[tíkso]

glue	**лепило** (с)	[lepílo]
sandpaper	**шмиргелова хартия** (ж)	[ʃmírgelova hartíja]
spring	**пружина** (ж)	[pruʒína]
magnet	**магнит** (м)	[magnít]
gloves	**ръкавици** (ж мн)	[rəkavítsi]
rope	**въже** (с)	[vəʒé]
cord	**шнур** (м)	[ʃnur]
wire (e.g. telephone ~)	**кабел** (м)	[kábel]
cable	**кабел** (м)	[kábel]
sledgehammer	**боен чук** (м)	[bóen ʧuk]
prybar	**лом** (м)	[lom]
ladder	**стълба** (ж)	[stəlba]
stepladder	**подвижна стълба** (ж)	[podvíʒna stəlba]
to screw (tighten)	**завъртам**	[zavərtam]
to unscrew (lid, filter, etc.)	**отвъртам**	[otvərtam]
to tighten (e.g. with a clamp)	**притискам**	[pritískam]
to glue, to stick	**залепвам**	[zalépvam]
to cut (vt)	**режа**	[réʒa]
malfunction (fault)	**неизправност** (ж)	[neisprávnost]
repair (mending)	**поправка** (ж)	[popráfka]
to repair, to fix (vt)	**ремонтирам**	[remontíram]
to adjust (machine, etc.)	**регулирам**	[regulíram]
to check (to examine)	**проверявам**	[proverʲávam]
checking	**проверка** (ж)	[provérka]
readings	**показание** (с)	[pokazánie]
reliable, solid (machine)	**сигурен**	[síguren]
complex (adj)	**сложен**	[slóʒen]
to rust (get rusted)	**ръждясвам**	[rəʒdʲásvam]
rusty (adj)	**ръждясал**	[rəʒdʲásal]
rust	**ръжда** (ж)	[rəʒdá]

Transport

169. Aeroplane

aeroplane	**самолет** (м)	[samolét]
air ticket	**самолетен билет** (м)	[samoléten bilét]
airline	**авиокомпания** (ж)	[aviokompánija]
airport	**летище** (с)	[letíʃte]
supersonic (adj)	**свръхзвуков**	[svrəh·zvúkov]
captain	**командир** (м) **на самолет**	[komandír na samolét]
crew	**екипаж** (м)	[ekipáʒ]
pilot	**пилот** (м)	[pilót]
stewardess	**стюардеса** (ж)	[stʲuardésa]
navigator	**щурман** (м)	[ʃtúrman]
wings	**крила** (мн)	[krilá]
tail	**опашка** (ж)	[opáʃka]
cockpit	**кабина** (ж)	[kabína]
engine	**двигател** (м)	[dvigátel]
undercarriage (landing gear)	**шаси** (мн)	[ʃasí]
turbine	**турбина** (ж)	[turbína]
propeller	**перка** (ж)	[pérka]
black box	**черна кутия** (ж)	[ʧérna kutíja]
yoke (control column)	**кормило** (с)	[kormílo]
fuel	**гориво** (с)	[gorívo]
safety card	**инструкция** (ж)	[instrúktsija]
oxygen mask	**кислородна маска** (ж)	[kisloródna máska]
uniform	**униформа** (ж)	[unifórma]
lifejacket	**спасителна жилетка** (ж)	[spasítelna ʒilétka]
parachute	**парашут** (м)	[paraʃút]
takeoff	**излитане** (с)	[izlítane]
to take off (vi)	**излитам**	[izlítam]
runway	**писта** (ж) **за излитане**	[písta za izlítane]
visibility	**видимост** (ж)	[vídimost]
flight (act of flying)	**полет** (м)	[pólet]
altitude	**височина** (ж)	[visoʧiná]
air pocket	**въздушна яма** (ж)	[vəzdúʃna jáma]
seat	**място** (с)	[mʲásto]
headphones	**слушалки** (ж мн)	[sluʃálki]
folding tray (tray table)	**прибираща се масичка** (ж)	[pribíraʃta se másiʧka]
airplane window	**илюминатор** (м)	[ilʲuminátor]
aisle	**проход** (м)	[próhot]

170. Train

train	**влак** (м)	[vlak]
commuter train	**електрически влак** (м)	[elektrítʃeski vlak]
express train	**бърз влак** (м)	[bərz vlak]
diesel locomotive	**дизелов локомотив** (м)	[dízelof lokomotíf]
steam locomotive	**парен локомотив** (м)	[páren lokomotíf]
coach, carriage	**вагон** (м)	[vagón]
buffet car	**вагон-ресторант** (м)	[vagón-restoránt]
rails	**релси** (ж мн)	[rélsi]
railway	**железница** (ж)	[ʒeléznitsa]
sleeper (track support)	**траверса** (ж)	[travérsa]
platform (railway ~)	**платформа** (ж)	[platfórma]
platform (~ 1, 2, etc.)	**коловоз** (м)	[kolovós]
semaphore	**семафор** (м)	[semafór]
station	**гара** (ж)	[gára]
train driver	**машинист** (м)	[maʃiníst]
porter (of luggage)	**носач** (м)	[nosátʃ]
carriage attendant	**стюард** (м)	[stʲuárt]
passenger	**пътник** (м)	[pətnik]
ticket inspector	**контрольор** (м)	[kontrolʲór]
corridor (in train)	**коридор** (м)	[koridór]
emergency brake	**аварийна спирачка** (ж)	[avaríjna spirátʃka]
compartment	**купе** (с)	[kupé]
berth	**легло** (с)	[legló]
upper berth	**горно легло** (с)	[górno legló]
lower berth	**долно легло** (с)	[dólno legló]
bed linen, bedding	**спално бельо** (с)	[spálno belʲó]
ticket	**билет** (м)	[bilét]
timetable	**разписание** (с)	[raspisánie]
information display	**табло** (с)	[tabló]
to leave, to depart	**заминавам**	[zaminávam]
departure (of a train)	**заминаване** (с)	[zaminávane]
to arrive (ab. train)	**пристигам**	[pristígam]
arrival	**пристигане** (с)	[pristígane]
to arrive by train	**пристигна с влак**	[pristígna s vlak]
to get on the train	**качвам се във влак**	[kátʃvam se vəf vlak]
to get off the train	**слизам от влак**	[slízam ot vlak]
train crash	**катастрофа** (ж)	[katastrófa]
to derail (vi)	**дерайлирам**	[derajlíram]
steam locomotive	**парен локомотив** (м)	[páren lokomotíf]
stoker, fireman	**огняр** (м)	[ognʲár]
firebox	**пещ** (м) **на локомотив**	[peʃt na lokomotíf]
coal	**въглища** (ж)	[vəgliʃta]

171. Ship

ship	**кораб** (м)	[kórap]
vessel	**плавателен съд** (м)	[plavátelen sət]
steamship	**параход** (м)	[parahót]
riverboat	**моторен кораб** (м)	[motóren kórap]
cruise ship	**рейсов кораб** (м)	[réjsov kórap]
cruiser	**крайцер** (м)	[krájtser]
yacht	**яхта** (ж)	[jáhta]
tugboat	**влекач** (м)	[vlekátʃ]
barge	**шлеп** (м)	[ʃlep]
ferry	**сал** (м)	[sal]
sailing ship	**платноходка** (ж)	[platnohótka]
brigantine	**бригантина** (ж)	[brigantína]
ice breaker	**ледоразбивач** (м)	[ledo·razbivátʃ]
submarine	**подводница** (ж)	[podvódnitsa]
boat (flat-bottomed ~)	**лодка** (ж)	[lótka]
dinghy (lifeboat)	**лодка** (ж)	[lótka]
lifeboat	**спасителна лодка** (ж)	[spasítelna lótka]
motorboat	**катер** (м)	[káter]
captain	**капитан** (м)	[kapitán]
seaman	**матрос** (м)	[matrós]
sailor	**моряк** (м)	[morʲák]
crew	**екипаж** (м)	[ekipáʒ]
boatswain	**боцман** (м)	[bótsman]
ship's boy	**юнга** (м)	[júnga]
cook	**корабен готвач** (м)	[kóraben gotvátʃ]
ship's doctor	**корабен лекар** (м)	[kóraben lékar]
deck	**палуба** (ж)	[páluba]
mast	**мачта** (ж)	[mátʃta]
sail	**корабно платно** (с)	[kórabno platnó]
hold	**трюм** (м)	[trʲum]
bow (prow)	**нос** (м)	[nos]
stern	**кърма** (ж)	[kərmá]
oar	**гребло** (с)	[grebló]
screw propeller	**витло** (с)	[vitló]
cabin	**каюта** (ж)	[kajúta]
wardroom	**каюткомпания** (ж)	[kajut kompánija]
engine room	**машинно отделение** (с)	[maʃínno otdelénie]
bridge	**капитански мостик** (м)	[kapitánski móstik]
radio room	**радиобудка** (ж)	[rádiobútka]
wave (radio)	**вълна** (ж)	[vəlná]
logbook	**корабен дневник** (м)	[kóraben dnévnik]
spyglass	**далекоглед** (м)	[dalekoglét]
bell	**камбана** (ж)	[kambána]

flag	**знаме** (с)	[známe]
hawser (mooring ~)	**дебело въже** (с)	[debélo vǝʒé]
knot (bowline, etc.)	**възел** (м)	[vǝ́zel]
deckrails	**дръжка** (ж)	[drǝ́ʃka]
gangway	**трап** (м)	[trap]
anchor	**котва** (ж)	[kótva]
to weigh anchor	**вдигна котва**	[vdígna kótva]
to drop anchor	**хвърля котва**	[hvǝ́rlʲa kótva]
anchor chain	**котвена верига** (ж)	[kótvena veríga]
port (harbour)	**пристанище** (с)	[pristániʃte]
quay, wharf	**кей** (м)	[kej]
to berth (moor)	**акостирам**	[akostíram]
to cast off	**отплувам**	[otplúvam]
trip, voyage	**пътешествие** (с)	[pǝteʃéstvie]
cruise (sea trip)	**морско пътешествие** (с)	[mórsko pǝteʃéstvie]
course (route)	**курс** (м)	[kurs]
route (itinerary)	**маршрут** (м)	[marʃrút]
fairway (safe water channel)	**фарватер** (м)	[farváter]
shallows	**плитчина** (ж)	[plitʧiná]
to run aground	**заседна на плитчина**	[zasédna na plitʧiná]
storm	**буря** (ж)	[búrʲa]
signal	**сигнал** (м)	[signál]
to sink (vi)	**потъвам**	[potǝ́vam]
SOS (distress signal)	**SOS**	[sos]
ring buoy	**спасителен пояс** (м)	[spasítilen pójas]

172. Airport

airport	**летище** (с)	[letíʃte]
aeroplane	**самолет** (м)	[samolét]
airline	**авиокомпания** (ж)	[aviokompánija]
air traffic controller	**авиодиспечер** (м)	[aviodispéʧer]
departure	**излитане** (с)	[izlítane]
arrival	**кацане** (с)	[kátsane]
to arrive (by plane)	**кацна**	[kátsna]
departure time	**време** (с) **на излитане**	[vréme na izlítane]
arrival time	**време** (с) **на кацане**	[vréme na kátsane]
to be delayed	**закъснявам**	[zakǝsnʲávam]
flight delay	**закъснение** (с) **на излитане**	[zakǝsnénie na izlítane]
information board	**информационно табло** (с)	[informatsiónno tabló]
information	**информация** (ж)	[informátsija]
to announce (vt)	**обявявам**	[obʲavʲávam]
flight (e.g. next ~)	**рейс** (м)	[rejs]
customs	**митница** (ж)	[mítnitsa]

customs officer	**митничар** (м)	[mitnitʃár]
customs declaration	**декларация** (ж)	[deklarátsija]
to fill in (vt)	**попълня**	[popəlnʲa]
to fill in the declaration	**попълня декларация**	[popəlnʲa deklarátsija]
passport control	**паспортен контрол** (м)	[paspórten kontról]
luggage	**багаж** (м)	[bagáʃ]
hand luggage	**ръчен багаж** (м)	[rətʃen bagáʃ]
luggage trolley	**количка** (ж)	[kolítʃka]
landing	**кацане** (с)	[kátsane]
landing strip	**писта** (ж) **за кацане**	[písta za kátsane]
to land (vi)	**кацам**	[kátsam]
airstair (passenger stair)	**стълба** (ж)	[stəlba]
check-in	**регистрация** (ж)	[registrátsija]
check-in counter	**гише** (с) **за регистрация**	[giʃé za registrátsija]
to check-in (vi)	**регистрирам се**	[registríram se]
boarding card	**бордна карта** (ж)	[bórdna kárta]
departure gate	**излизане** (с)	[izlízane]
transit	**транзит** (м)	[tranzít]
to wait (vt)	**чакам**	[tʃákam]
departure lounge	**чакалня** (ж)	[tʃakálnʲa]
to see off	**изпращам**	[ispráʃtam]
to say goodbye	**сбогувам се**	[sbogúvam se]

173. Bicycle. Motorcycle

bicycle	**колело** (с)	[koleló]
scooter	**мотороллер** (м)	[motoróler]
motorbike	**мотоциклет** (м)	[mototsiklét]
to go by bicycle	**карам колело**	[káram koleló]
handlebars	**волан** (м)	[volán]
pedal	**педал** (м)	[pedál]
brakes	**спирачки** (ж мн)	[spirátʃki]
bicycle seat (saddle)	**седло** (с)	[sedló]
pump	**помпа** (ж)	[pómpa]
pannier rack	**багажник** (м)	[bagáʒnik]
front lamp	**фенер** (м)	[fenér]
helmet	**шлем** (м)	[ʃlem]
wheel	**колело** (с)	[koleló]
mudguard	**калник** (с)	[kálnik]
rim	**джанта** (ж)	[dʒánta]
spoke	**спица** (ж)	[spítsa]

Cars

174. Types of cars

car	**автомобил** (м)	[aftomobíl]
sports car	**спортен автомобил** (м)	[spórten aftomobíl]
limousine	**лимузина** (ж)	[limuzína]
off-road vehicle	**джип** (м)	[dʒip]
drophead coupé (convertible)	**кабриолет** (м)	[kabriolét]
minibus	**микробус** (м)	[mikrobús]
ambulance	**бърза помощ** (ж)	[bérza pómoʃt]
snowplough	**снегорин** (м)	[snegorín]
lorry	**камион** (м)	[kamión]
road tanker	**автоцистерна** (ж)	[aftotsistérna]
van (small truck)	**фургон** (м)	[furgón]
tractor unit	**влекач** (м)	[vlekátʃ]
trailer	**ремарке** (с)	[remarké]
comfortable (adj)	**комфортен**	[komfórten]
used (adj)	**употребяван**	[upotrebʲávan]

175. Cars. Bodywork

bonnet	**капак** (м)	[kapák]
wing	**калник** (м)	[kálnik]
roof	**покрив** (м)	[pókriv]
windscreen	**предно стъкло** (с)	[prédno stəkló]
rear-view mirror	**огледало** (с) **за задно виждане**	[ogledálo za zádno víʒdane]
windscreen washer	**стъкломиячка** (ж)	[stəklomijátʃka]
windscreen wipers	**чистачки** (ж мн)	[tʃistátʃki]
side window	**странично стъкло** (с)	[stranítʃno stəkló]
electric window	**стъклоповдигач** (м)	[stəklo·povdigátʃ]
aerial	**антена** (ж)	[anténa]
sunroof	**шибидах** (м)	[ʃibidáh]
bumper	**броня** (ж)	[brónʲa]
boot	**багажник** (м)	[bagáʒnik]
roof luggage rack	**багажник** (м) **на покрива**	[bagáʒnik na pókriva]
door	**врата** (ж)	[vratá]
door handle	**дръжка** (ж)	[dréʃka]
door lock	**ключалка** (ж)	[klʲutʃálka]
number plate	**номер** (м)	[nómer]

silencer	**гърне** (с)	[gərné]
petrol tank	**резервоар** (м) **за бензин**	[rezervoár za benzín]
exhaust pipe	**ауспух** (м)	[áuspuh]
accelerator	**газ** (м)	[gas]
pedal	**педал** (м)	[pedál]
accelerator pedal	**газ** (м)	[gas]
brake	**спирачки** (ж мн)	[spirátʃki]
brake pedal	**спирачка** (ж)	[spirátʃka]
to brake (use the brake)	**удрям спирачка**	[údrʲam spirátʃka]
handbrake	**ръчна спирачка** (ж)	[rətʃna spirátʃka]
clutch	**съединител** (м)	[səedinítel]
clutch pedal	**педал** (м) **на съединител**	[pedál na səedinítel]
clutch disc	**диск** (м) **на съединител**	[disk na səedinítel]
shock absorber	**амортизатор** (м)	[amortizátor]
wheel	**колело** (с)	[koleló]
spare tyre	**резервна гума** (ж)	[rezérvna gúma]
tyre	**гума** (ж)	[gúma]
wheel cover (hubcap)	**капак** (м)	[kapák]
driving wheels	**водещи колела** (мн)	[vódeʃti kolelá]
front-wheel drive (as adj)	**с предно задвижване**	[s prédno zadvíʒvane]
rear-wheel drive (as adj)	**със задно задвижване**	[səs zádno zadvíʒvane]
all-wheel drive (as adj)	**с пълно задвижване**	[s pəlno zadvíʒvane]
gearbox	**скоростна кутия** (ж)	[skórostna kutíja]
automatic (adj)	**автоматичен**	[aftomatítʃen]
mechanical (adj)	**механически**	[mehanítʃeski]
gear lever	**лост** (м) **на скоростна кутия**	[lost na skórostna kutíja]
headlamp	**фар** (м)	[far]
headlights	**фарове** (м мн)	[fárove]
dipped headlights	**къси светлини** (ж мн)	[kəsi svetliní]
full headlights	**дълги светлини** (ж мн)	[dəlgi svetliní]
brake light	**сигнал** (м) **стоп**	[signál stop]
sidelights	**габаритни светлини** (ж мн)	[gabarítni svetliní]
hazard lights	**аварийни светлини** (ж мн)	[avaríjni svetliní]
fog lights	**фарове** (м мн) **за мъгла**	[fárove za məglá]
turn indicator	**мигач** (м)	[migátʃ]
reversing light	**заден ход** (м)	[záden hot]

176. Cars. Passenger compartment

car interior	**салон** (м)	[salón]
leather (as adj)	**кожен**	[kóʒen]
velour (as adj)	**велурен**	[velúren]
upholstery	**тапицерия** (ж)	[tapitsérija]
instrument (gage)	**уред** (м)	[úret]

dashboard	**бордово табло** (с)	[bórdovo tabló]
speedometer	**скоростомер** (м)	[skorostomér]
needle (pointer)	**стрелка** (ж)	[strelká]
mileometer	**километраж** (м)	[kilometráʃ]
indicator (sensor)	**датчик** (м)	[dáttʃik]
level	**ниво** (с)	[nivó]
warning light	**крушка** (ж)	[krúʃka]
steering wheel	**волан** (м)	[volán]
horn	**сигнал** (м)	[signál]
button	**бутон** (м)	[butón]
switch	**превключвател** (м)	[prefklʲutʃvátel]
seat	**седалка** (ж)	[sedálka]
backrest	**облегалка** (ж)	[oblegálka]
headrest	**подглавник** (м)	[podglávnik]
seat belt	**предпазен колан** (м)	[predpázen kolán]
to fasten the belt	**слагам колан**	[slágam kolán]
adjustment (of seats)	**регулиране** (с)	[regulírane]
airbag	**въздушна възглавница** (ж)	[vəzdúʃna vəzglávnitsa]
air-conditioner	**климатик** (м)	[klimatík]
radio	**радио** (с)	[rádio]
CD player	**CD плейър** (м)	[sidí pléər]
to turn on	**включа**	[fklʲútʃa]
aerial	**антена** (ж)	[anténa]
glove box	**жабка** (ж)	[ʒábka]
ashtray	**пепелник** (м)	[pepelník]

177. Cars. Engine

engine	**двигател** (м)	[dvigátel]
motor	**мотор** (м)	[motór]
diesel (as adj)	**дизелов**	[dízelof]
petrol (as adj)	**бензинов**	[benzínov]
engine volume	**обем** (м) **на двигателя**	[obém na dvigátelʲa]
power	**мощност** (ж)	[móʃtnost]
horsepower	**конска сила** (ж)	[kónska síla]
piston	**бутало** (с)	[butálo]
cylinder	**цилиндър** (м)	[tsilíndər]
valve	**клапа** (ж)	[klápa]
injector	**инжектор** (м)	[inʒéktor]
generator (alternator)	**генератор** (м)	[generátor]
carburettor	**карбуратор** (м)	[karburátor]
motor oil	**моторно масло** (с)	[motórno masló]
radiator	**радиатор** (м)	[radiátor]
coolant	**охлаждаща течност** (ж)	[ohláʒdaʃta tétʃnost]
cooling fan	**вентилатор** (м)	[ventilátor]
battery (accumulator)	**акумулатор** (м)	[akumulátor]

starter	**стартер** (м)	[stárter]
ignition	**запалване** (с)	[zapálvane]
sparking plug	**запалителна свещ** (ж)	[zapalítelna sveʃt]
terminal (battery ~)	**клема** (ж)	[kléma]
positive terminal	**плюс** (м)	[plʲus]
negative terminal	**минус** (м)	[mínus]
fuse	**предпазител** (м)	[predpázitel]
air filter	**въздушен филтър** (м)	[vəzdúʃen fíltər]
oil filter	**маслен филтър** (м)	[máslen fíltər]
fuel filter	**филтър** (м) **за гориво**	[fíltər za gorívo]

178. Cars. Crash. Repair

car crash	**катастрофа** (ж)	[katastrófa]
traffic accident	**пътно-транспортно произшествие** (с)	[pétno-transpórtno proisʃéstvie]
to crash (into the wall, etc.)	**блъсна се в ...**	[blésna se v]
to get smashed up	**катастрофирам**	[katastrofíram]
damage	**повреда** (ж)	[povréda]
intact (unscathed)	**цял**	[tsʲal]
breakdown	**счупване** (с)	[stʃúpvane]
to break down (vi)	**счупя се**	[stʃúpʲa se]
towrope	**автомобилно въже** (с)	[aftomobílno vəʒé]
puncture	**спукване** (с)	[spúkvane]
to have a puncture	**спусна**	[spúsna]
to pump up	**напомпвам**	[napómpvam]
pressure	**налягане** (с)	[nalʲágane]
to check (to examine)	**проверя**	[proverʲá]
repair	**ремонт** (м)	[remónt]
garage (auto service shop)	**автосервиз** (м)	[aftoservís]
spare part	**резервна част** (ж)	[rezérvna tʃast]
part	**детайл** (м)	[detájl]
bolt (with nut)	**болт** (м)	[bolt]
screw (fastener)	**винт** (м)	[vint]
nut	**гайка** (ж)	[gájka]
washer	**шайба** (ж)	[ʃájba]
bearing (e.g. ball ~)	**лагер** (м)	[láger]
tube	**тръба** (ж)	[trəbá]
gasket (head ~)	**уплътнение** (с)	[uplətnénie]
cable, wire	**кабел** (м)	[kábel]
jack	**крик** (м)	[krik]
spanner	**гаечен ключ** (м)	[gáetʃen klʲutʃ]
hammer	**чук** (м)	[tʃuk]
pump	**помпа** (ж)	[pómpa]
screwdriver	**отвертка** (ж)	[otvértka]
fire extinguisher	**пожарогасител** (м)	[poʒarogasítel]

warning triangle	**авариен триъгълник** (м)	[avaríen triógəlnik]
to stall (vi)	**заглъхвам**	[zagləhvam]
stall (n)	**спиране** (с)	[spírane]
to be broken	**счупен съм**	[stʃúpen səm]
to overheat (vi)	**прегря се**	[pregrʲá se]
to be clogged up	**запуша се**	[zapúʃa se]
to freeze up (pipes, etc.)	**замръзна**	[zamrəzna]
to burst (vi, ab. tube)	**спука се**	[spúka se]
pressure	**налягане** (с)	[nalʲágane]
level	**ниво** (с)	[nivó]
slack (~ belt)	**слаб**	[slap]
dent	**вдлъбнатина** (ж)	[vdləbnatiná]
knocking noise (engine)	**тракане** (с)	[trákane]
crack	**пукнатина** (ж)	[puknatiná]
scratch	**драскотина** (ж)	[draskotína]

179. Cars. Road

road	**път** (м)	[pət]
motorway	**автомагистрала** (ж)	[aftomagistrála]
highway	**шосе** (с)	[ʃosé]
direction (way)	**посока** (ж)	[posóka]
distance	**разстояние** (с)	[rastojánie]
bridge	**мост** (м)	[most]
car park	**паркинг** (м)	[párking]
square	**площад** (м)	[ploʃtát]
road junction	**кръстовище** (с)	[krəstóviʃte]
tunnel	**тунел** (м)	[tunél]
petrol station	**бензиностанция** (ж)	[benzino·stántsija]
car park	**паркинг** (м)	[párking]
petrol pump	**колонка** (ж)	[kolónka]
auto repair shop	**автосервиз** (м)	[aftoservís]
to fill up	**заредя**	[zaredʲá]
fuel	**гориво** (с)	[gorívo]
jerrycan	**туба** (ж)	[túba]
asphalt, tarmac	**асфалт** (м)	[asfált]
road markings	**маркировка** (ж)	[markirófka]
kerb	**бордюр** (м)	[bordʲúr]
crash barrier	**мантинела** (ж)	[mantinéla]
ditch	**канавка** (ж)	[kanáfka]
roadside (shoulder)	**банкет** (м)	[bankét]
lamppost	**стълб** (м)	[stəlp]
to drive (a car)	**карам**	[káram]
to turn (e.g., ~ left)	**завивам**	[zavívam]
to make a U-turn	**обръщам се**	[obréʃtam se]
reverse (~ gear)	**заден ход** (м)	[záden hot]
to honk (vi)	**сигнализирам**	[signalizíram]

honk (sound)	**звуков сигнал** (м)	[zvúkof signál]
to get stuck (in the mud, etc.)	**заседна**	[zasédna]
to spin the wheels	**буксувам**	[buksúvam]
to cut, to turn off (vt)	**гася**	[gasʲá]
speed	**скорост** (ж)	[skórost]
to exceed the speed limit	**превиша скорост**	[previʃá skórost]
to give a ticket	**глобявам**	[globʲávam]
traffic lights	**светофар** (м)	[svetofár]
driving licence	**шофьорска книжка** (ж)	[ʃofʲórska kníʃka]
level crossing	**прелез** (м)	[prélez]
crossroads	**кръстовище** (с)	[krəstóviʃte]
zebra crossing	**пешеходна пътека** (ж)	[peʃehódna pətéka]
bend, curve	**завой** (м)	[zavój]
pedestrian precinct	**пешеходна зона** (ж)	[peʃehódna zóna]

180. Signs

Highway Code	**правила** (с мн) **за улично движение**	[pravilá za úlitʃno dviʒénie]
road sign (traffic sign)	**пътен знак** (м)	[pəten znak]
overtaking	**изпреварване** (с)	[isprevárvane]
curve	**завой** (м)	[zavój]
U-turn	**обръщане** (с)	[obrəʃtane]
roundabout	**кръгово движение** (с)	[krəgovo dviʒənie]
No entry	**влизането забранено**	[vlízaneto zabranéno]
All vehicles prohibited	**движението забранено**	[dviʒénieto zabranéno]
No overtaking	**изпреварването забранено**	[isprevárvaneto zabranéno]
No parking	**паркирането забранено**	[parkíraneto zabranéno]
No stopping	**спирането забранено**	[spíraneto zabranéno]
dangerous curve	**остър завой** (м)	[óstər zavój]
steep descent	**стръмно спускане** (с)	[strəmno spúskane]
one-way traffic	**еднопосочно движение** (с)	[ednoposótʃno dviʒénie]
zebra crossing	**пешеходна пътека** (ж)	[peʃehódna pətéka]
slippery road	**хлъзгав път** (м)	[hləzgaf pət]
GIVE WAY	**дай път**	[daj pət]

PEOPLE. LIFE EVENTS

181. Holidays. Event

celebration, holiday	**празник** (м)	[práznik]
national day	**национален празник** (м)	[natsionálen práznik]
public holiday	**празничен ден** (м)	[prázniʧen den]
to commemorate (vt)	**празнувам**	[praznúvam]
event (happening)	**събитие** (с)	[səbítie]
event (organized activity)	**мероприятие** (с)	[meroprijátie]
banquet (party)	**банкет** (м)	[bankét]
reception (formal party)	**прием** (м)	[príem]
feast	**пир** (м)	[pir]
anniversary	**годишнина** (ж)	[godíʃnina]
jubilee	**юбилей** (м)	[jubiléj]
to celebrate (vt)	**отбележа**	[otbeléʒa]
New Year	**Нова година** (ж)	[nóva godína]
Happy New Year!	**Честита нова година!**	[ʧestíta nóva godína]
Christmas	**Коледа**	[kóleda]
Merry Christmas!	**Весела Коледа!**	[vésela kóleda]
Christmas tree	**коледна елха** (ж)	[kóledna elhá]
fireworks (fireworks show)	**заря** (ж)	[zarʲá]
wedding	**сватба** (ж)	[svátba]
groom	**годеник** (м)	[godeník]
bride	**годеница** (ж)	[godenítsa]
to invite (vt)	**каня**	[kánʲa]
invitation card	**покана** (ж)	[pokána]
guest	**гост** (м)	[gost]
to visit (~ your parents, etc.)	**отивам на гости**	[otívam na gósti]
to meet the guests	**посрещам гости**	[posréʃtam gósti]
gift, present	**подарък** (м)	[podárək]
to give (sth as present)	**подарявам**	[podarʲávam]
to receive gifts	**получавам подаръци**	[poluʧávam podárətsi]
bouquet (of flowers)	**букет** (м)	[bukét]
congratulations	**поздравление** (с)	[pozdravlénie]
to congratulate (vt)	**поздравявам**	[pozdravʲávam]
greetings card	**поздравителна картичка** (ж)	[pozdravítelna kártiʧka]
to send a postcard	**изпратя картичка**	[isprátʲa kártiʧka]
to get a postcard	**получа картичка**	[polúʧa kártiʧka]

toast	**тост** (м)	[tost]
to offer (a drink, etc.)	**черпя**	[ʧérpʲa]
champagne	**шампанско** (с)	[ʃampánsko]
to enjoy oneself	**веселя се**	[veselʲá se]
merriment (gaiety)	**веселба** (ж)	[veselbá]
joy (emotion)	**радост** (ж)	[rádost]
dance	**танц** (м)	[tɑntѕ]
to dance (vi, vt)	**танцувам**	[tantsúvam]
waltz	**валс** (м)	[vals]
tango	**танго** (с)	[tangó]

182. Funerals. Burial

cemetery	**гробища** (мн)	[gróbiʃta]
grave, tomb	**гроб** (м)	[grop]
cross	**кръст** (м)	[krəst]
gravestone	**надгробен паметник** (м)	[nadgróben pámetnik]
fence	**ограда** (ж)	[ográda]
chapel	**параклис** (м)	[paráklis]
death	**смърт** (ж)	[smərt]
to die (vi)	**умра**	[umrá]
the deceased	**покойник** (м)	[pokójnik]
mourning	**траур** (м)	[tráur]
to bury (vt)	**погребвам**	[pogrébvam]
undertakers	**погребални услуги** (мн)	[pogrebálni uslúgi]
funeral	**погребение** (с)	[pogrebénie]
wreath	**венец** (м)	[venéts]
coffin	**ковчег** (м)	[kofʧék]
hearse	**катафалка** (ж)	[katafálka]
shroud	**саван** (м)	[saván]
funeral procession	**погребално шествие** (с)	[pogrebálno ʃéstvie]
funerary urn	**урна** (ж)	[úrna]
crematorium	**крематориум** (м)	[krematórium]
obituary	**некролог** (м)	[nekrolók]
to cry (weep)	**плача**	[pláʧa]
to sob (vi)	**ридая**	[ridája]

183. War. Soldiers

platoon	**взвод** (м)	[vzvot]
company	**рота** (ж)	[róta]
regiment	**полк** (м)	[polk]
army	**армия** (ж)	[ármija]
division	**дивизия** (ж)	[divízija]

section, squad	**отряд** (м)	[otrʲát]
host (army)	**войска** (ж)	[vojská]
soldier	**войник** (м)	[vojník]
officer	**офицер** (м)	[ofitsér]
private	**редник** (м)	[rédnik]
sergeant	**сержант** (м)	[serʒánt]
lieutenant	**лейтенант** (м)	[lejtenánt]
captain	**капитан** (м)	[kapitán]
major	**майор** (м)	[majór]
colonel	**полковник** (м)	[polkóvnik]
general	**генерал** (м)	[generál]
sailor	**моряк** (м)	[morʲák]
captain	**капитан** (м)	[kapitán]
boatswain	**боцман** (м)	[bótsman]
artilleryman	**артилерист** (м)	[artilerníst]
paratrooper	**десантчик** (м)	[desánttʃik]
pilot	**летец** (м)	[letéts]
navigator	**щурман** (м)	[ʃtúrman]
mechanic	**механик** (м)	[mehánik]
pioneer (sapper)	**сапьор** (м)	[sapʲór]
parachutist	**парашутист** (м)	[paraʃutíst]
reconnaissance scout	**разузнавач** (м)	[razuznavátʃ]
sniper	**снайперист** (м)	[snajperíst]
patrol (group)	**патрул** (м)	[patrúl]
to patrol (vt)	**патрулирам**	[patrulíram]
sentry, guard	**часови** (м)	[tʃasoví]
warrior	**войник** (м)	[vojník]
patriot	**патриот** (м)	[patriót]
hero	**герой** (м)	[gerój]
heroine	**героиня** (ж)	[geroínʲa]
traitor	**предател** (м)	[predátel]
to betray (vt)	**предавам**	[predávam]
deserter	**дезертьор** (м)	[dezertʲór]
to desert (vi)	**дезертирам**	[dezertíram]
mercenary	**наемник** (м)	[naémnik]
recruit	**новобранец** (м)	[novobránets]
volunteer	**доброволец** (м)	[dobrovólets]
dead (n)	**убит** (м)	[ubít]
wounded (n)	**ранен** (м)	[ranén]
prisoner of war	**пленник** (м)	[plénnik]

184. War. Military actions. Part 1

war	**война** (ж)	[vojná]
to be at war	**воювам**	[vojúvam]

civil war **гражданска война** (ж) [gráʒdanska vojná]
treacherously (adv) **вероломно** [verolómno]
declaration of war **обявяване** (с) [obʲavʲávane]
to declare (~ war) **обявя** [obʲavʲá]
aggression **агресия** (ж) [agrésija]
to attack (invade) **нападам** [napádam]

to invade (vt) **завземам** [zavzémam]
invader **окупатор** (м) [okupátor]
conqueror **завоевател** (м) [zavoevátel]

defence **отбрана** (ж) [otbrána]
to defend (a country, etc.) **отбранявам** [otbranʲávam]
to defend (against ...) **отбранявам се** [otbranʲávam se]

enemy **враг** (м) [vrak]
foe, adversary **противник** (м) [protívnik]
enemy (as adj) **вражески** [vráʒeski]

strategy **стратегия** (ж) [stratégija]
tactics **тактика** (ж) [táktika]

order **заповед** (ж) [zápovet]
command (order) **команда** (ж) [kománda]
to order (vt) **заповядвам** [zapovʲádvam]
mission **задача** (ж) [zadátʃa]
secret (adj) **секретен** [sekréten]

battle **сражение** (с) [sraʒénie]
combat **бой** (м) [boj]

attack **атака** (ж) [atáka]
charge (assault) **щурм** (м) [ʃturm]
to storm (vt) **щурмувам** [ʃturmúvam]
siege (to be under ~) **обсада** (ж) [obsáda]

offensive (n) **настъпление** (с) [nastəplénie]
to go on the offensive **настъпвам** [nastə́pvam]

retreat **отстъпление** (с) [otstəplénie]
to retreat (vi) **отстъпвам** [otstə́pvam]

encirclement **обкръжение** (с) [opkrəʒénie]
to encircle (vt) **обкръжавам** [opkrəʒávam]

bombing (by aircraft) **бомбардиране** (с) [bombardírane]
to drop a bomb **хвърлям бомба** [hvə́rlʲam bómba]
to bomb (vt) **бомбардирам** [bombardíram]
explosion **експлозия** (ж) [eksplózija]

shot **изстрел** (м) [ísstrel]
to fire (~ a shot) **изстрелям** [isstrélʲam]
firing (burst of ~) **стрелба** (ж) [strelbá]

to aim (to point a weapon) **целя се** [tsélʲa se]
to point (a gun) **насоча** [nasótʃa]

to hit (the target)	**улуча**	[ulútʃa]
to sink (~ a ship)	**потопя**	[potopʲá]
hole (in a ship)	**дупка** (ж)	[dúpka]
to founder, to sink (vi)	**потъвам**	[potə́vam]
front (war ~)	**фронт** (м)	[front]
evacuation	**евакуация** (ж)	[evakuátsija]
to evacuate (vt)	**евакуирам**	[evakuíram]
barbed wire	**бодлив тел** (м)	[bodlív tel]
barrier (anti tank ~)	**заграждение** (с)	[zagraʒdénie]
watchtower	**кула** (ж)	[kúla]
military hospital	**военна болница** (ж)	[voénna bólnitsa]
to wound (vt)	**раня**	[ranʲá]
wound	**рана** (ж)	[rána]
wounded (n)	**ранен** (м)	[ranén]
to be wounded	**получа нараняване**	[polútʃa naranʲávane]
serious (wound)	**тежък**	[téʒək]

185. War. Military actions. Part 2

captivity	**плен** (м)	[plen]
to take captive	**пленявам**	[plenʲávam]
to be held captive	**намирам се в плен**	[namíram se v plen]
to be taken captive	**попадна в плен**	[popádna v plen]
concentration camp	**концлагер** (м)	[kóntsláger]
prisoner of war	**пленник** (м)	[plénnik]
to escape (vi)	**бягам**	[bʲágam]
to betray (vt)	**предам**	[predám]
betrayer	**предател** (м)	[predátel]
betrayal	**предателство** (с)	[predátelstvo]
to execute (by firing squad)	**разстрелям**	[rasstrélʲam]
execution (by firing squad)	**разстрелване** (с)	[rasstrélvane]
equipment (military gear)	**военна униформа** (ж)	[voénna unifórma]
shoulder board	**пагон** (м)	[pagón]
gas mask	**противогаз** (м)	[protivogás]
field radio	**радиостанция** (ж)	[radiostántsija]
cipher, code	**шифър** (м)	[ʃífər]
secrecy	**конспирация** (ж)	[konspirátsija]
password	**парола** (ж)	[paróla]
land mine	**мина** (ж)	[mína]
to mine (road, etc.)	**минирам**	[miníram]
minefield	**минно поле** (с)	[mínno polé]
air-raid warning	**въздушна тревога** (ж)	[vəzdúʃna trevóga]
alarm (alert signal)	**тревога** (ж)	[trevóga]
signal	**сигнал** (м)	[signál]

signal flare	**сигнална ракета** (ж)	[signálna rakéta]
headquarters	**щаб** (м)	[ʃtap]
reconnaissance	**разузнаване** (с)	[razuznávane]
situation	**обстановка** (ж)	[opstanófka]
report	**рапорт** (м)	[ráport]
ambush	**засада** (ж)	[zasáda]
reinforcement (army)	**подкрепа** (ж)	[potkrépa]
target	**мишена** (ж)	[miʃéna]
training area	**полигон** (м)	[poligón]
military exercise	**маневри** (м мн)	[manévri]
panic	**паника** (ж)	[pánika]
devastation	**разруха** (ж)	[razrúha]
destruction, ruins	**разрушения** (с мн)	[razruʃénija]
to destroy (vt)	**разрушавам**	[razruʃávam]
to survive (vi, vt)	**оцелея**	[otseléja]
to disarm (vt)	**обезоръжа**	[obezorəʒá]
to handle (~ a gun)	**служа си**	[slúʒa si]
Attention!	**Мирно!**	[mírno]
At ease!	**Свободно!**	[svobódno]
feat, act of courage	**подвиг** (м)	[pódvik]
oath (vow)	**клетва** (ж)	[klétva]
to swear (an oath)	**заклевам се**	[zaklévam se]
decoration (medal, etc.)	**награда** (ж)	[nagráda]
to award (give a medal to)	**награждавам**	[nagraʒdávam]
medal	**медал** (м)	[medál]
order (e.g. ~ of Merit)	**орден** (м)	[órden]
victory	**победа** (ж)	[pobéda]
defeat	**поражение** (с)	[poraʒénie]
armistice	**примирие** (с)	[primírie]
standard (battle flag)	**знаме** (с)	[známe]
glory (honour, fame)	**слава** (ж)	[sláva]
parade	**парад** (м)	[parát]
to march (on parade)	**марширувам**	[marʃirúvam]

186. Weapons

weapons	**оръжие** (с)	[orə́ʒie]
firearms	**огнестрелно оръжие** (с)	[ognestrélno orə́ʒie]
cold weapons (knives, etc.)	**хладно оръжие** (с)	[hládno orə́ʒie]
chemical weapons	**химическо оръжие** (с)	[himítʃesko orə́ʒie]
nuclear (adj)	**ядрен**	[jádren]
nuclear weapons	**ядрено оръжие** (с)	[jádreno orə́ʒie]
bomb	**бомба** (ж)	[bómba]
atomic bomb	**атомна бомба** (ж)	[átomna bómba]

pistol (gun) **пистолет** (м) [pistolét]
rifle **пушка** (ж) [púʃka]
submachine gun **автомат** (м) [aftomát]
machine gun **картечница** (ж) [kartétʃnitsa]

muzzle **дуло** (с) [dúlo]
barrel **цев** (м) [tsev]
calibre **калибър** (м) [kalíbər]

trigger **спусък** (м) [spúsək]
sight (aiming device) **мерник** (м) [mérnik]
magazine **магазин** (м) [magazín]
butt (shoulder stock) **приклад** (м) [priklát]

hand grenade **граната** (ж) [granáta]
explosive **експлозив** (с) [eksplozíf]

bullet **куршум** (м) [kurʃúm]
cartridge **патрон** (м) [patrón]
charge **заряд** (м) [zarʲát]
ammunition **боеприпаси** (мн) [boeprípasi]

bomber (aircraft) **бомбардировач** (м) [bombardirovátʃ]
fighter **изтребител** (м) [istrebítel]
helicopter **хеликоптер** (м) [helikópter]

anti-aircraft gun **зенитно оръдие** (с) [zenítno orədie]
tank **танк** (м) [tank]
tank gun **оръдие** (с) [orədie]

artillery **артилерия** (ж) [artilérija]
to lay (a gun) **насоча** [nasótʃa]

shell (projectile) **снаряд** (м) [snarʲát]
mortar bomb **мина** (ж) [mína]

mortar **миномет** (м) [minomét]
splinter (shell fragment) **парче** (с) [partʃé]

submarine **подводница** (ж) [podvódnitsa]
torpedo **торпедо** (с) [torpédo]
missile **ракета** (ж) [rakéta]

to load (gun) **зареждам** [zaréʒdam]
to shoot (vi) **стрелям** [strélʲam]

to point at (the cannon) **целя се в ...** [tsélʲa se v]
bayonet **щик** (м) [ʃtik]

rapier **шпага** (ж) [ʃpága]
sabre (e.g. cavalry ~) **сабя** (ж) [sábʲa]
spear (weapon) **копие** (с) [kópie]
bow **лък** (м) [lək]
arrow **стрела** (ж) [strelá]
musket **мускет** (м) [muskét]
crossbow **арбалет** (м) [arbalét]

187. Ancient people

primitive (prehistoric)	**първобитен**	[pərvobíten]
prehistoric (adj)	**доисторически**	[doistoríʧeski]
ancient (~ civilization)	**древен**	[dréven]
Stone Age	**Каменен век** (м)	[kámenen vek]
Bronze Age	**бронзова епоха** (ж)	[brónzova epóha]
Ice Age	**ледникова епоха** (ж)	[lédnikova epóha]
tribe	**племе** (с)	[pléme]
cannibal	**човекоядец** (м)	[ʧovekojádets]
hunter	**ловец** (м)	[lovéts]
to hunt (vi, vt)	**ловувам**	[lovúvam]
mammoth	**мамут** (м)	[mamút]
cave	**пещера** (ж)	[peʃterá]
fire	**огън** (м)	[ógən]
campfire	**клада** (ж)	[kláda]
cave painting	**скална рисунка** (ж)	[skálna risúnka]
tool (e.g. stone axe)	**оръдие** (с) **на труда**	[orədie na trudá]
spear	**копие** (с)	[kópie]
stone axe	**каменна брадва** (ж)	[kámenna brádva]
to be at war	**воювам**	[vojúvam]
to domesticate (vt)	**опитомявам**	[opitomʲávam]
idol	**идол** (м)	[ídol]
to worship (vt)	**покланям се**	[poklánʲam se]
superstition	**суеверие** (с)	[suevérie]
evolution	**еволюция** (ж)	[evolʲútsija]
development	**развитие** (с)	[razvítie]
disappearance (extinction)	**изчезване** (с)	[izʧézvane]
to adapt oneself	**приспособявам се**	[prisposobʲávam se]
archaeology	**археология** (ж)	[arheológija]
archaeologist	**археолог** (м)	[arheolók]
archaeological (adj)	**археологически**	[arheologíʧeski]
excavation site	**разкопки** (мн)	[raskópki]
excavations	**разкопки** (мн)	[raskópki]
find (object)	**находка** (ж)	[nahótka]
fragment	**фрагмент** (м)	[fragmént]

188. Middle Ages

people (ethnic group)	**народ** (м)	[narót]
peoples	**народи** (м мн)	[naródi]
tribe	**племе** (с)	[pléme]
tribes	**племена** (с мн)	[plemená]
barbarians	**варвари** (м мн)	[várvari]
Gauls	**гали** (м мн)	[gáli]

Goths	**готи** (м мн)	[góti]
Slavs	**славяни** (м мн)	[slav'áni]
Vikings	**викинги** (м мн)	[víkingi]
Romans	**римляни** (м мн)	[ríml'ani]
Roman (adj)	**римски**	[rímski]
Byzantines	**византийци** (м мн)	[vizantíjtsi]
Byzantium	**Византия** (ж)	[vizántija]
Byzantine (adj)	**византийски**	[vizantíjski]
emperor	**император** (м)	[imperátor]
leader, chief (tribal ~)	**вожд** (м)	[voʒt]
powerful (~ king)	**могъщ**	[mogéʃt]
king	**крал** (м)	[kral]
ruler (sovereign)	**владетел** (м)	[vladétel]
knight	**рицар** (м)	[rítsar]
feudal lord	**феодал** (м)	[feodál]
feudal (adj)	**феодален**	[feodálen]
vassal	**васал** (м)	[vasál]
duke	**херцог** (м)	[hertsók]
earl	**граф** (м)	[graf]
baron	**барон** (м)	[barón]
bishop	**епископ** (м)	[episkóp]
armour	**доспехи** (мн)	[dospéhi]
shield	**щит** (м)	[ʃtit]
sword	**меч** (м)	[metʃ]
visor	**забрало** (с)	[zabrálo]
chainmail	**ризница** (ж)	[ríznitsa]
Crusade	**кръстоносен поход** (м)	[krəstonósen póhot]
crusader	**кръстоносец** (м)	[krəstonósets]
territory	**територия** (ж)	[teritórija]
to attack (invade)	**нападам**	[napádam]
to conquer (vt)	**завоювам**	[zavojúvam]
to occupy (invade)	**завзема**	[zavzéma]
siege (to be under ~)	**обсада** (ж)	[obsáda]
besieged (adj)	**обсаден**	[opsadén]
to besiege (vt)	**обсаждам**	[opsáʒdam]
inquisition	**инквизиция** (ж)	[inkvizítsija]
inquisitor	**инквизитор** (м)	[inkvizítor]
torture	**измъчване** (с)	[izmə́tʃvane]
cruel (adj)	**жесток**	[ʒestók]
heretic	**еретик** (м)	[eretík]
heresy	**ерес** (ж)	[éres]
seafaring	**мореплаване** (с)	[moreplávane]
pirate	**пират** (м)	[pirát]
piracy	**пиратство** (с)	[pirátstvo]
boarding (attack)	**абордаж** (м)	[abordáʒ]

loot, booty	**плячка** (ж)	[plʲátʃka]
treasure	**съкровища** (с мн)	[səkróviʃta]
discovery	**откритие** (с)	[otkrítie]
to discover (new land, etc.)	**откривам**	[otkrívam]
expedition	**експедиция** (ж)	[ekspedítsija]
musketeer	**мускетар** (м)	[musketár]
cardinal	**кардинал** (м)	[kardinál]
heraldry	**хералдика** (ж)	[heráldika]
heraldic (adj)	**хералдически**	[heraldítʃeski]

189. Leader. Chief. Authorities

king	**крал** (м)	[kral]
queen	**кралица** (ж)	[kralítsa]
royal (adj)	**кралски**	[králski]
kingdom	**кралство** (с)	[králstvo]
prince	**принц** (м)	[prints]
princess	**принцеса** (ж)	[printsésa]
president	**президент** (м)	[prezidént]
vice-president	**вицепрезидент** (м)	[vítse·prezidént]
senator	**сенатор** (м)	[senátor]
monarch	**монарх** (м)	[monárh]
ruler (sovereign)	**владетел** (м)	[vladétel]
dictator	**диктатор** (м)	[diktátor]
tyrant	**тиранин** (м)	[tiránin]
magnate	**магнат** (м)	[magnát]
director	**директор** (м)	[diréktor]
chief	**шеф** (м)	[ʃef]
manager (director)	**управител** (м)	[uprávitel]
boss	**бос** (м)	[bos]
owner	**собственик** (м)	[sóbstvenik]
head (~ of delegation)	**глава** (ж)	[glavá]
authorities	**власти** (ж мн)	[vlásti]
superiors	**началство** (с)	[natʃálstvo]
governor	**губернатор** (м)	[gubernátor]
consul	**консул** (м)	[kónsul]
diplomat	**дипломат** (м)	[diplomát]
mayor	**кмет** (м)	[kmet]
sheriff	**шериф** (м)	[ʃeríf]
emperor	**император** (м)	[imperátor]
tsar, czar	**цар** (м)	[tsar]
pharaoh	**фараон** (м)	[faraón]
khan	**хан** (м)	[han]

190. Road. Way. Directions

road	**път** (м)	[pət]
way (direction)	**път** (м)	[pət]
highway	**шосе** (с)	[ʃosé]
motorway	**автомагистрала** (ж)	[aftomagistrála]
trunk road	**първостепенен път** (м)	[pərvostépenen pət]
main road	**главен път** (м)	[gláven pət]
dirt road	**междуселски път** (м)	[meʒdusélski pət]
pathway	**пътека** (ж)	[pətéka]
footpath (troddenpath)	**пътечка** (ж)	[pətéʧka]
Where?	**Къде?**	[kədé]
Where (to)?	**Къде?**	[kədé]
From where?	**Откъде?**	[otkədé]
direction (way)	**посока** (ж)	[posóka]
to point (~ the way)	**посочвам**	[posóʧvam]
to the left	**наляво**	[nalʲávo]
to the right	**вдясно**	[vdʲásno]
straight ahead (adv)	**направо**	[naprávo]
back (e.g. to turn ~)	**назад**	[nazát]
bend, curve	**завой** (м)	[zavój]
to turn (e.g., ~ left)	**завивам**	[zavívam]
to make a U-turn	**обръщам се**	[obréʃtam se]
to be visible (mountains, castle, etc.)	**виждам се**	[víʒdam se]
to appear (come into view)	**покажа се**	[pokáʒa se]
stop, halt (e.g., during a trip)	**спиране** (с)	[spírane]
to rest, to pause (vi)	**почивам си**	[poʧívam si]
rest (pause)	**почивка** (ж)	[poʧífka]
to lose one's way	**загубя се**	[zagúbʲa se]
to lead to … (ab. road)	**водя към …**	[vódʲa kəm]
to came out (e.g., on the highway)	**изляза на …**	[izlʲáza na]
stretch (of the road)	**отрязък** (м)	[otrʲázək]
asphalt	**асфалт** (м)	[asfált]
kerb	**бордюр** (м)	[bordʲúr]
ditch	**канавка** (ж)	[kanáfka]
manhole	**капак** (м)	[kapák]
roadside (shoulder)	**банкет** (м)	[bankét]
pit, pothole	**дупка** (ж)	[dúpka]
to go (on foot)	**вървя**	[vərvʲá]
to overtake (vt)	**изпреваря**	[isprevárʲa]
step (footstep)	**крачка** (ж)	[kráʧka]

on foot (adv)	**пеш**	[peʃ]
to block (road)	**преградя**	[pregradʲá]
boom gate	**бариера** (ж)	[bariéra]
dead end	**задънена улица** (ж)	[zadənena úlitsa]

191. Breaking the law. Criminals. Part 1

bandit	**бандит** (м)	[bandít]
crime	**престъпление** (с)	[prestəplénie]
criminal (person)	**престъпник** (м)	[prestəpnik]
thief	**крадец** (м)	[kradéts]
to steal (vi, vt)	**крада**	[kradá]
stealing, theft	**кражба** (ж)	[kráʒba]
to kidnap (vt)	**отвлека**	[otvleká]
kidnapping	**отвличане** (с)	[otvlíʧane]
kidnapper	**похитител** (м)	[pohitítel]
ransom	**откуп** (м)	[ótkup]
to demand ransom	**искам откуп**	[ískam ótkup]
to rob (vt)	**грабя**	[grábʲa]
robber	**грабител** (м)	[grabítel]
to extort (vt)	**изнудвам**	[iznúdvam]
extortionist	**изнудвач** (м)	[iznudváʧ]
extortion	**изнудване** (с)	[iznúdvane]
to murder, to kill	**убия**	[ubíja]
murder	**убийство** (с)	[ubíjstvo]
murderer	**убиец** (м)	[ubíets]
gunshot	**изстрел** (м)	[ísstrel]
to fire (~ a shot)	**изстрелям**	[isstrélʲam]
to shoot to death	**застрелям**	[zastrélʲam]
to shoot (vi)	**стрелям**	[strélʲam]
shooting	**стрелба** (ж)	[strelbá]
incident (fight, etc.)	**произшествие** (с)	[proisʃéstvie]
fight, brawl	**сбиване** (с)	[zbívane]
Help!	**Помогнете!**	[pomognéte]
victim	**жертва** (ж)	[ʒértva]
to damage (vt)	**повредя**	[povredʲá]
damage	**щета** (ж)	[ʃtetá]
dead body, corpse	**труп** (м)	[trup]
grave (~ crime)	**тежък**	[téʒək]
to attack (vt)	**нападна**	[napádna]
to beat (to hit)	**бия**	[bíja]
to beat up	**набия**	[nabíja]
to take (rob of sth)	**отнема**	[otnéma]
to stab to death	**заколя**	[zakólʲa]

to maim (vt)	**осакатя**	[osakatʲá]
to wound (vt)	**раня**	[ranʲá]
blackmail	**шантаж** (м)	[ʃantáʒ]
to blackmail (vt)	**шантажирам**	[ʃantaʒíram]
blackmailer	**шантажист** (м)	[ʃantaʒíst]
protection racket	**рекет** (м)	[réket]
racketeer	**рекетьор** (м)	[reketʲór]
gangster	**гангстер** (м)	[gángster]
mafia	**мафия** (ж)	[máfija]
pickpocket	**джебчия** (м)	[dʒebʧíja]
burglar	**разбивач** (м) **на врати**	[razbiváʧ na vratí]
smuggling	**контрабанда** (ж)	[kontrabánda]
smuggler	**контрабандист** (м)	[kontrabandíst]
forgery	**фалшификат** (м)	[falʃifikát]
to forge (counterfeit)	**фалшифицирам**	[falʃifitsíram]
fake (forged)	**фалшив**	[falʃív]

192. Breaking the law. Criminals. Part 2

rape	**изнасилване** (с)	[iznasílvane]
to rape (vt)	**изнасиля**	[iznasílʲa]
rapist	**насилник** (м)	[nasílnik]
maniac	**маниак** (м)	[maniák]
prostitute (fem.)	**проститутка** (ж)	[prostitútka]
prostitution	**проституция** (ж)	[prostitútsija]
pimp	**сутеньор** (м)	[sutenʲór]
drug addict	**наркоман** (м)	[narkomán]
drug dealer	**наркотрафикант** (м)	[narkotrafikánt]
to blow up (bomb)	**взривя**	[vzrivʲá]
explosion	**експлозия** (ж)	[eksplózija]
to set fire	**подпаля**	[podpálʲa]
arsonist	**подпалвач** (м)	[podpalváʧ]
terrorism	**тероризъм** (м)	[terorízəm]
terrorist	**терорист** (м)	[teroríst]
hostage	**заложник** (м)	[zalóʒnik]
to swindle (deceive)	**измамя**	[izmámʲa]
swindle, deception	**измама** (ж)	[izmáma]
swindler	**мошеник** (м)	[moʃénik]
to bribe (vt)	**подкупя**	[podkúpʲa]
bribery	**подкуп** (м)	[pótkup]
bribe	**рушвет** (м)	[ruʃvét]
poison	**отрова** (ж)	[otróva]
to poison (vt)	**отровя**	[otróvʲa]

to poison oneself	**отровя се**	[otróv^ja se]
suicide (act)	**самоубийство** (с)	[samoubíjstvo]
suicide (person)	**самоубиец** (м)	[samoubíets]
to threaten (vt)	**заплашвам**	[zapláʃvam]
threat	**заплаха** (ж)	[zapláha]
to make an attempt	**покушавам се**	[pokuʃávam se]
attempt (attack)	**покушение** (с)	[pokuʃénie]
to steal (a car)	**открадна**	[otkrádna]
to hijack (a plane)	**отвлека**	[otvleká]
revenge	**отмъщение** (с)	[otməʃténie]
to avenge (get revenge)	**отмъщавам**	[otməʃtávam]
to torture (vt)	**изтезавам**	[istezávam]
torture	**измъчване** (с)	[izmə́tʃvane]
to torment (vt)	**измъчвам**	[izmə́tʃvam]
pirate	**пират** (м)	[pirát]
hooligan	**хулиган** (м)	[huligán]
armed (adj)	**въоръжен**	[vəorəʒén]
violence	**насилие** (с)	[nasílie]
illegal (unlawful)	**незаконен**	[nezakónen]
spying (espionage)	**шпионаж** (м)	[ʃpionáʒ]
to spy (vi)	**шпионирам**	[ʃpioníram]

193. Police. Law. Part 1

justice	**правосъдие** (с)	[pravosə́die]
court (see you in ~)	**съд** (м)	[sət]
judge	**съдия** (м)	[sədijá]
jurors	**съдебни заседатели** (м мн)	[sədébni zasedáteli]
jury trial	**съд** (м) **със съдебни заседатели**	[sət səs sədébni zasedáteli]
to judge, to try (vt)	**съдя**	[sə́d^ja]
lawyer, barrister	**адвокат** (м)	[advokát]
defendant	**подсъдим** (м)	[potsədím]
dock	**подсъдима скамейка** (ж)	[potsədíma skaméjka]
charge	**обвинение** (с)	[obvinénie]
accused	**обвиняем** (м)	[obvin^jáem]
sentence	**присъда** (ж)	[prisə́da]
to sentence (vt)	**осъдя**	[osə́d^ja]
guilty (culprit)	**виновник** (м)	[vinóvnik]
to punish (vt)	**накажа**	[nakáʒa]
punishment	**наказание** (с)	[nakazánie]
fine (penalty)	**глоба** (ж)	[glóba]
life imprisonment	**доживотен затвор** (м)	[doʒivóten zatvór]

death penalty	**смъртно наказание** (с)	[smərtno nakazánie]
electric chair	**електрически стол** (м)	[elektrítʃeski stol]
gallows	**бесилка** (ж)	[besílka]
to execute (vt)	**екзекутирам**	[ekzekutíram]
execution	**екзекуция** (ж)	[ekzekútsija]
prison	**затвор** (м)	[zatvór]
cell	**килия** (ж)	[kilíja]
escort (convoy)	**караул** (м)	[karaúl]
prison officer	**надзирател** (м)	[nadzirátel]
prisoner	**затворник** (м)	[zatvórnik]
handcuffs	**белезници** (мн)	[beleznítsi]
to handcuff (vt)	**сложа белезници**	[slóʒa beleznítsi]
prison break	**бягство** (с)	[bʲákstvo]
to break out (vi)	**избягам**	[izbʲágam]
to disappear (vi)	**изчезна**	[iztʃézna]
to release (from prison)	**освободя**	[osvobodʲá]
amnesty	**амнистия** (ж)	[amnístija]
police	**полиция** (ж)	[polítsija]
police officer	**полицай** (м)	[politsáj]
police station	**полицейско управление** (с)	[politséjsko upravlénie]
truncheon	**палка** (ж)	[pálka]
megaphone (loudhailer)	**рупор** (м)	[rúpor]
patrol car	**патрулка** (ж)	[patrúlka]
siren	**сирена** (ж)	[siréna]
to turn on the siren	**включа сирена**	[fklʲútʃa siréna]
siren call	**звук** (м) **на сирена**	[zvuk na siréna]
crime scene	**място** (с) **на произшествието**	[mʲásto na proisʃéstvieto]
witness	**свидетел** (м)	[svidétel]
freedom	**свобода** (ж)	[svobodá]
accomplice	**съучастник** (м)	[səutʃásnik]
to flee (vi)	**скрия се**	[skríja sé]
trace (to leave a ~)	**следа** (ж)	[sledá]

194. Police. Law. Part 2

search (investigation)	**издирване** (с)	[izdírvane]
to look for ...	**издирвам**	[izdírvam]
suspicion	**подозрение** (с)	[podozrénie]
suspicious (e.g., ~ vehicle)	**подозрителен**	[podozrítelen]
to stop (cause to halt)	**спра**	[spra]
to detain (keep in custody)	**задържа**	[zadərʒá]
case (lawsuit)	**дело** (с)	[délo]
investigation	**следствие** (с)	[slétstvie]

English	Bulgarian	Pronunciation
detective	**детектив** (м)	[detektíf]
investigator	**следовател** (м)	[sledovátel]
hypothesis	**версия** (ж)	[vérsija]
motive	**мотив** (м)	[motív]
interrogation	**разпит** (м)	[ráspit]
to interrogate (vt)	**разпитвам**	[raspítvam]
to question (~ neighbors, etc.)	**разпитвам**	[raspítvam]
check (identity ~)	**проверка** (ж)	[provérka]
round-up (raid)	**хайка** (ж)	[hájka]
search (~ warrant)	**обиск** (м)	[óbisk]
chase (pursuit)	**преследване** (с)	[preslédvane]
to pursue, to chase	**преследвам**	[preslédvam]
to track (a criminal)	**следя**	[sled^já]
arrest	**арест** (м)	[árest]
to arrest (sb)	**арестувам**	[arestúvam]
to catch (thief, etc.)	**заловя**	[zalov^já]
capture	**залавяне** (с)	[zaláv^jane]
document	**документ** (м)	[dokumént]
proof (evidence)	**доказателство** (с)	[dokazátelstvo]
to prove (vt)	**доказвам**	[dokázvam]
footprint	**следа** (ж)	[sledá]
fingerprints	**отпечатъци на пръстите** (м мн)	[otpetʃátətsi na prə́stite]
piece of evidence	**улика** (ж)	[úlika]
alibi	**алиби** (с)	[alíbi]
innocent (not guilty)	**невиновен**	[nevinóven]
injustice	**несправедливост** (ж)	[nespravedlívost]
unjust, unfair (adj)	**несправедлив**	[nespravedlív]
criminal (adj)	**криминален**	[kriminálen]
to confiscate (vt)	**конфискувам**	[konfiskúvam]
drug (illegal substance)	**наркотик** (м)	[narkotík]
weapon, gun	**оръжие** (с)	[orə́ʒie]
to disarm (vt)	**обезоръжа**	[obezorəʒá]
to order (command)	**заповядвам**	[zapov^jádvam]
to disappear (vi)	**изчезна**	[iztʃézna]
law	**закон** (м)	[zakón]
legal, lawful (adj)	**законен**	[zakónen]
illegal, illicit (adj)	**незаконен**	[nezakónen]
responsibility (blame)	**отговорност** (ж)	[otgovórnost]
responsible (adj)	**отговорен**	[otgovóren]

NATURE

The Earth. Part 1

195. Outer space

space	**космос** (м)	[kósmos]
space (as adj)	**космически**	[kosmítʃeski]
outer space	**космическо пространство** (с)	[kosmítʃesko prostránstvo]
world	**свят** (м)	[svʲat]
universe	**вселена** (ж)	[fseléna]
galaxy	**галактика** (ж)	[galáktika]
star	**звезда** (ж)	[zvezdá]
constellation	**съзвездие** (с)	[səzvézdie]
planet	**планета** (ж)	[planéta]
satellite	**спътник** (м)	[spétnik]
meteorite	**метеорит** (м)	[meteorít]
comet	**комета** (ж)	[kométa]
asteroid	**астероид** (м)	[asteroít]
orbit	**орбита** (ж)	[órbita]
to revolve (~ around the Earth)	**въртя се**	[vərtʲá se]
atmosphere	**атмосфера** (ж)	[atmosféra]
the Sun	**Слънце**	[slə́ntse]
solar system	**Слънчева система** (ж)	[slə́ntʃeva sistə́ma]
solar eclipse	**слънчево затъмнение** (с)	[slə́ntʃevo zatəmnə́nie]
the Earth	**Земя**	[zemʲá]
the Moon	**Луна**	[luná]
Mars	**Марс**	[mars]
Venus	**Венера**	[venéra]
Jupiter	**Юпитер**	[júpiter]
Saturn	**Сатурн**	[satúrn]
Mercury	**Меркурий**	[merkúrij]
Uranus	**Уран**	[urán]
Neptune	**Нептун**	[neptún]
Pluto	**Плутон**	[plutón]
Milky Way	**Млечен Път**	[mlétʃen pət]
Great Bear (Ursa Major)	**Голяма Мечка**	[golʲáma métʃka]
North Star	**Полярна Звезда**	[polʲárna zvezdá]

Martian	**марсианец** (м)	[marsiánets]
extraterrestrial (n)	**извънземен** (м)	[izvənzémen]
alien	**пришелец** (м)	[priʃeléts]
flying saucer	**летяща чиния** (ж)	[letʲáʃta ʧiníja]
spaceship	**космически кораб** (м)	[kosmíʧeski kórap]
space station	**орбитална станция** (ж)	[orbitálna stántsija]
blast-off	**старт** (м)	[start]
engine	**двигател** (м)	[dvigátel]
nozzle	**дюза** (ж)	[dʲúza]
fuel	**гориво** (с)	[gorívo]
cockpit, flight deck	**кабина** (ж)	[kabína]
aerial	**антена** (ж)	[anténa]
porthole	**илюминатор** (м)	[ilʲuminátor]
solar panel	**слънчева батерия** (ж)	[slənʧeva batərija]
spacesuit	**скафандър** (м)	[skafándər]
weightlessness	**безтегловност** (ж)	[besteglóvnost]
oxygen	**кислород** (м)	[kislorót]
docking (in space)	**свързване** (с)	[svərzvane]
to dock (vi, vt)	**свързвам се**	[svərzvam se]
observatory	**обсерватория** (ж)	[opservatórija]
telescope	**телескоп** (м)	[teleskóp]
to observe (vt)	**наблюдавам**	[nablʲudávam]
to explore (vt)	**изследвам**	[isslédvam]

196. The Earth

the Earth	**Земя** (ж)	[zemʲá]
the globe (the Earth)	**земно кълбо** (с)	[zémno kəlbó]
planet	**планета** (ж)	[planéta]
atmosphere	**атмосфера** (ж)	[atmosféra]
geography	**география** (ж)	[geográfija]
nature	**природа** (ж)	[priróda]
globe (table ~)	**глобус** (м)	[glóbus]
map	**карта** (ж)	[kárta]
atlas	**атлас** (м)	[atlás]
Europe	**Европа**	[evrópa]
Asia	**Азия**	[ázija]
Africa	**Африка**	[áfrika]
Australia	**Австралия**	[afstrálija]
America	**Америка**	[amérika]
North America	**Северна Америка**	[séverna amérika]
South America	**Южна Америка**	[júʒna amérika]
Antarctica	**Антарктида**	[antarktída]
the Arctic	**Арктика**	[árktika]

197. Cardinal directions

north	**север** (м)	[séver]
to the north	**на север**	[na séver]
in the north	**на север**	[na séver]
northern (adj)	**северен**	[séveren]
south	**юг** (м)	[juk]
to the south	**на юг**	[na juk]
in the south	**на юг**	[na juk]
southern (adj)	**южен**	[júʒen]
west	**запад** (м)	[západ]
to the west	**на запад**	[na zápat]
in the west	**на запад**	[na zápat]
western (adj)	**западен**	[západen]
east	**изток** (м)	[ístok]
to the east	**на изток**	[na ístok]
in the east	**на изток**	[na ístok]
eastern (adj)	**източен**	[ístotʃen]

198. Sea. Ocean

sea	**море** (с)	[moré]
ocean	**океан** (м)	[okeán]
gulf (bay)	**залив** (м)	[zálif]
straits	**пролив** (м)	[próliv]
continent (mainland)	**материк** (м)	[materík]
island	**остров** (м)	[óstrov]
peninsula	**полуостров** (м)	[poluóstrov]
archipelago	**архипелаг** (м)	[arhipelák]
bay, cove	**залив** (м)	[zálif]
harbour	**залив** (м)	[zálif]
lagoon	**лагуна** (ж)	[lagúna]
cape	**нос** (м)	[nos]
atoll	**атол** (м)	[atól]
reef	**риф** (м)	[rif]
coral	**корал** (м)	[korál]
coral reef	**коралов риф** (м)	[korálov rif]
deep (adj)	**дълбок**	[dəlbók]
depth (deep water)	**дълбочина** (ж)	[dəlbotʃiná]
abyss	**бездна** (ж)	[bézna]
trench (e.g. Mariana ~)	**падина** (ж)	[padiná]
current (Ocean ~)	**течение** (с)	[tetʃénie]
to surround (bathe)	**мия**	[míja]
shore	**бряг** (м)	[brʲak]
coast	**крайбрежие** (с)	[krajbréʒie]

flow (flood tide)	**прилив** (м)	[príliv]
ebb (ebb tide)	**отлив** (м)	[ótliv]
shoal	**плитчина** (ж)	[plittʃiná]
bottom (~ of the sea)	**дъно** (с)	[dә́no]
wave	**вълна** (ж)	[vәlná]
crest (~ of a wave)	**гребен** (м) **на вълна**	[grében na vәlná]
spume (sea foam)	**пяна** (ж)	[pʲána]
storm (sea storm)	**буря** (ж)	[búrʲa]
hurricane	**ураган** (м)	[uragán]
tsunami	**цунами** (с)	[tsunámi]
calm (dead ~)	**безветрие** (с)	[bezvétrie]
quiet, calm (adj)	**спокоен**	[spokóen]
pole	**полюс** (м)	[pólʲus]
polar (adj)	**полярен**	[polʲáren]
latitude	**ширина** (ж)	[ʃiriná]
longitude	**дължина** (ж)	[dәlʒiná]
parallel	**паралел** (ж)	[paralél]
equator	**екватор** (м)	[ekvátor]
sky	**небе** (с)	[nebé]
horizon	**хоризонт** (м)	[horizónt]
air	**въздух** (м)	[vә́zduh]
lighthouse	**фар** (м)	[far]
to dive (vi)	**гмуркам се**	[gmúrkam se]
to sink (ab. boat)	**потъна**	[potә́na]
treasure	**съкровища** (с мн)	[sәkróviʃta]

199. Seas & Oceans names

Atlantic Ocean	**Атлантически океан**	[atlantítʃeski okeán]
Indian Ocean	**Индийски океан**	[indíjski okeán]
Pacific Ocean	**Тихи океан**	[tíhi okeán]
Arctic Ocean	**Северен Ледовит океан**	[séveren ledovít okeán]
Black Sea	**Черно море**	[tʃérno moré]
Red Sea	**Червено море**	[tʃervéno moré]
Yellow Sea	**Жълто море**	[ʒә́lto morә]
White Sea	**Бяло море**	[bʲálo moré]
Caspian Sea	**Каспийско море**	[káspijsko moré]
Dead Sea	**Мъртво море**	[mә́rtvo morә]
Mediterranean Sea	**Средиземно море**	[sredizémno moré]
Aegean Sea	**Егейско море**	[egéjsko moré]
Adriatic Sea	**Адриатическо море**	[adriatítʃesko moré]
Arabian Sea	**Арабско море**	[arápsko moré]
Sea of Japan	**Японско море**	[japónsko moré]
Bering Sea	**Берингово море**	[beríngovo moré]

South China Sea	**Южнокитайско море**	[juʒnokitájsko moré]
Coral Sea	**Коралово море**	[korálovo moré]
Tasman Sea	**Тасманово море**	[tasmánovo moré]
Caribbean Sea	**Карибско море**	[karíbsko moré]
Barents Sea	**Баренцово море**	[baréntsovo moré]
Kara Sea	**Карско море**	[kársko moré]
North Sea	**Северно море**	[séverno moré]
Baltic Sea	**Балтийско море**	[baltíjsko moré]
Norwegian Sea	**Норвежко море**	[norvéʃko moré]

200. Mountains

mountain	**планина** (ж)	[planiná]
mountain range	**планинска верига** (ж)	[planínska veríga]
mountain ridge	**планински хребет** (м)	[planínski hrebét]
summit, top	**връх** (м)	[vrəh]
peak	**пик** (м)	[pik]
foot (~ of the mountain)	**подножие** (с)	[podnóʒie]
slope (mountainside)	**склон** (м)	[sklon]
volcano	**вулкан** (м)	[vulkán]
active volcano	**действащ вулкан** (м)	[déjstvaʃt vulkán]
dormant volcano	**изгаснал вулкан** (м)	[izgásnal vulkán]
eruption	**изригване** (с)	[izrígvane]
crater	**кратер** (м)	[kráter]
magma	**магма** (ж)	[mágma]
lava	**лава** (ж)	[láva]
molten (~ lava)	**нажежен**	[naʒeʒén]
canyon	**каньон** (м)	[kanjón]
gorge	**дефиле** (с)	[defilé]
crevice	**тясна клисура** (ж)	[t'ásna klisúra]
abyss (chasm)	**пропаст** (ж)	[própast]
pass, col	**превал** (м)	[prevál]
plateau	**плато** (с)	[pláto]
cliff	**скала** (ж)	[skalá]
hill	**хълм** (м)	[həlm]
glacier	**ледник** (м)	[lédnik]
waterfall	**водопад** (м)	[vodopát]
geyser	**гейзер** (м)	[géjzer]
lake	**езеро** (с)	[ézero]
plain	**равнина** (ж)	[ravniná]
landscape	**пейзаж** (м)	[pejzáʒ]
echo	**ехо** (с)	[ého]
alpinist	**алпинист** (м)	[alpiníst]
rock climber	**катерач** (м)	[kateráʧ]

to conquer (in climbing)	**покорявам**	[pokorʲávam]
climb (an easy ~)	**възкачване** (с)	[vəskátʃvane]

201. Mountains names

The Alps	**Алпи**	[álpi]
Mont Blanc	**Мон Блан**	[mon blan]
The Pyrenees	**Пиринеи**	[pirinéi]
The Carpathians	**Карпати**	[karpáti]
The Ural Mountains	**Урал**	[urál]
The Caucasus Mountains	**Кавказ**	[kafkáz]
Mount Elbrus	**Елбрус**	[elbrús]
The Altai Mountains	**Алтай**	[altáj]
The Tian Shan	**Тяншан**	[tʲanʃan]
The Pamirs	**Памир**	[pamír]
The Himalayas	**Хималаи**	[himalái]
Mount Everest	**Еверест**	[everést]
The Andes	**Анди**	[ándi]
Mount Kilimanjaro	**Килиманджаро**	[kilimandʒáro]

202. Rivers

river	**река** (ж)	[reká]
spring (natural source)	**извор** (м)	[ízvor]
riverbed (river channel)	**корито** (с)	[koríto]
basin (river valley)	**басейн** (м)	[baséjn]
to flow into ...	**вливам се**	[vlívam se]
tributary	**приток** (м)	[prítok]
bank (river ~)	**бряг** (м)	[brʲak]
current (stream)	**течение** (с)	[tetʃénie]
downstream (adv)	**надолу по течението**	[nadólu po tetʃénieto]
upstream (adv)	**нагоре по течението**	[nagóre po tetʃénieto]
inundation	**наводнение** (с)	[navodnénie]
flooding	**пролетно пълноводие** (с)	[prolétno pəlnovódie]
to overflow (vi)	**разливам се**	[razlívam se]
to flood (vt)	**потопявам**	[potopʲávam]
shallow (shoal)	**плитчина** (ж)	[plittʃiná]
rapids	**праг** (м)	[prak]
dam	**яз** (м)	[jaz]
canal	**канал** (м)	[kanál]
reservoir (artificial lake)	**водохранилище** (с)	[vodohranílište]
sluice, lock	**шлюз** (м)	[ʃlʲuz]
water body (pond, etc.)	**водоем** (м)	[vodoém]
swamp (marshland)	**блато** (с)	[bláto]

bog, marsh	**тресавище** (с)	[tresáviʃte]
whirlpool	**водовъртеж** (м)	[vodovərtéʒ]
stream (brook)	**ручей** (м)	[rútʃej]
drinking (ab. water)	**питеен**	[pitéen]
fresh (~ water)	**сладководен**	[slatkovóden]
ice	**лед** (м)	[let]
to freeze over (ab. river, etc.)	**замръзна**	[zamrəzna]

203. Rivers names

Seine	**Сена**	[séna]
Loire	**Лоара**	[loára]
Thames	**Темза**	[témza]
Rhine	**Рейн**	[rejn]
Danube	**Дунав**	[dúnav]
Volga	**Волга**	[vólga]
Don	**Дон**	[don]
Lena	**Лена**	[léna]
Yellow River	**Хуанхъ**	[huanhə́]
Yangtze	**Яндзъ**	[jandzə́]
Mekong	**Меконг**	[mekónk]
Ganges	**Ганг**	[gang]
Nile River	**Нил**	[nil]
Congo River	**Конго**	[kóngo]
Okavango River	**Окаванго**	[okavángo]
Zambezi River	**Замбези**	[zambézi]
Limpopo River	**Лимпопо**	[limpopó]
Mississippi River	**Мисисипи**	[misisípi]

204. Forest

forest, wood	**гора** (ж)	[gorá]
forest (as adj)	**горски**	[górski]
thick forest	**гъсталак** (м)	[gəstalák]
grove	**горичка** (ж)	[gorítʃka]
forest clearing	**поляна** (ж)	[polʲána]
thicket	**гъсталак** (м)	[gəstalák]
scrubland	**храсталак** (м)	[hrastalák]
footpath (troddenpath)	**пътечка** (ж)	[pətétʃka]
gully	**овраг** (м)	[ovrák]
tree	**дърво** (с)	[dərvó]
leaf	**лист** (м)	[list]

leaves (foliage)	**шума** (ж)	[ʃúma]
fall of leaves	**листопад** (м)	[listopát]
to fall (ab. leaves)	**опадвам**	[opádvam]
top (of the tree)	**връх** (м)	[vrəh]
branch	**клонка** (м)	[klónka]
bough	**дебел клон** (м)	[debél klon]
bud (on shrub, tree)	**пъпка** (ж)	[pəpka]
needle (of the pine tree)	**игла** (ж)	[iglá]
fir cone	**шишарка** (ж)	[ʃiʃárka]
tree hollow	**хралупа** (ж)	[hralúpa]
nest	**гнездо** (с)	[gnezdó]
burrow (animal hole)	**дупка** (ж)	[dúpka]
trunk	**стъбло** (с)	[stəbló]
root	**корен** (м)	[kóren]
bark	**кора** (ж)	[korá]
moss	**мъх** (м)	[məh]
to uproot (remove trees or tree stumps)	**изкоренявам**	[izkorenʲávam]
to chop down	**сека**	[seká]
to deforest (vt)	**изсичам**	[issítʃam]
tree stump	**пън** (м)	[pən]
campfire	**клада** (ж)	[kláda]
forest fire	**пожар** (м)	[poʒár]
to extinguish (vt)	**загасявам**	[zagasʲávam]
forest ranger	**горски пазач** (м)	[górski pazátʃ]
protection	**опазване** (с)	[opázvane]
to protect (~ nature)	**опазвам**	[opázvam]
poacher	**бракониер** (м)	[brakoniér]
steel trap	**капан** (м)	[kapán]
to gather, to pick (vt)	**събирам**	[səbíram]
to lose one's way	**загубя се**	[zagúbʲa se]

205. Natural resources

natural resources	**природни ресурси** (м мн)	[priródni resúrsi]
minerals	**полезни изкопаеми** (с мн)	[polézni iskopáemi]
deposits	**залежи** (мн)	[zaléʒi]
field (e.g. oilfield)	**находище** (с)	[nahódiʃte]
to mine (extract)	**добивам**	[dobívam]
mining (extraction)	**добиване** (с)	[dobívane]
ore	**руда** (ж)	[rudá]
mine (e.g. for coal)	**рудник** (м)	[rúdnik]
shaft (mine ~)	**шахта** (ж)	[ʃáhta]
miner	**миньор** (м)	[minʲór]
gas (natural ~)	**газ** (м)	[gas]
gas pipeline	**газопровод** (м)	[gazoprovót]

oil (petroleum)	**нефт** (м)	[neft]
oil pipeline	**нефтопровод** (м)	[neftoprovót]
oil well	**нефтена кула** (ж)	[néftena kúla]
derrick (tower)	**сондажна кула** (ж)	[sondáʒna kúla]
tanker	**танкер** (м)	[tánker]
sand	**пясък** (м)	[pʲásək]
limestone	**варовик** (м)	[varóvik]
gravel	**дребен чакъл** (м)	[drében ʧakél]
peat	**торф** (м)	[torf]
clay	**глина** (ж)	[glína]
coal	**въглища** (мн)	[vəgliʃta]
iron (ore)	**желязо** (с)	[ʒelʲázo]
gold	**злато** (с)	[zláto]
silver	**сребро** (с)	[srebró]
nickel	**никел** (м)	[níkel]
copper	**мед** (ж)	[met]
zinc	**цинк** (м)	[tsink]
manganese	**манган** (м)	[mangán]
mercury	**живак** (м)	[ʒivák]
lead	**олово** (с)	[olóvo]
mineral	**минерал** (м)	[minerál]
crystal	**кристал** (м)	[kristál]
marble	**мрамор** (м)	[mrámor]
uranium	**уран** (м)	[urán]

The Earth. Part 2

206. Weather

weather	**време** (с)	[vréme]
weather forecast	**прогноза** (ж) **за времето**	[prognóza za vrémeto]
temperature	**температура** (ж)	[temperatúra]
thermometer	**термометър** (м)	[termométər]
barometer	**барометър** (м)	[barométər]
humid (adj)	**влажен**	[vláʒen]
humidity	**влажност** (ж)	[vláʒnost]
heat (extreme ~)	**пек** (м)	[pek]
hot (torrid)	**горещ**	[goréʃt]
it's hot	**горещо**	[goréʃto]
it's warm	**топло**	[tóplo]
warm (moderately hot)	**топъл**	[tópəl]
it's cold	**студено**	[studéno]
cold (adj)	**студен**	[studén]
sun	**слънце** (с)	[slántse]
to shine (vi)	**грея**	[gréja]
sunny (day)	**слънчев**	[slántʃev]
to come up (vi)	**изгрея**	[izgréja]
to set (vi)	**заляза**	[zalʲáza]
cloud	**облак** (м)	[óblak]
cloudy (adj)	**облачен**	[óblatʃen]
rain cloud	**голям облак** (м)	[golʲám óblak]
somber (gloomy)	**навъсен**	[navə́sen]
rain	**дъжд** (м)	[dəʒd]
it's raining	**вали дъжд**	[valí dəʒt]
rainy (~ day, weather)	**дъждовен**	[dəʒdóven]
to drizzle (vi)	**ръмя**	[rəmʲá]
pouring rain	**пороен дъжд** (м)	[poróen dəʒt]
downpour	**порой** (м)	[porój]
heavy (e.g. ~ rain)	**силен**	[sílen]
puddle	**локва** (ж)	[lókva]
to get wet (in rain)	**намокря се**	[namókrʲa se]
fog (mist)	**мъгла** (ж)	[məglá]
foggy	**мъглив**	[məglíf]
snow	**сняг** (м)	[snʲak]
it's snowing	**вали сняг**	[valí snʲak]

207. Severe weather. Natural disasters

thunderstorm	**гръмотевична буря** (ж)	[grəmotévitʃna búrʲa]
lightning (~ strike)	**мълния** (ж)	[məlnija]
to flash (vi)	**блясвам**	[blʲásvam]
thunder	**гръм** (м)	[grəm]
to thunder (vi)	**гърмя**	[gərmʲá]
it's thundering	**гърми**	[gərmí]
hail	**градушка** (ж)	[gradúʃka]
it's hailing	**пада градушка**	[páda gradúʃka]
to flood (vt)	**потопя**	[potopʲá]
flood, inundation	**наводнение** (с)	[navodnénie]
earthquake	**земетресение** (с)	[zemetresénie]
tremor, shoke	**трус** (м)	[trus]
epicentre	**епицентър** (м)	[epitséntər]
eruption	**изригване** (с)	[izrígvane]
lava	**лава** (ж)	[láva]
twister, tornado	**торнадо** (с)	[tornádo]
typhoon	**тайфун** (м)	[tajfún]
hurricane	**ураган** (м)	[uragán]
storm	**буря** (ж)	[búrʲa]
tsunami	**цунами** (с)	[tsunámi]
cyclone	**циклон** (м)	[tsiklón]
bad weather	**лошо време** (с)	[lóʃo vréme]
fire (accident)	**пожар** (м)	[poʒár]
disaster	**катастрофа** (ж)	[katastrófa]
meteorite	**метеорит** (м)	[meteorít]
avalanche	**лавина** (ж)	[lavína]
snowslide	**лавина** (ж)	[lavína]
blizzard	**виелица** (ж)	[viélitsa]
snowstorm	**снежна буря** (ж)	[snéʒna búrʲa]

208. Noises. Sounds

silence (quiet)	**тишина** (ж)	[tiʃiná]
sound	**звук** (м)	[zvuk]
noise	**шум** (м)	[ʃum]
to make noise	**шумя**	[ʃumʲá]
noisy (adj)	**шумен**	[ʃúmen]
loudly (to speak, etc.)	**силно**	[sílno]
loud (voice, etc.)	**силен**	[sílen]
constant (e.g., ~ noise)	**постоянен**	[postojánen]
cry, shout (n)	**вик** (м)	[vik]

to cry, to shout (vi)	**викам**	[víkam]
whisper	**шепот** (м)	[ʃépot]
to whisper (vi, vt)	**шептя**	[ʃeptʲá]
barking (dog's ~)	**лай** (м)	[laj]
to bark (vi)	**лая**	[lája]
groan (of pain, etc.)	**стон** (м)	[ston]
to groan (vi)	**стена**	[sténa]
cough	**кашлица** (ж)	[káʃlitsa]
to cough (vi)	**кашлям**	[káʃlʲam]
whistle	**свирене** (с)	[svírene]
to whistle (vi)	**свиря**	[svírʲa]
knock (at the door)	**тракане** (с)	[trákane]
to knock (on the door)	**чукам**	[ʧúkam]
to crack (vi)	**пращя**	[praʃtʲá]
crack (cracking sound)	**трясък** (м)	[trʲásək]
siren	**сирена** (ж)	[siréna]
whistle (factory ~, etc.)	**сирена** (ж)	[siréna]
to whistle (ab. train)	**буча**	[buʧá]
honk (car horn sound)	**клаксон** (м)	[klákson]
to honk (vi)	**сигнализирам**	[signalizíram]

209. Winter

winter (n)	**зима** (ж)	[zíma]
winter (as adj)	**зимен**	[zímen]
in winter	**през зимата**	[prez zímata]
snow	**сняг** (м)	[snʲak]
it's snowing	**вали сняг**	[valí snʲak]
snowfall	**снеговалеж** (м)	[snegovaléʒ]
snowdrift	**преспа** (ж)	[préspa]
snowflake	**снежинка** (ж)	[sneʒínka]
snowball	**снежна топка** (ж)	[snéʒna tópka]
snowman	**снежен човек** (м)	[snéʒen ʧovék]
icicle	**ледена висулка** (ж)	[lédena visúlka]
December	**декември** (м)	[dekémvri]
January	**януари** (м)	[januári]
February	**февруари** (м)	[fevruári]
frost (severe ~, freezing cold)	**мраз** (м)	[mraz]
frosty (weather, air)	**мразовит**	[mrazovít]
below zero (adv)	**под нулата**	[pot núlata]
first frost	**леко застудяване** (с)	[léko zastudʲávane]
hoarfrost	**скреж** (м)	[skreʒ]
cold (cold weather)	**студ** (м)	[stut]
it's cold	**студено**	[studéno]

fur coat	**кожено палто** (с)	[kóʒeno paltó]
mittens	**ръкавици** (ж мн) **с един пръст**	[rəkavítsi s edín pərst]
to fall ill	**разболявам**	[razbolʲávam]
cold (illness)	**настинка** (ж)	[nastínka]
to catch a cold	**настина**	[nastína]
ice	**лед** (м)	[let]
black ice	**поледица** (ж)	[poléditsa]
to freeze over (ab. river, etc.)	**замръзна**	[zamrə́zna]
ice floe	**леден блок** (м)	[léden blok]
skis	**ски** (мн)	[ski]
skier	**скиор** (м)	[skiór]
to ski (vi)	**карам ски**	[káram ski]
to skate (vi)	**пързалям се с кънки**	[pərzálʲam se s kə́nki]

Fauna

210. Mammals. Predators

predator	**хищник** (м)	[híʃtnik]
tiger	**тигър** (м)	[tígər]
lion	**лъв** (м)	[ləv]
wolf	**вълк** (м)	[vəlk]
fox	**лисица** (ж)	[lisítsa]
jaguar	**ягуар** (м)	[jaguár]
leopard	**леопард** (м)	[leopárt]
cheetah	**гепард** (м)	[gepárt]
black panther	**пантера** (ж)	[pantéra]
puma	**пума** (ж)	[púma]
snow leopard	**снежен барс** (м)	[snéʒen bars]
lynx	**рис** (м)	[ris]
coyote	**койот** (м)	[kojót]
jackal	**чакал** (м)	[ʧakál]
hyena	**хиена** (ж)	[hiéna]

211. Wild animals

animal	**животно** (с)	[ʒivótno]
beast (animal)	**звяр** (м)	[zv^jar]
squirrel	**катерица** (ж)	[káteritsa]
hedgehog	**таралеж** (м)	[taraléʒ]
hare	**заек** (м)	[záek]
rabbit	**питомен заек** (м)	[pítomen záek]
badger	**язовец** (м)	[jázovets]
raccoon	**енот** (м)	[enót]
hamster	**хамстер** (м)	[hámster]
marmot	**мармот** (м)	[marmót]
mole	**къртица** (ж)	[kərtítsa]
mouse	**мишка** (ж)	[míʃka]
rat	**плъх** (м)	[pləh]
bat	**прилеп** (м)	[prílep]
ermine	**хермелин** (м)	[hermelín]
sable	**самур** (м)	[samúr]
marten	**бялка** (ж)	[b^jálka]
weasel	**невестулка** (ж)	[nevestúlka]
mink	**норка** (ж)	[nórka]

beaver	**бобър** (м)	[bóbər]
otter	**видра** (ж)	[vídra]
horse	**кон** (м)	[kon]
moose	**лос** (м)	[los]
deer	**елен** (м)	[elén]
camel	**камила** (ж)	[kamíla]
bison	**бизон** (м)	[bizón]
wisent	**зубър** (м)	[zúbər]
buffalo	**бивол** (м)	[bívol]
zebra	**зебра** (ж)	[zébra]
antelope	**антилопа** (ж)	[antilópa]
roe deer	**сърна** (ж)	[sərná]
fallow deer	**лопатар** (м)	[lopatár]
chamois	**сърна** (ж)	[sərná]
wild boar	**глиган** (м)	[gligán]
whale	**кит** (м)	[kit]
seal	**тюлен** (м)	[tʲulén]
walrus	**морж** (м)	[morʒ]
fur seal	**морска котка** (ж)	[mórska kótka]
dolphin	**делфин** (м)	[delfín]
bear	**мечка** (ж)	[métʃka]
polar bear	**бяла мечка** (ж)	[bʲála métʃka]
panda	**панда** (ж)	[pánda]
monkey	**маймуна** (ж)	[majmúna]
chimpanzee	**шимпанзе** (с)	[ʃimpanzé]
orangutan	**орангутан** (м)	[orangután]
gorilla	**горила** (ж)	[goríla]
macaque	**макак** (м)	[makák]
gibbon	**гибон** (м)	[gibón]
elephant	**слон** (м)	[slon]
rhinoceros	**носорог** (м)	[nosorók]
giraffe	**жираф** (м)	[ʒiráf]
hippopotamus	**хипопотам** (м)	[hipopotám]
kangaroo	**кенгуру** (с)	[kénguru]
koala (bear)	**коала** (ж)	[koála]
mongoose	**мангуста** (ж)	[mangústa]
chinchilla	**чинчила** (ж)	[tʃintʃíla]
skunk	**скунс** (м)	[skuns]
porcupine	**бодливец** (м)	[bodlívets]

212. Domestic animals

cat	**котка** (ж)	[kótka]
tomcat	**котарак** (м)	[kotarák]
horse	**кон** (м)	[kon]

stallion (male horse)	**жребец** (м)	[ʒrebéts]
mare	**кобила** (ж)	[kobíla]
cow	**крава** (ж)	[kráva]
bull	**бик** (м)	[bik]
ox	**вол** (м)	[vol]
sheep (ewe)	**овца** (ж)	[ovtsá]
ram	**овен** (м)	[ovén]
goat	**коза** (ж)	[kozá]
billy goat, he-goat	**козел** (м)	[kozél]
donkey	**магаре** (с)	[magáre]
mule	**муле** (с)	[múle]
pig	**свиня** (ж)	[svinʲá]
piglet	**прасе** (с)	[prasé]
rabbit	**питомен заек** (м)	[pítomen záek]
hen (chicken)	**кокошка** (ж)	[kokóʃka]
cock	**петел** (м)	[petél]
duck	**патица** (ж)	[pátitsa]
drake	**паток** (м)	[patók]
goose	**гъсок** (м)	[gəsók]
tom turkey, gobbler	**пуяк** (м)	[pújak]
turkey (hen)	**пуйка** (ж)	[pújka]
domestic animals	**домашни животни** (с мн)	[domáʃni ʒivótni]
tame (e.g. ~ hamster)	**питомен**	[pítomen]
to tame (vt)	**опитомявам**	[opitomʲávam]
to breed (vt)	**отглеждам**	[otgléʒdam]
farm	**ферма** (ж)	[férma]
poultry	**домашна птица** (ж)	[domáʃna ptítsa]
cattle	**добитък** (м)	[dobítək]
herd (cattle)	**стадо** (с)	[stádo]
stable	**обор** (м)	[obór]
pigsty	**кочина** (ж)	[kóʧina]
cowshed	**краварник** (м)	[kravárnik]
rabbit hutch	**зайчарник** (м)	[zajʧárnik]
hen house	**курник** (м)	[kúrnik]

213. Dogs. Dog breeds

dog	**куче** (с)	[kúʧe]
sheepdog	**овчарско куче** (с)	[ofʧársko kúʧe]
German shepherd	**немска овчарка** (ж)	[némska ofʧárka]
poodle	**пудел** (м)	[púdel]
dachshund	**дакел** (м)	[dákel]
bulldog	**булдог** (м)	[buldók]
boxer	**боксер** (м)	[boksér]

mastiff	**мастиф** (м)	[mastíf]
Rottweiler	**ротвайлер** (м)	[rotvájler]
Doberman	**доберман** (м)	[dóberman]
basset	**басет** (м)	[báset]
bobtail	**бобтейл** (м)	[bóbtejl]
Dalmatian	**далматинец** (м)	[dalmatinéts]
cocker spaniel	**кокер шпаньол** (м)	[kóker ʃpanʲól]
Newfoundland	**нюфаундленд** (м)	[nʲufáundlend]
Saint Bernard	**санбернар** (м)	[sanbernár]
husky	**сибирско хъски** (с)	[sibírsko həski]
Chow Chow	**чау-чау** (с)	[ʧáu-ʧáu]
spitz	**шпиц** (м)	[ʃpits]
pug	**мопс** (м)	[mops]

214. Sounds made by animals

barking (n)	**лай** (м)	[laj]
to bark (vi)	**лая**	[lája]
to miaow (vi)	**мяукам**	[mʲaúkam]
to purr (vi)	**мъркам**	[mərkam]
to moo (vi)	**муча**	[muʧá]
to bellow (bull)	**рева**	[revá]
to growl (vi)	**ръмжа**	[rəmʒá]
howl (n)	**вой** (м)	[voj]
to howl (vi)	**вия**	[víja]
to whine (vi)	**скимтя**	[skimtʲá]
to bleat (sheep)	**блея**	[bléja]
to oink, to grunt (pig)	**грухтя**	[gruhtʲá]
to squeal (vi)	**вреща**	[vreʃtʲá]
to croak (vi)	**крякам**	[krʲákam]
to buzz (insect)	**бръмча**	[brəmʧá]
to chirp (crickets, grasshopper)	**цвърча**	[tsvərʧá]

215. Young animals

cub	**бебе, зверче** (с)	[bébe], [zverʧé]
kitten	**котенце** (с)	[kótentse]
baby mouse	**мишле** (с)	[miʃlé]
puppy	**кученце** (с)	[kúʧentse]
leveret	**зайче** (с)	[zájʧe]
baby rabbit	**зайче** (с)	[zájʧe]
wolf cub	**вълче** (с)	[vəlʧé]
fox cub	**лисиче** (с)	[lisíʧe]

bear cub	**мече** (с)	[metʃé]
lion cub	**лъвче** (с)	[lə́ftʃe]
tiger cub	**тигърче** (с)	[tígərtʃe]
elephant calf	**слонче** (с)	[slóntʃe]
piglet	**прасе** (с)	[prasé]
calf (young cow, bull)	**теле** (с)	[téle]
kid (young goat)	**яре** (с)	[járe]
lamb	**агне** (с)	[ágne]
fawn (young deer)	**еленче** (с)	[eléntʃe]
young camel	**камилче** (с)	[kamíltʃe]
snakelet (baby snake)	**змийче** (с)	[zmijtʃé]
froglet (baby frog)	**жабче** (с)	[ʒáptʃe]
baby bird	**пиле** (с)	[píle]
chick (of chicken)	**пиле** (с)	[píle]
duckling	**пате** (с)	[páte]

216. Birds

bird	**птица** (ж)	[ptítsa]
pigeon	**гълъб** (м)	[gə́ləp]
sparrow	**врабче** (с)	[vrabtʃé]
tit (great tit)	**синигер** (м)	[sinigér]
magpie	**сврака** (ж)	[svráka]
raven	**гарван** (м)	[gárvan]
crow	**врана** (ж)	[vrána]
jackdaw	**гарга** (ж)	[gárga]
rook	**полски гарван** (м)	[pólski gárvan]
duck	**патица** (ж)	[pátitsa]
goose	**гъсок** (м)	[gəsók]
pheasant	**фазан** (м)	[fazán]
eagle	**орел** (м)	[orél]
hawk	**ястреб** (м)	[jástrep]
falcon	**сокол** (м)	[sokól]
vulture	**гриф** (м)	[grif]
condor (Andean ~)	**кондор** (м)	[kondór]
swan	**лебед** (м)	[lébet]
crane	**жерав** (м)	[ʒérav]
stork	**щъркел** (м)	[ʃtə́rkel]
parrot	**папагал** (м)	[papagál]
hummingbird	**колибри** (с)	[kolíbri]
peacock	**паун** (м)	[paún]
ostrich	**щраус** (м)	[ʃtráus]
heron	**чапла** (ж)	[tʃápla]
flamingo	**фламинго** (с)	[flamíngo]
pelican	**пеликан** (м)	[pelikán]

nightingale	**славей** (м)	[slávej]
swallow	**лястовица** (ж)	[lʲástovitsa]
thrush	**дрозд** (м)	[drozd]
song thrush	**поен дрозд** (м)	[póen drozd]
blackbird	**кос, черен дрозд** (м)	[kos], [ʧéren drozd]
swift	**бързолет** (м)	[bərzolét]
lark	**чучулига** (ж)	[ʧuʧulíga]
quail	**пъдпъдък** (м)	[pədpədək]
woodpecker	**кълвач** (м)	[kəlváʧ]
cuckoo	**кукувица** (ж)	[kúkuvitsa]
owl	**сова** (ж)	[sóva]
eagle owl	**бухал** (м)	[búhal]
wood grouse	**глухар** (м)	[gluhár]
black grouse	**тетрев** (м)	[tétrev]
partridge	**яребица** (ж)	[járebitsa]
starling	**скорец** (м)	[skoréts]
canary	**канарче** (с)	[kanárʧe]
hazel grouse	**лещарка** (ж)	[leʃtárka]
chaffinch	**чинка** (ж)	[ʧínka]
bullfinch	**червенушка** (ж)	[ʧervenúʃka]
seagull	**чайка** (ж)	[ʧájka]
albatross	**албатрос** (м)	[albatrós]
penguin	**пингвин** (м)	[pingvín]

217. Birds. Singing and sounds

to sing (vi)	**пея**	[péja]
to call (animal, bird)	**крясакам**	[krʲáskam]
to crow (cock)	**кукуригам**	[kukurígam]
cock-a-doodle-doo	**кукуригу**	[kukurígu]
to cluck (hen)	**кудкудякам**	[kutkudʲákam]
to caw (crow call)	**грача**	[gráʧa]
to quack (duck call)	**крякам**	[krʲákam]
to cheep (vi)	**пищя**	[piʃtʲá]
to chirp, to twitter	**чуруликам**	[ʧurulíkam]

218. Fish. Marine animals

bream	**платика** (ж)	[platíka]
carp	**шаран** (м)	[ʃarán]
perch	**костур** (м)	[kostúr]
catfish	**сом** (м)	[som]
pike	**щука** (ж)	[ʃtúka]
salmon	**сьомга** (ж)	[sʲómga]
sturgeon	**есетра** (ж)	[esétra]

herring	**селда** (ж)	[sélda]
Atlantic salmon	**сьомга** (ж)	[sʲómga]
mackerel	**скумрия** (ж)	[skumríja]
flatfish	**калкан** (м)	[kalkán]
zander, pike perch	**бяла риба** (ж)	[bʲála ríba]
cod	**треска** (ж)	[tréska]
tuna	**риба тон** (м)	[ríba ton]
trout	**пъстърва** (ж)	[pəstérva]
eel	**змиорка** (ж)	[zmiórka]
electric ray	**електрически скат** (м)	[elektríʧeski skat]
moray eel	**мурена** (ж)	[muréna]
piranha	**пираня** (ж)	[piránʲa]
shark	**акула** (ж)	[akúla]
dolphin	**делфин** (м)	[delfín]
whale	**кит** (м)	[kit]
crab	**морски рак** (м)	[mórski rak]
jellyfish	**медуза** (ж)	[medúza]
octopus	**октопод** (м)	[oktopót]
starfish	**морска звезда** (ж)	[mórska zvezdá]
sea urchin	**морски таралеж** (м)	[mórski taraléʒ]
seahorse	**морско конче** (с)	[mórsko kónʧe]
oyster	**стрида** (ж)	[strída]
prawn	**скарида** (ж)	[skarída]
lobster	**омар** (м)	[omár]
spiny lobster	**лангуста** (ж)	[langústa]

219. Amphibians. Reptiles

snake	**змия** (ж)	[zmijá]
venomous (snake)	**отровен**	[otróven]
viper	**усойница** (ж)	[usójnitsa]
cobra	**кобра** (ж)	[kóbra]
python	**питон** (м)	[pitón]
boa	**боа** (ж)	[boá]
grass snake	**смок** (м)	[smok]
rattle snake	**гърмяща змия** (ж)	[gərmʲáʃta zmijá]
anaconda	**анаконда** (ж)	[anakónda]
lizard	**гущер** (м)	[gúʃter]
iguana	**игуана** (ж)	[iguána]
monitor lizard	**варан** (м)	[varán]
salamander	**саламандър** (м)	[salamándər]
chameleon	**хамелеон** (м)	[hameleón]
scorpion	**скорпион** (м)	[skorpión]
turtle	**костенурка** (ж)	[kostenúrka]
frog	**водна жаба** (ж)	[vódna ʒába]

toad	**жаба** (ж)	[ʒába]
crocodile	**крокодил** (м)	[krokodíl]

220. Insects

insect	**насекомо** (с)	[nasekómo]
butterfly	**пеперуда** (ж)	[peperúda]
ant	**мравка** (ж)	[mráfka]
fly	**муха** (ж)	[muhá]
mosquito	**комар** (м)	[komár]
beetle	**бръмбар** (м)	[brəmbar]
wasp	**оса** (ж)	[osá]
bee	**пчела** (ж)	[ptʃelá]
bumblebee	**земна пчела** (ж)	[zémna ptʃelá]
gadfly (botfly)	**щръклица** (ж), **овод** (м)	[ʃtrəklitsa], [óvot]
spider	**паяк** (м)	[pájak]
spider's web	**паяжина** (ж)	[pájaʒina]
dragonfly	**водно конче** (с)	[vódno kóntʃe]
grasshopper	**скакалец** (м)	[skakaléts]
moth (night butterfly)	**нощна пеперуда** (ж)	[nóʃtna peperúda]
cockroach	**хлебарка** (ж)	[hlebárka]
tick	**кърлеж** (м)	[kərleʃ]
flea	**бълха** (ж)	[bəlhá]
midge	**мушица** (ж)	[muʃítsa]
locust	**прелетен скакалец** (м)	[préleten skakaléts]
snail	**охлюв** (м)	[óhlʲuf]
cricket	**щурец** (м)	[ʃturéts]
firefly	**светулка** (ж)	[svetúlka]
ladybird	**калинка** (ж)	[kalínka]
cockchafer	**майски бръмбар** (м)	[májski brəmbar]
leech	**пиявица** (ж)	[pijávitsa]
caterpillar	**гъсеница** (ж)	[gəsénitsa]
earthworm	**червей** (м)	[tʃérvej]
larva	**буба** (ж)	[búba]

221. Animals. Body parts

beak	**клюн** (м)	[klʲun]
wings	**криле** (мн)	[krilé]
foot (of the bird)	**крак** (м)	[krak]
feathers (plumage)	**перушина** (ж)	[peruʃína]
feather	**перо** (с)	[peró]
crest	**качул** (с)	[katʃúl]
gills	**хриле** (с)	[hrilé]
spawn	**хайвер** (м)	[hajvér]

larva	**личинка** (ж)	[lítʃinka]
fin	**перка** (ж)	[pérka]
scales (of fish, reptile)	**люспа** (ж)	[lʲúspa]
fang (canine)	**зъб** (м)	[zəp]
paw (e.g. cat's ~)	**лапа** (ж)	[lápa]
muzzle (snout)	**муцуна** (ж)	[mutsúna]
mouth (cat's ~)	**уста** (ж)	[ustá]
tail	**опашка** (ж)	[opáʃka]
whiskers	**мустаци** (м мн)	[mustátsi]
hoof	**копито** (с)	[kopíto]
horn	**рог** (м)	[rok]
carapace	**черупка** (ж)	[tʃerúpka]
shell (mollusk ~)	**мида** (ж)	[mída]
eggshell	**черупка** (ж)	[tʃerúpka]
animal's hair (pelage)	**козина** (ж)	[kózina]
pelt (hide)	**кожа** (ж)	[kóʒa]

222. Actions of animals

to fly (vi)	**летя**	[letʲá]
to fly in circles	**вия се**	[víja se]
to fly away	**отлетя**	[otletʲá]
to flap (~ the wings)	**махам**	[máham]
to peck (vi)	**кълва**	[kəlvá]
to sit on eggs	**излюпвам**	[izlʲúpvam]
to hatch out (vi)	**излюпвам се**	[izlʲúpvam se]
to build a nest	**вия**	[víja]
to slither, to crawl	**пълзя**	[pəlzʲá]
to sting, to bite (insect)	**жиля**	[ʒílʲa]
to bite (ab. animal)	**хапя**	[hápʲɑ]
to sniff (vt)	**душа**	[dúʃa]
to bark (vi)	**лая**	[lája]
to hiss (snake)	**съска**	[sə́ska]
to scare (vt)	**плаша**	[pláʃa]
to attack (vt)	**нападам**	[napádam]
to gnaw (bone, etc.)	**гриза**	[grizá]
to scratch (with claws)	**драскам**	[dráskam]
to hide (vi)	**крия се**	[kríja se]
to play (kittens, etc.)	**играя**	[igrája]
to hunt (vi, vt)	**ловувам**	[lovúvam]
to hibernate (vi)	**изпадам в зимен сън**	[ispádam v zímen sən]
to go extinct	**измра**	[izmrá]

223. Animals. Habitats

habitat	**среда** (ж) **на обитаване**	[sredá na obitávane]
migration	**миграция** (ж)	[migrátsija]
mountain	**планина** (ж)	[planiná]
reef	**риф** (м)	[rif]
cliff	**скала** (ж)	[skalá]
forest	**гора** (ж)	[gorá]
jungle	**джунгла** (ж)	[dʒúngla]
savanna	**савана** (ж)	[savána]
tundra	**тундра** (ж)	[túndra]
steppe	**степ** (ж)	[step]
desert	**пустиня** (ж)	[pustínʲa]
oasis	**оазис** (м)	[oázis]
sea	**море** (с)	[moré]
lake	**езеро** (с)	[ézero]
ocean	**океан** (м)	[okeán]
swamp (marshland)	**блато** (с)	[bláto]
freshwater (adj)	**сладководен**	[slatkovóden]
pond	**изкуствен вир** (м)	[iskústven vir]
river	**река** (ж)	[reká]
den (bear's ~)	**бърлога** (ж)	[bərlóga]
nest	**гнездо** (с)	[gnezdó]
tree hollow	**хралупа** (ж)	[hralúpa]
burrow (animal hole)	**дупка** (ж)	[dúpka]
anthill	**мравуняк** (м)	[mravúnʲak]

224. Animal care

zoo	**зоологическа градина** (ж)	[zoologítʃeska gradína]
nature reserve	**резерват** (м)	[rezervát]
breeder (cattery, kennel, etc.)	**развъдник** (м)	[razvə́dnik]
open-air cage	**волиера** (ж)	[voliéra]
cage	**клетка** (ж)	[klétka]
kennel	**кучешка колибка** (ж)	[kútʃeʃka kolípka]
dovecot	**гълъбарник** (м)	[gələbárnik]
aquarium (fish tank)	**аквариум** (м)	[akvárium]
dolphinarium	**делфинариум** (м)	[delfinárium]
to breed (animals)	**развъждам**	[razvə́ʒdam]
brood, litter	**потомство** (с)	[potómstvo]
to tame (vt)	**опитомявам**	[opitomʲávam]
to train (animals)	**дресирам**	[dresíram]
feed (fodder, etc.)	**храна** (ж)	[hraná]
to feed (vt)	**храня**	[hránʲa]

pet shop	**зоомагазин** (м)	[zoomagazín]
muzzle (for dog)	**намордник** (м)	[namórdnik]
collar (e.g., dog ~)	**каишка** (ж)	[kaíʃka]
name (of an animal)	**име** (с)	[íme]
pedigree (dog's ~)	**родословие** (с)	[rodoslóvie]

225. Animals. Miscellaneous

pack (wolves)	**глутница** (ж)	[glútnitsa]
flock (birds)	**ято** (с)	[játo]
shoal, school (fish)	**пасаж** (м)	[pasáʒ]
herd (horses)	**табун** (м)	[tabún]
male (n)	**самец** (м)	[saméts]
female (n)	**самка** (ж)	[sámka]
hungry (adj)	**гладен**	[gláden]
wild (adj)	**див**	[div]
dangerous (adj)	**опасен**	[opásen]

226. Horses

horse	**кон** (м)	[kon]
breed (race)	**порода** (ж)	[poróda]
foal	**жребец** (м)	[ʒrebéts]
mare	**кобила** (ж)	[kobíla]
mustang	**мустанг** (м)	[mustáng]
pony	**пони** (с)	[póni]
draught horse	**товарен кон** (м)	[továren kon]
mane	**грива** (ж)	[gríva]
tail	**опашка** (ж)	[opáʃka]
hoof	**копито** (с)	[kopíto]
horseshoe	**подкова** (ж)	[potkóva]
to shoe (vt)	**подкова**	[potková]
blacksmith	**ковач** (м)	[kovátʃ]
saddle	**седло** (с)	[sedló]
stirrup	**стреме** (с)	[stréme]
bridle	**юзда** (ж)	[juzdá]
reins	**поводи** (м мн)	[póvodi]
whip (for riding)	**камшик** (м)	[kamʃík]
rider	**ездач** (м)	[ezdátʃ]
to saddle up (vt)	**яхна**	[jáhna]
to mount a horse	**седна в седло**	[sédna f sedló]
gallop	**галоп** (м)	[galóp]
to gallop (vi)	**галопирам**	[galopíram]

trot (n)	**тръс** (м)	[trəs]
at a trot (adv)	**в тръс**	[f trəs]
to go at a trot	**скачам в тръс**	[skátʃam f trəs]
racehorse	**състезателен кон** (м)	[səstezátelen kon]
horse racing	**конни надбягвания** (с мн)	[kónni nadbʲágvanija]
stable	**обор** (м)	[obór]
to feed (vt)	**храня**	[hránʲa]
hay	**сено** (с)	[senó]
to water (animals)	**поя**	[pojá]
to wash (horse)	**чистя**	[tʃístʲa]
horse-drawn cart	**каруца** (ж)	[karútsa]
to graze (vi)	**паса**	[pasá]
to neigh (vi)	**цвиля**	[tsvílʲa]
to kick (to buck)	**ритна**	[rítna]

Flora

227. Trees

tree	**дърво** (с)	[dərvó]
deciduous (adj)	**широколистно**	[ʃirokolístno]
coniferous (adj)	**иглолистно**	[iglolístno]
evergreen (adj)	**вечнозелено**	[vetʃnozeléno]
apple tree	**ябълка** (ж)	[jábəlka]
pear tree	**круша** (ж)	[krúʃa]
sweet cherry tree	**череша** (ж)	[tʃeréʃa]
sour cherry tree	**вишна** (ж)	[víʃna]
plum tree	**слива** (ж)	[slíva]
birch	**бреза** (ж)	[brezá]
oak	**дъб** (м)	[dəp]
linden tree	**липа** (ж)	[lipá]
aspen	**трепетлика** (ж)	[trepetlíka]
maple	**клен** (м)	[klen]
spruce	**ела** (ж)	[elá]
pine	**бор** (м)	[bor]
larch	**лиственица** (ж)	[lístvenitsa]
fir tree	**бяла ела** (ж)	[bʲála elá]
cedar	**кедър** (м)	[kédər]
poplar	**топола** (ж)	[topóla]
rowan	**офика** (ж)	[ofíka]
willow	**върба** (ж)	[vərbá]
alder	**елша** (ж)	[elʃá]
beech	**бук** (м)	[buk]
elm	**бряст** (м)	[brʲast]
ash (tree)	**ясен** (м)	[jásen]
chestnut	**кестен** (м)	[késtən]
magnolia	**магнолия** (ж)	[magnólija]
palm tree	**палма** (ж)	[pálma]
cypress	**кипарис** (м)	[kiparís]
mangrove	**мангрово дърво** (с)	[mangrovo dərvó]
baobab	**баобаб** (м)	[baobáp]
eucalyptus	**евкалипт** (м)	[efkalípt]
sequoia	**секвоя** (ж)	[sekvója]

228. Shrubs

bush	**храст** (м)	[hrast]
shrub	**храсталак** (м)	[hrastalák]

grapevine	**грозде** (с)	[grózde]
vineyard	**лозе** (с)	[lóze]
raspberry bush	**малина** (ж)	[malína]
blackcurrant bush	**черно френско грозде** (с)	[ʧérno frénsko grózde]
redcurrant bush	**червено френско грозде** (с)	[ʧervéno frénsko grózde]
gooseberry bush	**цариградско грозде** (с)	[tsarigrátsko grózde]
acacia	**акация** (ж)	[akátsija]
barberry	**кисел трън** (м)	[kísel trən]
jasmine	**жасмин** (м)	[ʒasmín]
juniper	**хвойна, смрика** (ж)	[hvójna], [smríka]
rosebush	**розов храст** (м)	[rózov hrast]
dog rose	**шипка** (ж)	[ʃípka]

229. Mushrooms

mushroom	**гъба** (ж)	[gəba]
edible mushroom	**ядлива гъба** (ж)	[jadlíva gəba]
poisonous mushroom	**отровна гъба** (ж)	[otróvna gəba]
cap	**шапка** (ж)	[ʃápka]
stipe	**пънче** (с)	[pənʧe]
cep, penny bun	**манатарка** (ж)	[manatárka]
orange-cap boletus	**червена брезовка** (ж)	[ʧervéna brézofka]
birch bolete	**брезова манатарка** (ж)	[brézova manatárka]
chanterelle	**пачи крак** (м)	[páʧi krak]
russula	**гълъбка** (ж)	[gələpka]
morel	**пумпалка** (ж)	[púmpalka]
fly agaric	**мухоморка** (ж)	[muhomórka]
death cap	**зелена мухоморка** (ж)	[zeléna muhómorka]

230. Fruits. Berries

fruit	**плод** (м)	[plot]
fruits	**плодове** (м мн)	[plodové]
apple	**ябълка** (ж)	[jábəlka]
pear	**круша** (ж)	[krúʃa]
plum	**слива** (ж)	[slíva]
strawberry (garden ~)	**ягода** (ж)	[jágoda]
sour cherry	**вишна** (ж)	[víʃna]
sweet cherry	**череша** (ж)	[ʧeréʃa]
grape	**грозде** (с)	[grózde]
raspberry	**малина** (ж)	[malína]
blackcurrant	**черно френско грозде** (с)	[ʧérno frénsko grózde]
redcurrant	**червено френско грозде** (с)	[ʧervéno frénsko grózde]

gooseberry	**цариградско грозде** (с)	[tsarigrátsko grózde]
cranberry	**клюква** (ж)	[klʲúkva]
orange	**портокал** (м)	[portokál]
tangerine	**мандарина** (ж)	[mandarína]
pineapple	**ананас** (м)	[ananás]
banana	**банан** (м)	[banán]
date	**фурма** (ж)	[furmá]
lemon	**лимон** (м)	[limón]
apricot	**кайсия** (ж)	[kajsíja]
peach	**праскова** (ж)	[práskova]
kiwi	**киви** (с)	[kívi]
grapefruit	**грейпфрут** (м)	[gréjpfrut]
berry	**горски плод** (м)	[górski plot]
berries	**горски плодове** (м мн)	[górski plodové]
cowberry	**червена боровинка** (ж)	[ʧervéna borovínka]
wild strawberry	**горска ягода** (ж)	[górska jágoda]
bilberry	**черна боровинка** (ж)	[ʧérna borovínka]

231. Flowers. Plants

flower	**цвете** (с)	[tsvéte]
bouquet (of flowers)	**букет** (м)	[bukét]
rose (flower)	**роза** (ж)	[róza]
tulip	**лале** (с)	[lalé]
carnation	**карамфил** (м)	[karamfíl]
gladiolus	**гладиола** (ж)	[gladióla]
cornflower	**метличина** (ж)	[metliʧína]
harebell	**камбанка** (ж)	[kambánka]
dandelion	**глухарче** (с)	[gluhárʧe]
camomile	**лайка** (ж)	[lájka]
aloe	**алое** (с)	[alóe]
cactus	**кактус** (м)	[káktus]
rubber plant, ficus	**фикус** (м)	[fíkus]
lily	**лилиум** (м)	[lílium]
geranium	**мушкато** (с)	[muʃkáto]
hyacinth	**зюмбюл** (м)	[zʲúmbʲúl]
mimosa	**мимоза** (ж)	[mimóza]
narcissus	**нарцис** (м)	[nartsís]
nasturtium	**латинка** (ж)	[latínka]
orchid	**орхидея** (ж)	[orhidéja]
peony	**божур** (м)	[boʒúr]
violet	**теменуга** (ж)	[temenúga]
pansy	**трицветна теменуга** (ж)	[tritsvétna temenúga]
forget-me-not	**незабравка** (ж)	[nezabráfka]

daisy	**маргаритка** (ж)	[margarítka]
poppy	**мак** (м)	[mak]
hemp	**коноп** (м)	[konóp]
mint	**мента** (ж)	[ménta]
lily of the valley	**момина сълза** (ж)	[mómina səlzá]
snowdrop	**кокиче** (с)	[kokítʃe]
nettle	**коприва** (ж)	[kopríva]
sorrel	**киселец** (м)	[kíselets]
water lily	**водна лилия** (ж)	[vódna lílija]
fern	**папрат** (м)	[páprat]
lichen	**лишей** (м)	[líʃej]
conservatory (greenhouse)	**оранжерия** (ж)	[oranʒérija]
lawn	**тревна площ** (ж)	[trévna ploʃt]
flowerbed	**цветна леха** (ж)	[tsvétna lehá]
plant	**растение** (с)	[rasténie]
grass	**трева** (ж)	[trevá]
blade of grass	**тревичка** (ж)	[trevítʃka]
leaf	**лист** (м)	[list]
petal	**венчелистче** (с)	[ventʃelísttʃe]
stem	**стъбло** (с)	[stəbló]
tuber	**грудка** (ж)	[grútka]
young plant (shoot)	**кълн** (м)	[kəln]
thorn	**бодил** (м)	[bodíl]
to blossom (vi)	**цъфтя**	[tsəftʲá]
to fade, to wither	**увяхвам**	[uvʲáhvam]
smell (odour)	**мирис** (м)	[míris]
to cut (flowers)	**отрежа**	[otréʒa]
to pick (a flower)	**откъсна**	[otkə́sna]

232. Cereals, grains

grain	**зърно** (с)	[zə́rno]
cereal crops	**житни култури** (ж мн)	[ʒítni kultúri]
ear (of barley, etc.)	**клас** (м)	[klas]
wheat	**пшеница** (ж)	[pʃenítsa]
rye	**ръж** (ж)	[rəʒ]
oats	**овес** (м)	[ovés]
millet	**просо** (с)	[prosó]
barley	**ечемик** (м)	[etʃemík]
maize	**царевица** (ж)	[tsárevitsa]
rice	**ориз** (м)	[oríz]
buckwheat	**елда** (ж)	[élda]
pea plant	**грах** (м)	[grah]
kidney bean	**фасул** (м)	[fasúl]

soya	**соя** (ж)	[sója]
lentil	**леща** (ж)	[léʃta]
beans (pulse crops)	**боб** (м)	[bop]

233. Vegetables. Greens

vegetables	**зеленчуци** (м мн)	[zelentʃútsi]
greens	**зарзават** (м)	[zarzavát]
tomato	**домат** (м)	[domát]
cucumber	**краставица** (ж)	[krástavitsa]
carrot	**морков** (м)	[mórkof]
potato	**картофи** (мн)	[kartófi]
onion	**лук** (м)	[luk]
garlic	**чесън** (м)	[tʃésən]
cabbage	**зеле** (с)	[zéle]
cauliflower	**карфиол** (м)	[karfiól]
Brussels sprouts	**брюкселско зеле** (с)	[brʲúkselsko zéle]
broccoli	**броколи** (с)	[brókoli]
beetroot	**цвекло** (с)	[tsvekló]
aubergine	**патладжан** (м)	[patladʒán]
marrow	**тиквичка** (ж)	[tíkvitʃka]
pumpkin	**тиква** (ж)	[tíkva]
turnip	**ряпа** (ж)	[rʲápa]
parsley	**магданоз** (м)	[magdanóz]
dill	**копър** (м)	[kópər]
lettuce	**салата** (ж)	[saláta]
celery	**целина** (ж)	[tsélina]
asparagus	**аспержа** (ж)	[aspérʒa]
spinach	**спанак** (м)	[spanák]
pea	**грах** (м)	[grah]
beans	**боб** (м)	[bop]
maize	**царевица** (ж)	[tsárevitsa]
kidney bean	**фасул** (м)	[fasúl]
pepper	**пипер** (м)	[pipér]
radish	**репичка** (ж)	[répitʃka]
artichoke	**ангинар** (м)	[anginár]

REGIONAL GEOGRAPHY

234. Western Europe

Europe	**Европа**	[evrópa]
European Union	**Европейски Съюз** (м)	[evropéjski səjúz]
European (n)	**европеец** (м)	[evropéets]
European (adj)	**европейски**	[evropéjski]
Austria	**Австрия**	[áfstrija]
Austrian (masc.)	**австриец** (м)	[afstríets]
Austrian (fem.)	**австрийка** (ж)	[afstríjka]
Austrian (adj)	**австрийски**	[afstríjski]
Great Britain	**Великобритания**	[velikobritánija]
England	**Англия**	[ánglija]
British (masc.)	**англичанин** (м)	[angliʧánin]
British (fem.)	**англичанка** (ж)	[angliʧánka]
English, British (adj)	**английски**	[anglíjski]
Belgium	**Белгия**	[bélgija]
Belgian (masc.)	**белгиец** (м)	[belgíets]
Belgian (fem.)	**белгийка** (ж)	[belgíjka]
Belgian (adj)	**белгийски**	[belgíjski]
Germany	**Германия**	[germánija]
German (masc.)	**германец** (м)	[germánets]
German (fem.)	**германка** (ж)	[germánka]
German (adj)	**немски**	[némski]
Netherlands	**Нидерландия**	[niderlándija]
Holland	**Холандия** (ж)	[holándija]
Dutch (masc.)	**холандец** (м)	[holándets]
Dutch (fem.)	**холандка** (ж)	[holántka]
Dutch (adj)	**холандски**	[holántski]
Greece	**Гърция**	[gə́rtsija]
Greek (masc.)	**грък** (м)	[grək]
Greek (fem.)	**гъркиня** (ж)	[gərkínʲa]
Greek (adj)	**гръцки**	[grə́tski]
Denmark	**Дания**	[dánija]
Dane (masc.)	**датчанин** (м)	[datʧánin]
Dane (fem.)	**датчанка** (ж)	[datʧánka]
Danish (adj)	**датски**	[dátski]
Ireland	**Ирландия**	[irlándija]
Irish (masc.)	**ирландец** (м)	[irlándets]
Irish (fem.)	**ирландка** (ж)	[irlántka]
Irish (adj)	**ирландски**	[irlántski]

Iceland **Исландия** [islándija]
Icelander (masc.) **исландец** (м) [islándets]
Icelander (fem.) **исландка** (ж) [islántka]
Icelandic (adj) **исландски** [islántski]

Spain **Испания** [ispánija]
Spaniard (masc.) **испанец** (м) [ispánets]
Spaniard (fem.) **испанка** (ж) [ispánka]
Spanish (adj) **испански** [ispánski]

Italy **Италия** [itálija]
Italian (masc.) **италианец** (м) [italiánets]
Italian (fem.) **италианка** (ж) [italiánka]
Italian (adj) **италиански** [italiánski]

Cyprus **Кипър** [kípər]
Cypriot (masc.) **кипърец** (м) [kípərets]
Cypriot (fem.) **кипърка** (ж) [kípərka]
Cypriot (adj) **кипърски** [kípərski]

Malta **Малта** [málta]
Maltese (masc.) **малтиец** (м) [maltíets]
Maltese (fem.) **малтийка** (ж) [maltíjka]
Maltese (adj) **малтийски** [maltíjski]

Norway **Норвегия** [norvégija]
Norwegian (masc.) **норвежец** (м) [norvéʒets]
Norwegian (fem.) **норвежка** (ж) [norvéʃka]
Norwegian (adj) **норвежки** [norvéʃki]

Portugal **Португалия** [portugálija]
Portuguese (masc.) **португалец** (м) [portugálets]
Portuguese (fem.) **португалка** (ж) [portugálka]
Portuguese (adj) **португалски** [portugálski]

Finland **Финландия** [finlándija]
Finn (masc.) **финландец** (м) [finlándets]
Finn (fem.) **финландка** (ж) [finlántka]
Finnish (adj) **фински** [fínski]

France **Франция** [frántsija]
French (masc.) **французин** (м) [frantsúzin]
French (fem.) **французойка** (ж) [frantsuzójka]
French (adj) **френски** [frénski]

Sweden **Швеция** [ʃvétsija]
Swede (masc.) **швед** (м) [ʃvet]
Swede (fem.) **шведка** (ж) [ʃvétka]
Swedish (adj) **шведски** [ʃvétski]

Switzerland **Швейцария** [ʃvejtsárija]
Swiss (masc.) **швейцарец** (м) [ʃvejtsárets]
Swiss (fem.) **швейцарка** (ж) [ʃvejtsárka]
Swiss (adj) **швейцарски** [ʃvejtsárski]
Scotland **Шотландия** [ʃotlándija]
Scottish (masc.) **шотландец** (м) [ʃotlándets]

Scottish (fem.)	**шотландка** (ж)	[ʃotlántka]
Scottish (adj)	**шотландски**	[ʃotlántski]
Vatican City	**Ватикана**	[vatikána]
Liechtenstein	**Лихтенщайн**	[líhtenʃtajn]
Luxembourg	**Люксембург**	[lʲúksemburg]
Monaco	**Монако**	[monáko]

235. Central and Eastern Europe

Albania	**Албания**	[albánija]
Albanian (masc.)	**албанец** (м)	[albánets]
Albanian (fem.)	**албанка** (ж)	[albánka]
Albanian (adj)	**албански**	[albánski]
Bulgaria	**България**	[bəlgárija]
Bulgarian (masc.)	**българин** (м)	[bə́lgarin]
Bulgarian (fem.)	**българка** (ж)	[bə́lgarka]
Bulgarian (adj)	**български**	[bə́lgarski]
Hungary	**Унгария**	[ungárija]
Hungarian (masc.)	**унгарец** (м)	[ungárets]
Hungarian (fem.)	**унгарка** (ж)	[ungárka]
Hungarian (adj)	**унгарски**	[ungárski]
Latvia	**Латвия**	[látvija]
Latvian (masc.)	**латвиец** (м)	[latvíets]
Latvian (fem.)	**латвийка** (ж)	[latvíjka]
Latvian (adj)	**латвийски**	[latvíjski]
Lithuania	**Литва**	[lítva]
Lithuanian (masc.)	**литовец** (м)	[litóvets]
Lithuanian (fem.)	**литовка** (ж)	[litófka]
Lithuanian (adj)	**литовски**	[litófski]
Poland	**Полша**	[pólʃa]
Pole (masc.)	**поляк** (м)	[polʲák]
Pole (fem.)	**полякиня** (ж)	[polʲakínʲa]
Polish (adj)	**полски**	[pólski]
Romania	**Румъния**	[rumə́nija]
Romanian (masc.)	**румънец** (м)	[rumə́nets]
Romanian (fem.)	**румънка** (ж)	[rumə́nka]
Romanian (adj)	**румънски**	[rumə́nski]
Serbia	**Сърбия**	[sə́rbija]
Serbian (masc.)	**сърбин** (м)	[sə́rbin]
Serbian (fem.)	**сръбкиня** (ж)	[srəpkínʲa]
Serbian (adj)	**сръбски**	[srə́pski]
Slovakia	**Словакия**	[slovákija]
Slovak (masc.)	**словак** (м)	[slovák]
Slovak (fem.)	**словачка** (ж)	[slovátʃka]
Slovak (adj)	**словашки**	[slováʃki]

Croatia	**Хърватия**	[hərvátija]
Croatian (masc.)	**хърватин** (м)	[hərvátin]
Croatian (fem.)	**хърватка** (ж)	[hərvátka]
Croatian (adj)	**хърватски**	[hərvátski]
Czech Republic	**Чехия**	[ʧéhija]
Czech (masc.)	**чех** (м)	[ʧeh]
Czech (fem.)	**чехкиня** (ж)	[ʧehkín'a]
Czech (adj)	**чешки**	[ʧéʃki]
Estonia	**Естония**	[estónija]
Estonian (masc.)	**естонец** (м)	[estónets]
Estonian (fem.)	**естонка** (ж)	[estónka]
Estonian (adj)	**естонски**	[estónski]
Bosnia and Herzegovina	**Босна и Херцеговина**	[bósna i hertsegóvina]
North Macedonia	**Македония**	[makedónija]
Slovenia	**Словения**	[slovénija]
Montenegro	**Черна гора**	[ʧérna gorá]

236. Former USSR countries

Azerbaijan	**Азербайджан**	[azerbajdʒán]
Azerbaijani (masc.)	**азербайджанец** (м)	[azerbajdʒánets]
Azerbaijani (fem.)	**азербайджанка** (ж)	[azerbajdʒánka]
Azerbaijani, Azeri (adj)	**азербайджански**	[azerbajdʒánski]
Armenia	**Армения**	[arménija]
Armenian (masc.)	**арменец** (м)	[arménets]
Armenian (fem.)	**арменка** (ж)	[arménka]
Armenian (adj)	**арменски**	[arménski]
Belarus	**Беларус**	[belarús]
Belarusian (masc.)	**беларусин** (м)	[belarúsin]
Belarusian (fem.)	**беларускиня** (ж)	[belaruskín'a]
Belarusian (adj)	**беларуски**	[belarúski]
Georgia	**Грузия**	[grúzija]
Georgian (masc.)	**грузинец** (м)	[gruzínets]
Georgian (fem.)	**грузинка** (ж)	[gruzínka]
Georgian (adj)	**грузински**	[gruzínski]
Kazakhstan	**Казахстан**	[kazahstán]
Kazakh (masc.)	**казах** (м)	[kazáh]
Kazakh (fem.)	**казашка** (ж)	[kazáʃka]
Kazakh (adj)	**казахски**	[kazáhski]
Kirghizia	**Киргизстан**	[kirgistán]
Kirghiz (masc.)	**киргиз** (м)	[kirgíz]
Kirghiz (fem.)	**киргизка** (ж)	[kirgíska]
Kirghiz (adj)	**киргизки**	[kirgíski]
Moldova, Moldavia	**Молдова**	[moldóva]
Moldavian (masc.)	**молдовец** (м)	[moldóvets]

Moldavian (fem.)	**молдовка** (ж)	[moldófka]
Moldavian (adj)	**молдавски**	[moldáfski]
Russia	**Русия**	[rusíja]
Russian (masc.)	**руснак** (м)	[rusnák]
Russian (fem.)	**рускиня** (ж)	[ruskínʲa]
Russian (adj)	**руски**	[rúski]
Tajikistan	**Таджикистан**	[tadʒikistán]
Tajik (masc.)	**таджик** (м)	[tadʒík]
Tajik (fem.)	**таджикистанка** (ж)	[tadʒikistánka]
Tajik (adj)	**таджикски**	[tadʒíkski]
Turkmenistan	**Туркменистан**	[turkmenistán]
Turkmen (masc.)	**туркмен** (м)	[turkmén]
Turkmen (fem.)	**туркменка** (ж)	[turkménka]
Turkmenian (adj)	**туркменски**	[turkménski]
Uzbekistan	**Узбекистан**	[uzbekistán]
Uzbek (masc.)	**узбек** (м)	[uzbék]
Uzbek (fem.)	**узбечка** (ж)	[uzbétʃka]
Uzbek (adj)	**узбекски**	[uzbékski]
Ukraine	**Украйна**	[ukrájna]
Ukrainian (masc.)	**украинец** (м)	[ukraínets]
Ukrainian (fem.)	**украинка** (ж)	[ukraínka]
Ukrainian (adj)	**украински**	[ukraínski]

237. Asia

Asia	**Азия**	[ázija]
Asian (adj)	**азиатски**	[aziátski]
Vietnam	**Виетнам**	[vietnám]
Vietnamese (masc.)	**виетнамец** (м)	[vietnámets]
Vietnamese (fem.)	**виетнамка** (ж)	[vietnámka]
Vietnamese (adj)	**виетнамски**	[vietnámski]
India	**Индия**	[índija]
Indian (masc.)	**индиец** (м)	[indíets]
Indian (fem.)	**индийка** (ж)	[indíjka]
Indian (adj)	**индийски**	[indíjski]
Israel	**Израел**	[izráel]
Israeli (masc.)	**израилтянин** (м)	[izrailtʲánin]
Israeli (fem.)	**израилтянка** (ж)	[izrailtʲánka]
Israeli (adj)	**израелски**	[izráelski]
Jew (n)	**евреин** (м)	[evréin]
Jewess (n)	**еврейка** (ж)	[evréjka]
Jewish (adj)	**еврейски**	[evréjski]
China	**Китай**	[kitáj]
Chinese (masc.)	**китаец** (м)	[kitáets]

Chinese (fem.)	**китайка** (ж)	[kitájka]
Chinese (adj)	**китайски**	[kitájski]
Korean (masc.)	**кореец** (м)	[koréets]
Korean (fem.)	**корейка** (ж)	[koréjka]
Korean (adj)	**корейски**	[koréjski]
Lebanon	**Ливан**	[liván]
Lebanese (masc.)	**ливанец** (м)	[livánets]
Lebanese (fem.)	**ливанка** (ж)	[livánka]
Lebanese (adj)	**ливански**	[livánski]
Mongolia	**Монголия**	[mongólija]
Mongolian (masc.)	**монголец** (м)	[mongólets]
Mongolian (fem.)	**монголка** (ж)	[mongólka]
Mongolian (adj)	**монголски**	[mongólski]
Malaysia	**Малайзия**	[malájzija]
Malaysian (masc.)	**малайзиец** (м)	[malajzíets]
Malaysian (fem.)	**малайзийка** (ж)	[malajzíjka]
Malaysian (adj)	**малайски**	[malájski]
Pakistan	**Пакистан**	[pakistán]
Pakistani (masc.)	**пакистанец** (м)	[pakistánets]
Pakistani (fem.)	**пакистанка** (ж)	[pakistánka]
Pakistani (adj)	**пакистански**	[pakistánski]
Saudi Arabia	**Саудитска Арабия**	[saudítska arábija]
Arab (masc.)	**арабин** (м)	[arábin]
Arab (fem.)	**арабка** (ж)	[arápka]
Arabic, Arabian (adj)	**арабски**	[arápski]
Thailand	**Тайланд**	[tajlánt]
Thai (masc.)	**тайландец** (м)	[tajlándets]
Thai (fem.)	**тайландка** (ж)	[tajlántka]
Thai (adj)	**тайландски**	[tajlántski]
Taiwan	**Тайван**	[tajván]
Taiwanese (masc.)	**тайванец** (м)	[tajvánets]
Taiwanese (fem.)	**тайванка** (ж)	[tajvánka]
Taiwanese (adj)	**тайвански**	[tajvánski]
Turkey	**Турция**	[túrtsija]
Turk (masc.)	**турчин** (м)	[túrʧin]
Turk (fem.)	**туркиня** (ж)	[turkínʲa]
Turkish (adj)	**турски**	[túrski]
Japan	**Япония**	[japónija]
Japanese (masc.)	**японец** (м)	[japónets]
Japanese (fem.)	**японка** (ж)	[japónka]
Japanese (adj)	**японски**	[japónski]
Afghanistan	**Афганистан**	[afganistán]
Bangladesh	**Бангладеш**	[bangladéʃ]
Indonesia	**Индонезия**	[indonézija]
Jordan	**Йордания**	[jordánija]

Iraq	**Ирак**	[irák]
Iran	**Иран**	[irán]
Cambodia	**Камбоджа**	[kambódʒa]
Kuwait	**Кувейт**	[kuvéjt]
Laos	**Лаос**	[laós]
Myanmar	**Мянма**	[mʲánma]
Nepal	**Непал**	[nepál]
United Arab Emirates	**Обединени арабски емирства**	[obedinéni arápski emírstva]
Syria	**Сирия**	[sírija]
Palestine	**Палестинска автономия**	[palestínska aftonómija]
South Korea	**Южна Корея**	[júʒna koréja]
North Korea	**Северна Корея**	[séverna koréja]

238. North America

United States of America	**Съединени американски щати**	[səedinéni amerikánski ʃtáti]
American (masc.)	**американец** (м)	[amerikánets]
American (fem.)	**американка** (ж)	[amerikánka]
American (adj)	**американски**	[amerikánski]
Canada	**Канада**	[kanáda]
Canadian (masc.)	**канадец** (м)	[kanádets]
Canadian (fem.)	**канадка** (ж)	[kanátka]
Canadian (adj)	**канадски**	[kanátski]
Mexico	**Мексико**	[méksiko]
Mexican (masc.)	**мексиканец** (м)	[meksikánets]
Mexican (fem.)	**мексиканка** (ж)	[meksikánka]
Mexican (adj)	**мексикански**	[meksikánski]

239. Central and South America

Argentina	**Аржентина**	[arʒentína]
Argentinian (masc.)	**аржентинец** (м)	[arʒentínets]
Argentinian (fem.)	**аржентинка** (ж)	[arʒentínka]
Argentinian (adj)	**аржентински**	[arʒentínski]
Brazil	**Бразилия**	[brazílija]
Brazilian (masc.)	**бразилец** (м)	[brazílets]
Brazilian (fem.)	**бразилка** (ж)	[brazílka]
Brazilian (adj)	**бразилски**	[brazílski]
Colombia	**Колумбия**	[kolúmbija]
Colombian (masc.)	**колумбиец** (м)	[kolumbíets]
Colombian (fem.)	**колумбийка** (ж)	[kolumbíjka]
Colombian (adj)	**колумбийски**	[kolumbíjski]
Cuba	**Куба**	[kúba]
Cuban (masc.)	**кубинец** (м)	[kubínets]

Cuban (fem.)	**кубинка** (ж)	[kubínka]
Cuban (adj)	**кубински**	[kubínski]
Chile	**Чили**	[ʧíli]
Chilean (masc.)	**чилиец** (м)	[ʧilíets]
Chilean (fem.)	**чилийка** (ж)	[ʧilíjka]
Chilean (adj)	**чилийски**	[ʧilíjski]
Bolivia	**Боливия**	[bolívija]
Venezuela	**Венецуела**	[venetsuéla]
Paraguay	**Парагвай**	[paragváj]
Peru	**Перу**	[perú]
Suriname	**Суринам**	[surinám]
Uruguay	**Уругвай**	[urugváj]
Ecuador	**Еквадор**	[ekvadór]
The Bahamas	**Бахамски острови**	[bahámski óstrovi]
Haiti	**Хаити**	[haíti]
Dominican Republic	**Доминиканска република**	[dominikánska repúblika]
Panama	**Панама**	[panáma]
Jamaica	**Ямайка**	[jamájka]

240. Africa

Egypt	**Египет**	[egípet]
Egyptian (masc.)	**египтянин** (м)	[egíptʲanin]
Egyptian (fem.)	**египтянка** (ж)	[egíptʲanka]
Egyptian (adj)	**египетски**	[egípetski]
Morocco	**Мароко**	[maróko]
Moroccan (masc.)	**мароканец** (м)	[marokánets]
Moroccan (fem.)	**мароканка** (ж)	[marokánka]
Moroccan (adj)	**марокански**	[marokánski]
Tunisia	**Тунис**	[túnis]
Tunisian (masc.)	**тунисец** (м)	[tunísets]
Tunisian (fem.)	**туниска** (ж)	[tuníska]
Tunisian (adj)	**туниски**	[tuníski]
Ghana	**Гана**	[gána]
Zanzibar	**Занзибар**	[zanzibár]
Kenya	**Кения**	[kénija]
Libya	**Либия**	[líbija]
Madagascar	**Мадагаскар**	[madagaskár]
Namibia	**Намибия**	[namíbija]
Senegal	**Сенегал**	[senegál]
Tanzania	**Танзания**	[tanzánija]
South Africa	**Южноафриканска република**	[juʒno·afrikánska repúblika]
African (masc.)	**африканец** (м)	[afrikánets]
African (fem.)	**африканка** (ж)	[afrikánka]
African (adj)	**африкански**	[afrikánski]

241. Australia. Oceania

Australia	**Австралия**	[afstrálija]
Australian (masc.)	**австралиец** (м)	[afstralíets]
Australian (fem.)	**австралийка** (ж)	[afstralíjka]
Australian (adj)	**австралийски**	[afstralíjski]
New Zealand	**Нова Зеландия**	[nóva zelándija]
New Zealander (masc.)	**новозеландец** (м)	[novozelándets]
New Zealander (fem.)	**новозеландка** (ж)	[novozelántka]
New Zealand (as adj)	**новозеландски**	[novozelántski]
Tasmania	**Тасмания**	[tasmánija]
French Polynesia	**Френска Полинезия**	[frénska polinézija]

242. Cities

Amsterdam	**Амстердам**	[amsterdám]
Ankara	**Анкара**	[ánkara]
Athens	**Атина**	[átina]
Baghdad	**Багдад**	[bagdád]
Bangkok	**Банкок**	[bankók]
Barcelona	**Барселона**	[barselóna]
Beijing	**Пекин**	[pekín]
Beirut	**Бейрут**	[bejrút]
Berlin	**Берлин**	[berlín]
Mumbai (Bombay)	**Мумбай**	[mumbáj]
Bonn	**Бон**	[bon]
Bordeaux	**Бордо**	[bordó]
Bratislava	**Братислава**	[bratisláva]
Brussels	**Брюксел**	[brʲúksel]
Bucharest	**Букурещ**	[búkureʃt]
Budapest	**Будапеща**	[budapéʃta]
Cairo	**Кайро**	[kájro]
Kolkata (Calcutta)	**Калкута**	[kalkúta]
Chicago	**Чикаго**	[ʧikágo]
Copenhagen	**Копенхаген**	[kopenhágen]
Dar-es-Salaam	**Дар ес Салам**	[dar es salám]
Delhi	**Делхи**	[délhi]
Dubai	**Дубай**	[dubáj]
Dublin	**Дъблин**	[dəblin]
Düsseldorf	**Дюселдорф**	[dʲúseldorf]
Florence	**Флоренция**	[floréntsija]
Frankfurt	**Франкфурт**	[fránkfurt]
Geneva	**Женева**	[ʒenéva]
The Hague	**Хага**	[hága]
Hamburg	**Хамбург**	[hámburk]

Hanoi	**Ханой**	[hanój]
Havana	**Хавана**	[havána]
Helsinki	**Хелзинки**	[hélzinki]
Hiroshima	**Хирошима**	[hiroʃíma]
Hong Kong	**Хонконг**	[honkóng]
Istanbul	**Истанбул**	[istanbúl]
Jerusalem	**Ерусалим**	[érusalim]
Kyiv	**Киев**	[kíev]
Kuala Lumpur	**Куала Лумпур**	[kuála lumpúr]
Lisbon	**Лисабон**	[lisabón]
London	**Лондон**	[lóndon]
Los Angeles	**Лос Анджелис**	[los ándʒelis]
Lyons	**Лион**	[lión]
Madrid	**Мадрид**	[madrít]
Marseille	**Марсилия**	[marsílija]
Mexico City	**Мексико**	[méksiko]
Miami	**Маями**	[majámi]
Montreal	**Монреал**	[monreál]
Moscow	**Москва**	[moskvá]
Munich	**Мюнхен**	[mʲúnhen]
Nairobi	**Найроби**	[najróbi]
Naples	**Неапол**	[neápol]
New York	**Ню Йорк**	[nʲu jórk]
Nice	**Ница**	[nítsa]
Oslo	**Осло**	[óslo]
Ottawa	**Отава**	[otáva]
Paris	**Париж**	[paríʒ]
Prague	**Прага**	[prága]
Rio de Janeiro	**Рио де Жанейро**	[río de ʒanéjro]
Rome	**Рим**	[rim]
Saint Petersburg	**Санкт Петербург**	[sankt péterburk]
Seoul	**Сеул**	[seúl]
Shanghai	**Шанхай**	[ʃanháj]
Singapore	**Сингапур**	[singapúr]
Stockholm	**Стокхолм**	[stokhólm]
Sydney	**Сидни**	[sídni]
Taipei	**Тайпе**	[tajpé]
Tokyo	**Токио**	[tókio]
Toronto	**Торонто**	[torónto]
Venice	**Венеция**	[venétsija]
Vienna	**Виена**	[viéna]
Warsaw	**Варшава**	[varʃáva]
Washington	**Вашингтон**	[váʃinkton]

243. Politics. Government. Part 1

politics	**политика** (ж)	[politíka]
political (adj)	**политически**	[politítʃeski]

politician	**политик** (м)	[politík]
state (country)	**държава** (ж)	[dərʒáva]
citizen	**гражданин** (м)	[gráʒdanin]
citizenship	**гражданство** (с)	[gráʒdanstvo]
national emblem	**национален герб** (м)	[natsionálen gerp]
national anthem	**държавен химн** (м)	[dərʒáven himn]
government	**правителство** (с)	[pravítelstvo]
head of state	**държавен глава** (м)	[dərʒáven glavá]
parliament	**парламент** (м)	[parlamént]
party	**партия** (ж)	[pártija]
capitalism	**капитализъм** (м)	[kapitalízəm]
capitalist (adj)	**капиталистически**	[kapitalistítʃeski]
socialism	**социализъм** (м)	[sotsialízəm]
socialist (adj)	**социалистически**	[sotsialistítʃeski]
communism	**комунизъм** (м)	[komunízəm]
communist (adj)	**комунистически**	[komunistítʃeski]
communist (n)	**комунист** (м)	[komuníst]
democracy	**демокрация** (ж)	[demokrátsija]
democrat	**демократ** (м)	[demokrát]
democratic (adj)	**демократически**	[demokratítʃeski]
Democratic party	**демократическа партия** (ж)	[demokratítʃeska pártija]
liberal (n)	**либерал** (м)	[liberál]
Liberal (adj)	**либерален**	[liberálen]
conservative (n)	**консерватор** (м)	[konservátor]
conservative (adj)	**консервативен**	[konservatíven]
republic (n)	**република** (ж)	[repúblika]
republican (n)	**републиканец** (м)	[republikánets]
Republican party	**републиканска партия** (ж)	[republikánska pártija]
elections	**избори** (мн)	[ízbori]
to elect (vt)	**избирам**	[izbíram]
elector, voter	**избирател** (м)	[izbirátel]
election campaign	**избирателна кампания** (ж)	[izbirátelna kampánija]
voting (n)	**гласуване** (с)	[glasúvane]
to vote (vi)	**гласувам**	[glasúvam]
suffrage, right to vote	**право** (с) **на глас**	[právo na glas]
candidate	**кандидат** (м)	[kandidát]
to run for (~ President)	**балотирам се**	[balotíram se]
campaign	**кампания** (ж)	[kampánija]
opposition (as adj)	**опозиционен**	[opozitsiónen]
opposition (n)	**опозиция** (ж)	[opozítsija]
visit	**визита** (ж)	[vizíta]
official visit	**официална визита** (ж)	[ofitsiálna vizíta]

international (adj)	**международен**	[meʒdunaróden]
negotiations	**преговори** (мн)	[prégovori]
to negotiate (vi)	**водя преговори**	[vódʲa prégovori]

244. Politics. Government. Part 2

society	**общество** (с)	[obʃtestvó]
constitution	**конституция** (ж)	[konstitútsija]
power (political control)	**власт** (ж)	[vlast]
corruption	**корупция** (ж)	[korúptsija]
law (justice)	**закон** (м)	[zakón]
legal (legitimate)	**законен**	[zakónen]
justice (fairness)	**справедливост** (ж)	[spravedlívost]
just (fair)	**справедлив**	[spravedlív]
committee	**комитет** (м)	[komitét]
bill (draft law)	**законопроект** (м)	[zakonoproékt]
budget	**бюджет** (м)	[bʲudʒét]
policy	**политика** (ж)	[polítika]
reform	**реформа** (ж)	[refórma]
radical (adj)	**радикален**	[radikálen]
power (strength, force)	**сила** (ж)	[síla]
powerful (adj)	**силен**	[sílen]
supporter	**привърженик** (м)	[privərʒenik]
influence	**влияние** (с)	[vlijánie]
regime (e.g. military ~)	**режим** (м)	[reʒím]
conflict	**конфликт** (м)	[konflíkt]
conspiracy (plot)	**заговор** (м)	[zágovor]
provocation	**провокация** (ж)	[provokátsija]
to overthrow (regime, etc.)	**сваля**	[svalʲá]
overthrow (of a government)	**сваляне** (с)	[sválʲane]
revolution	**революция** (ж)	[revolʲútsija]
coup d'état	**преврат** (м)	[prevrát]
military coup	**военен преврат** (м)	[voénen prevrát]
crisis	**криза** (ж)	[kríza]
economic recession	**икономически спад** (м)	[ikonomítʃeski spat]
demonstrator (protester)	**демонстрант** (м)	[demonstránt]
demonstration	**демонстрация** (ж)	[demonstrátsija]
martial law	**военно положение** (с)	[voénno poloʒénie]
military base	**база** (ж)	[báza]
stability	**стабилност** (ж)	[stabílnost]
stable (adj)	**стабилен**	[stabílen]
exploitation	**експлоатация** (ж)	[eksploatátsija]
to exploit (workers)	**експлоатирам**	[eksploatíram]
racism	**расизъм** (м)	[rasízəm]

racist	**расист** (м)	[rasíst]
fascism	**фашизъм** (м)	[faʃízəm]
fascist	**фашист** (м)	[faʃíst]

245. Countries. Miscellaneous

foreigner	**чужденец** (м)	[ʧuʒdenéts]
foreign (adj)	**чуждестранен**	[ʧuʒdestránen]
abroad (in a foreign country)	**в чужбина**	[v ʧuʒbína]
emigrant	**емигрант** (м)	[emigránt]
emigration	**емиграция** (ж)	[emigrátsija]
to emigrate (vi)	**емигрирам**	[emigríram]
the West	**Запад**	[zápat]
the East	**Изток**	[ístok]
the Far East	**Далечният Изток**	[dalétʃnijat ístok]
civilization	**цивилизация** (ж)	[tsivilizátsija]
humanity (mankind)	**човечество** (с)	[ʧovétʃestvo]
the world (earth)	**свят** (м)	[svʲat]
peace	**мир** (м)	[mir]
worldwide (adj)	**световен**	[svetóven]
homeland	**родина** (ж)	[rodína]
people (population)	**народ** (м)	[narót]
population	**население** (с)	[naselénie]
people (a lot of ~)	**хора** (мн)	[hóra]
nation (people)	**нация** (ж)	[nátsija]
generation	**поколение** (с)	[pokolénie]
territory (area)	**територия** (ж)	[teritórija]
region	**регион** (м)	[región]
state (part of a country)	**щат** (м)	[ʃtat]
tradition	**традиция** (ж)	[tradítsija]
custom (tradition)	**обичай** (м)	[obitʃáj]
ecology	**екология** (ж)	[ekológija]
Indian (Native American)	**индианец** (м)	[indiánets]
Gypsy (masc.)	**циганин** (м)	[tsíganin]
Gypsy (fem.)	**циганка** (ж)	[tsíganka]
Gypsy (adj)	**цигански**	[tsíganski]
empire	**империя** (ж)	[impérija]
colony	**колония** (ж)	[kolónija]
slavery	**робство** (с)	[rópstvo]
invasion	**нашествие** (с)	[naʃéstvie]
famine	**глад** (м)	[glat]

246. Major religious groups. Confessions

religion	**религия** (ж)	[relígija]
religious (adj)	**религиозен**	[religiózen]

faith, belief	**вяра** (ж)	[vʲára]
to believe (in God)	**вярвам**	[vʲárvam]
believer	**вярващ** (м)	[vʲárvaʃt]
atheism	**атеизъм** (м)	[ateízəm]
atheist	**атеист** (м)	[ateíst]
Christianity	**християнство** (с)	[hristijánstvo]
Christian (n)	**християнин** (м)	[hristijánin]
Christian (adj)	**християнски**	[hristijánski]
Catholicism	**Католицизъм** (м)	[katolitsízəm]
Catholic (n)	**католик** (м)	[katolík]
Catholic (adj)	**католически**	[katolítʃeski]
Protestantism	**протестантство** (с)	[protestántstvo]
Protestant Church	**протестантска църква** (ж)	[protestántska tsərkva]
Protestant (n)	**протестант** (м)	[protestánt]
Orthodoxy	**Православие** (с)	[pravoslávie]
Orthodox Church	**Православна църква** (ж)	[pravoslávna tsərkva]
Orthodox (n)	**православен**	[pravosláven]
Presbyterianism	**Презвитерианство** (с)	[prezviteriánstvo]
Presbyterian Church	**Презвитерианска църква** (ж)	[prezviteriánska tsə́rkva]
Presbyterian (n)	**презвитерианец** (м)	[prezviteriánets]
Lutheranism	**Лютеранска църква** (ж)	[lʲuteránska tsərkva]
Lutheran (n)	**лютеран** (м)	[lʲuterán]
Baptist Church	**Баптизъм** (м)	[baptízəm]
Baptist (n)	**баптист** (м)	[baptíst]
Anglican Church	**Англиканска църква** (ж)	[anglikánska tsərkva]
Anglican (n)	**англиканец** (м)	[anglikánets]
Mormonism	**мормонство** (с)	[mormónstvo]
Mormon (n)	**мормон** (м)	[mormón]
Judaism	**Юдаизъм** (м)	[judaízəm]
Jew (n)	**юдей** (м)	[judéj]
Buddhism	**Будизъм** (м)	[budízəm]
Buddhist (n)	**будист** (м)	[budíst]
Hinduism	**Индуизъм** (м)	[induízəm]
Hindu (n)	**индус** (м)	[indús]
Islam	**Ислям** (м)	[islʲám]
Muslim (n)	**мюсюлманин** (м)	[mʲusʲulmánin]
Muslim (adj)	**мюсюлмански**	[mʲusʲulmánski]
Shiah Islam	**шиизъм** (м)	[ʃiízəm]
Shiite (n)	**шиит** (м)	[ʃiít]
Sunni Islam	**сунизъм** (м)	[sunízəm]
Sunnite (n)	**сунит** (м)	[sunít]

247. Religions. Priests

priest	**свещеник** (м)	[sveʃténik]
the Pope	**Папа Римски** (м)	[pápa rímski]
monk, friar	**монах** (м)	[monáh]
nun	**монахиня** (ж)	[monahínʲa]
pastor	**пастор** (м)	[pástor]
abbot	**абат** (м)	[abát]
vicar (parish priest)	**викарий** (м)	[vikárij]
bishop	**епископ** (м)	[episkóp]
cardinal	**кардинал** (м)	[kardinál]
preacher	**проповедник** (м)	[propovédnik]
preaching	**проповед** (м)	[própovet]
parishioners	**енориаши** (мн)	[enoriáʃi]
believer	**вярващ** (м)	[vʲárvaʃt]
atheist	**атеист** (м)	[ateíst]

248. Faith. Christianity. Islam

Adam	**Адам**	[adám]
Eve	**Ева**	[éva]
God	**Бог**	[bok]
the Lord	**Господ**	[góspot]
the Almighty	**Всемогъщ**	[fsemogə́ʃt]
sin	**грях** (м)	[grʲah]
to sin (vi)	**греша**	[greʃá]
sinner (masc.)	**грешник** (м)	[gréʃnik]
sinner (fem.)	**грешница** (ж)	[gréʃnitsa]
hell	**ад** (м)	[at]
paradise	**рай** (м)	[raj]
Jesus	**Исус**	[isús]
Jesus Christ	**Исус Христос**	[isús hristós]
the Holy Spirit	**Светия Дух**	[svetíja duh]
the Saviour	**Спасител**	[spasítel]
the Virgin Mary	**Богородица**	[bogoróditsa]
the Devil	**Дявол**	[dʲávol]
devil's (adj)	**дяволски**	[dʲávolski]
Satan	**Сатана**	[sataná]
satanic (adj)	**сатанински**	[sataninski]
angel	**ангел** (м)	[ángel]
guardian angel	**ангел-пазител** (м)	[ángel-pazítel]
angelic (adj)	**ангелски**	[ángelski]

apostle	**апостол** (м)	[apóstol]
archangel	**архангел** (м)	[arhángel]
the Antichrist	**антихрист** (м)	[antíhrist]
Church	**Църква** (ж)	[tsərkva]
Bible	**библия** (ж)	[bíblija]
biblical (adj)	**библейски**	[bibléjski]
Old Testament	**Старият Завет** (м)	[stárija zavét]
New Testament	**Новия Завет** (м)	[nóvija zavét]
Gospel	**Евангелие** (с)	[evángelie]
Holy Scripture	**Свещено Писание** (с)	[sveʃténo pisánie]
Heaven	**Небе** (с)	[nebé]
Commandment	**заповед** (ж)	[zápovet]
prophet	**пророк** (м)	[prorók]
prophecy	**пророчество** (с)	[proróʧestvo]
Allah	**Алах**	[aláh]
Mohammed	**Мохамед**	[mohamét]
the Koran	**Коран**	[korán]
mosque	**джамия** (ж)	[dʒamíja]
mullah	**молла** (м)	[mollá]
prayer	**молитва** (ж)	[molítva]
to pray (vi, vt)	**моля се**	[mólʲa se]
pilgrimage	**поклонничество** (с)	[poklónniʧestvo]
pilgrim	**поклонник** (м)	[poklónnik]
Mecca	**Мека**	[méka]
church	**църква** (ж)	[tsərkva]
temple	**храм** (м)	[hram]
cathedral	**катедрала** (ж)	[katedrála]
Gothic (adj)	**готически**	[gotíʧeski]
synagogue	**синагога** (ж)	[sinagóga]
mosque	**джамия** (ж)	[dʒamíja]
chapel	**параклис** (м)	[paráklis]
abbey	**абатство** (с)	[abátstvo]
convent	**манастир** (м)	[manastír]
monastery	**манастир** (м)	[manastír]
bell (church ~s)	**камбана** (ж)	[kambána]
bell tower	**камбанария** (ж)	[kambanaríja]
to ring (ab. bells)	**бия**	[bíja]
cross	**кръст** (м)	[krəst]
cupola (roof)	**купол** (м)	[kúpol]
icon	**икона** (ж)	[ikóna]
soul	**душа** (ж)	[duʃá]
fate (destiny)	**съдба** (ж)	[sədbá]
evil (n)	**зло** (с)	[zlo]
good (n)	**добро** (с)	[dobró]
vampire	**вампир** (м)	[vampír]

witch (evil ~)	**вещица** (ж)	[véʃtitsa]
demon	**демон** (м)	[démon]
spirit	**дух** (м)	[duh]
redemption (giving us ~)	**изкупление** (с)	[iskuplénie]
to redeem (vt)	**изкупя**	[iskúpʲa]
church service	**служба** (ж)	[slúʒba]
to say mass	**служа**	[slúʒa]
confession	**изповед** (ж)	[íspovet]
to confess (vi)	**изповядвам се**	[ispovʲádvam se]
saint (n)	**светец** (м)	[svetéts]
sacred (holy)	**свещен**	[sveʃtén]
holy water	**света вода** (ж)	[svetá vodá]
ritual (n)	**ритуал** (м)	[rituál]
ritual (adj)	**ритуален**	[rituálen]
sacrifice	**жертвоприношение** (с)	[ʒertvoprinoʃénie]
superstition	**суеверие** (с)	[suevérie]
superstitious (adj)	**суеверен**	[suevéren]
afterlife	**задгробен живот** (м)	[zadgróben ʒivót]
eternal life	**вечен живот** (м)	[vétʃen ʒivót]

MISCELLANEOUS

249 Various useful words

background (green ~)	**фон** (м)	[fon]
balance (of the situation)	**баланс** (м)	[baláns]
barrier (obstacle)	**преграда** (ж)	[pregráda]
base (basis)	**база** (ж)	[báza]
beginning	**начало** (с)	[natʃálo]
category	**категория** (ж)	[kategórija]
cause (reason)	**причина** (ж)	[pritʃína]
choice	**избор** (м)	[ízbor]
coincidence	**съвпадение** (с)	[səfpadénie]
comfortable (~ chair)	**удобен**	[udóben]
comparison	**сравнение** (с)	[sravnénie]
compensation	**компенсация** (ж)	[kompensátsija]
degree (extent, amount)	**степен** (ж)	[stépen]
development	**развитие** (с)	[razvítie]
difference	**различие** (с)	[razlítʃie]
effect (e.g. of drugs)	**ефект** (м)	[efékt]
effort (exertion)	**усилие** (с)	[usílie]
element	**елемент** (м)	[elemént]
end (finish)	**край** (м)	[kraj]
example (illustration)	**пример** (м)	[prímer]
fact	**факт** (м)	[fakt]
frequent (adj)	**чест**	[tʃest]
growth (development)	**ръст** (м)	[rəst]
help	**помощ** (ж)	[pómoʃt]
ideal	**идеал** (м)	[ideál]
kind (sort, type)	**вид** (м)	[vit]
labyrinth	**лабиринт** (м)	[labirínt]
mistake, error	**грешка** (ж)	[gréʃka]
moment	**момент** (м)	[momént]
object (thing)	**обект** (м)	[obékt]
obstacle	**пречка** (ж)	[prétʃka]
original (original copy)	**оригинал** (м)	[originál]
part (~ of sth)	**част** (ж)	[tʃast]
particle, small part	**частица** (ж)	[tʃastítsa]
pause (break)	**пауза** (ж)	[páuza]
position	**позиция** (ж)	[pozítsija]
principle	**принцип** (м)	[príntsip]
problem	**проблем** (м)	[problém]
process	**процес** (м)	[protsés]

progress	**прогрес** (м)	[progrés]
property (quality)	**свойство** (с)	[svójstvo]
reaction	**реакция** (ж)	[reáktsija]
risk	**риск** (м)	[risk]
secret	**тайна** (ж)	[tájna]
series	**серия** (ж)	[sérija]
shape (outer form)	**форма** (ж)	[fórma]
situation	**ситуация** (ж)	[situátsija]
solution	**решение** (с)	[reʃénie]
standard (adj)	**стандартен**	[standárten]
standard (level of quality)	**стандарт** (м)	[standárt]
stop (pause)	**почивка** (ж)	[potʃífka]
style	**стил** (м)	[stil]
system	**система** (ж)	[sistéma]
table (chart)	**таблица** (ж)	[táblitsa]
tempo, rate	**темпо** (с)	[témpo]
term (word, expression)	**термин** (м)	[términ]
thing (object, item)	**вещ** (ж)	[veʃt]
truth (e.g. moment of ~)	**истина** (ж)	[ístina]
turn (please wait your ~)	**ред** (м)	[ret]
type (sort, kind)	**тип** (м)	[tip]
urgent (adj)	**срочен**	[sróʧen]
urgently	**срочно**	[sróʧno]
utility (usefulness)	**полза** (ж)	[pólza]
variant (alternative)	**вариант** (м)	[variánt]
way (means, method)	**начин** (м)	[náʧin]
zone	**зона** (ж)	[zóna]

250. Modifiers. Adjectives. Part 1

additional (adj)	**допълнителен**	[dopəlnítelen]
ancient (~ civilization)	**древен**	[dréven]
artificial (adj)	**изкуствен**	[iskústven]
back, rear (adj)	**заден**	[záden]
bad (adj)	**лош**	[loʃ]
beautiful (~ palace)	**прекрасен**	[prekrásen]
beautiful (person)	**хубав**	[húbav]
big (in size)	**голям**	[golʲám]
bitter (taste)	**горчив**	[gorʧív]
blind (sightless)	**сляп**	[slʲap]
calm, quiet (adj)	**спокоен**	[spokóen]
careless (negligent)	**немарлив**	[nemarlív]
caring (~ father)	**грижлив**	[griʒlív]
central (adj)	**централен**	[tsentrálen]
cheap (low-priced)	**евтин**	[éftin]
cheerful (adj)	**весел**	[vésel]

children's (adj)	**детски**	[détski]
civil (~ law)	**граждански**	[gráʒdanski]
clandestine (secret)	**нелегален**	[nelegálen]
clean (free from dirt)	**чист**	[ʧist]
clear (explanation, etc.)	**понятен**	[pon^játen]
clever (intelligent)	**умен**	[úmen]
close (near in space)	**близък**	[blízək]
closed (adj)	**затворен**	[zatvóren]
cloudless (sky)	**безоблачен**	[bezóblaʧen]
cold (drink, weather)	**студен**	[studén]
compatible (adj)	**съвместим**	[səvmestím]
contented (satisfied)	**доволен**	[dovólen]
continuous (uninterrupted)	**непрекъснат**	[neprekə́snat]
cool (weather)	**прохладен**	[prohláden]
dangerous (adj)	**опасен**	[opásen]
dark (room)	**тъмен**	[tə́men]
dead (not alive)	**мъртъв**	[mə́rtəv]
dense (fog, smoke)	**гъст**	[gəst]
destitute (extremely poor)	**беден**	[béden]
different (not the same)	**различен**	[razlíʧen]
difficult (decision)	**труден**	[trúden]
difficult (problem, task)	**сложен**	[slóʒen]
dim, faint (light)	**блед**	[blet]
dirty (not clean)	**мръсен**	[mrə́sen]
distant (in space)	**далечен**	[daléʧen]
dry (clothes, etc.)	**сух**	[suh]
easy (not difficult)	**лесен**	[lésen]
empty (glass, room)	**празен**	[prázen]
even (e.g. ~ surface)	**равен**	[ráven]
exact (amount)	**точен**	[tóʧen]
excellent (adj)	**отличен**	[otlíʧen]
excessive (adj)	**прекален**	[prekalén]
expensive (adj)	**скъп**	[skəp]
exterior (adj)	**външен**	[və́nʃen]
far (the ~ East)	**далечен**	[daléʧen]
fast (quick)	**бърз**	[bərz]
fatty (food)	**мазен**	[mázen]
fertile (land, soil)	**плодороден**	[plodoróden]
flat (~ panel display)	**плосък**	[plósək]
foreign (adj)	**чуждестранен**	[ʧuʒdestránen]
fragile (china, glass)	**крехък**	[kréhək]
free (at no cost)	**безплатен**	[bespláten]
free (unrestricted)	**свободен**	[svobóden]
fresh (~ water)	**сладък**	[sládək]
fresh (e.g. ~ bread)	**пресен**	[présen]
frozen (food)	**замразен**	[zamrazén]
full (completely filled)	**пълен**	[pə́len]

gloomy (house, forecast)	**мрачен**	[mrátʃen]
good (book, etc.)	**добър**	[dobər]
good, kind (kindhearted)	**добър**	[dobər]
grateful (adj)	**благодарен**	[blagodáren]
happy (adj)	**щастлив**	[ʃtastlív]
hard (not soft)	**твърд**	[tvərt]
heavy (in weight)	**тежък**	[téʒək]
hostile (adj)	**враждебен**	[vraʒdében]
hot (adj)	**горещ**	[goréʃt]
huge (adj)	**огромен**	[ogrómen]
humid (adj)	**влажен**	[vláʒen]
hungry (adj)	**гладен**	[gláden]
ill (sick, unwell)	**болен**	[bólen]
immobile (adj)	**неподвижен**	[nepodvíʒen]
important (adj)	**важен**	[váʒen]
impossible (adj)	**невъзможен**	[nevəzmóʒen]
incomprehensible	**непонятен**	[nepon^játen]
indispensable (adj)	**необходим**	[neobhodím]
inexperienced (adj)	**неопитен**	[neópiten]
insignificant (adj)	**незначителен**	[neznatʃítelen]
interior (adj)	**вътрешен**	[vətreʃen]
joint (~ decision)	**съвместен**	[səvmésten]
last (e.g. ~ week)	**минал**	[mínal]
last (final)	**последен**	[posléden]
left (e.g. ~ side)	**ляв**	[l^jav]
legal (legitimate)	**законен**	[zakónen]
light (in weight)	**лек**	[lek]
light (pale color)	**светъл**	[svétəl]
limited (adj)	**ограничен**	[ogranitʃén]
liquid (fluid)	**течен**	[tétʃen]
long (e.g. ~ hair)	**дълъг**	[dələk]
loud (voice, etc.)	**силен**	[sílen]
low (voice)	**тих**	[tih]

251. Modifiers. Adjectives. Part 2

main (principal)	**главен**	[gláven]
matt, matte	**матов**	[mátov]
meticulous (job)	**акуратен**	[akuráten]
mysterious (adj)	**загадъчен**	[zagádətʃen]
narrow (street, etc.)	**тесен**	[tésen]
native (~ country)	**роден**	[róden]
nearby (adj)	**ближен**	[blíʒen]
needed (necessary)	**нужен**	[núʒen]
negative (~ response)	**отрицателен**	[otritsátelen]
neighbouring (adj)	**съседен**	[səséden]
nervous (adj)	**нервен**	[nérven]

new (adj)	**нов**	[nov]
next (e.g. ~ week)	**следващ**	[slédvaʃt]
nice (agreeable)	**мил**	[mil]
pleasant (voice)	**приятен**	[prijáten]
normal (adj)	**нормален**	[normálen]
not big (adj)	**неголям**	[negolʲám]
not difficult (adj)	**лесен**	[lésen]
obligatory (adj)	**обезателен**	[obezátelen]
old (house)	**стар**	[star]
open (adj)	**отворен**	[otvóren]
opposite (adj)	**противоположен**	[protivopolóʒen]
ordinary (usual)	**обикновен**	[obiknovén]
original (unusual)	**оригинален**	[originálen]
past (recent)	**минал**	[mínal]
permanent (adj)	**постоянен**	[postojánen]
personal (adj)	**частен**	[ʧásten]
polite (adj)	**вежлив**	[veʒlív]
poor (not rich)	**беден**	[béden]
possible (adj)	**възможен**	[vəzmóʒen]
present (current)	**настоящ**	[nastojáʃt]
previous (adj)	**предишен**	[predíʃen]
principal (main)	**основен**	[osnóven]
private (~ jet)	**частен**	[ʧásten]
probable (adj)	**вероятен**	[verojáten]
prolonged (e.g. ~ applause)	**продължителен**	[prodəlʒítelen]
public (open to all)	**обществен**	[obʃtéstven]
punctual (person)	**пунктуален**	[punktuálen]
quiet (tranquil)	**тих**	[tih]
rare (adj)	**рядък**	[rʲádək]
raw (uncooked)	**суров**	[suróf]
right (not left)	**десен**	[désen]
right, correct (adj)	**правилен**	[právilen]
ripe (fruit)	**зрял**	[zrʲal]
risky (adj)	**рискован**	[riskóvan]
sad (~ look)	**печален**	[peʧálen]
sad (depressing)	**тъжен**	[təʒen]
safe (not dangerous)	**безопасен**	[bezopásen]
salty (food)	**солен**	[solén]
satisfied (customer)	**удовлетворен**	[udovletvorén]
second hand (adj)	**употребяван**	[upotrebʲávan]
shallow (water)	**плитък**	[plítək]
sharp (blade, etc.)	**остър**	[óstər]
short (in length)	**къс**	[kəs]
short, short-lived (adj)	**краткотраен**	[kratkotráen]
short-sighted (adj)	**късоглед**	[kəsoglét]
significant (notable)	**значителен**	[znaʧítelen]

similar (adj)	**приличащ**	[prilítʃaʃt]
simple (easy)	**лесен**	[lésen]
skinny	**кльощав**	[klʲóʃtaf]
small (in size)	**малък**	[málək]
smooth (surface)	**гладък**	[gládək]
soft (~ toys)	**мек**	[mek]
solid (~ wall)	**стабилен**	[stabílen]
sour (flavour, taste)	**кисел**	[kísel]
spacious (house, etc.)	**просторен**	[prostóren]
special (adj)	**специален**	[spetsiálen]
straight (line, road)	**прав**	[prav]
strong (person)	**силен**	[sílen]
stupid (foolish)	**глупав**	[glúpav]
suitable (e.g. ~ for drinking)	**пригоден**	[prigóden]
sunny (day)	**слънчев**	[slə́ntʃev]
superb, perfect (adj)	**превъзходен**	[prevəshóden]
swarthy (dark-skinned)	**мургав**	[múrgav]
sweet (sugary)	**сладък**	[sládək]
tanned (adj)	**почернял**	[potʃernʲál]
tasty (delicious)	**вкусен**	[fkúsen]
tender (affectionate)	**нежен**	[néʒen]
the highest (adj)	**висш**	[visʃ]
the most important	**най-важен**	[naj-váʒen]
the nearest	**най-близък**	[naj-blízək]
the same, equal (adj)	**еднакъв**	[ednákəv]
thick (e.g. ~ fog)	**гъст**	[gəst]
thick (wall, slice)	**дебел**	[debél]
thin (person)	**слаб**	[slap]
tight (~ shoes)	**тесен**	[tésen]
tired (exhausted)	**изморен**	[izmorén]
tiring (adj)	**изморителен**	[izmorítelen]
transparent (adj)	**бистър**	[bístər]
unclear (adj)	**неясен**	[nejásen]
unique (exceptional)	**уникален**	[unikálen]
various (adj)	**различен, разни**	[razlítʃen], [rázni]
warm (moderately hot)	**топъл**	[tópəl]
wet (e.g. ~ clothes)	**мокър**	[mókər]
whole (entire, complete)	**цял**	[tsʲal]
wide (e.g. ~ road)	**широк**	[ʃirók]
young (adj)	**млад**	[mlat]

MAIN 500 VERBS

252. Verbs A-C

to accompany (vt)	**придружавам**	[pridruʒávam]
to accuse (vt)	**обвинявам**	[obvinʲávam]
to acknowledge (admit)	**признавам**	[priznávam]
to act (take action)	**действам**	[déjstvam]
to add (supplement)	**добавям**	[dobávʲam]
to address (speak to)	**обръщам се**	[obrə́ʃtam se]
to admire (vi)	**възхищавам се**	[vəshiʃtávam se]
to advertise (vt)	**рекламирам**	[reklamíram]
to advise (vt)	**съветвам**	[səvétvam]
to affirm (assert)	**утвърждавам**	[utvərʒdávam]
to agree (say yes)	**съгласявам се**	[səglasʲávam se]
to aim (to point a weapon)	**целя се**	[tsélʲa se]
to allow (sb to do sth)	**позволявам**	[pozvolʲávam]
to amputate (vt)	**ампутирам**	[amputíram]
to answer (vi, vt)	**отговарям**	[otgovárʲam]
to apologize (vi)	**извинявам се**	[izvinʲávam se]
to appear (come into view)	**появявам се**	[pojavʲávam se]
to applaud (vi, vt)	**аплодирам**	[aplodíram]
to appoint (assign)	**назначавам**	[naznaʧávam]
to approach (come closer)	**доближавам (се)**	[dobliʒávam se]
to arrive (ab. train)	**пристигам**	[pristígam]
to ask (~ sb to do sth)	**моля**	[mólʲa]
to aspire to …	**стремя се**	[stremʲá se]
to assist (help)	**асистирам**	[asistíram]
to attack (mil.)	**атакувам**	[atakúvam]
to attain (objectives)	**достигам**	[dostígam]
to avenge (get revenge)	**отмъщавам**	[otməʃtávam]
to avoid (danger, task)	**избягвам**	[izbʲágvam]
to award (give a medal to)	**наградя**	[nagradʲá]
to battle (vi)	**сражавам се**	[sraʒávam se]
to be (vi)	**съм, бъда**	[səm], [bə́da]
to be a cause of …	**да бъда причина**	[da bə́da priʧína]
to be afraid	**страхувам се**	[strahúvam se]
to be angry (with …)	**сърдя се на …**	[sə́rdʲa se na]
to be at war	**воювам**	[vojúvam]
to be based (on …)	**базирам се на …**	[bazíram se na]
to be bored	**скучая**	[skuʧája]

to be convinced **убеждавам се** [ubeʒdávam se]
to be enough **стигам** [stígam]
to be envious **завиждам** [zavíʒdam]
to be indignant **възмущавам се** [vəzmuʃtávam se]
to be interested in ... **интересувам се** [interesúvam se]

to be lost in thought **замисля се** [zamíslʲa se]
to be lying (~ on the table) **лежа** [leʒá]
to be needed **трябвам** [trʲábvam]
to be perplexed (puzzled) **недоумявам** [nedoumʲávam]

to be preserved **запазвам се** [zapázvam se]
to be required **трябвам** [trʲábvam]
to be surprised **учудвам се** [utʃúdvam se]
to be worried **безпокоя се** [bespokojá se]

to beat (to hit) **бия** [bíja]
to become (e.g. ~ old) **ставам** [stávam]
to behave (vi) **държа се** [dərʒá se]
to believe (think) **вярвам** [vʲárvam]

to belong to ... **принадлежа** [prinadleʒá]
to berth (moor) **акостирам** [akostíram]
to blind (other drivers) **ослепявам** [oslepʲávam]
to blow (wind) **надувам** [nadúvam]

to blush (vi) **изчервявам се** [istʃervʲávam se]
to boast (vi) **хваля се** [hválʲa se]
to borrow (money) **взимам на заем** [vzímam na záem]
to break (branch, toy, etc.) **чупя** [tʃúpʲa]

to breathe (vi) **дишам** [díʃam]
to bring (sth) **докарвам** [dokárvam]
to burn (paper, logs) **изгарям** [izgárʲam]
to buy (purchase) **купувам** [kupúvam]

to call (~ for help) **викам** [víkam]
to call (yell for sb) **повикам** [povíkam]
to calm down (vt) **успокоявам** [uspokojávam]
can (v aux) **мога** [móga]

to cancel (call off) **отменям** [otménʲam]
to cast off (of a boat or ship) **отплувам** [otplúvam]
to catch (e.g. ~ a ball) **ловя** [lovʲá]
to change (~ one's opinion) **сменям** [sménʲam]
to change (exchange) **сменям** [sménʲam]

to charm (vt) **очаровам** [otʃaróvam]
to choose (select) **избирам** [izbíram]
to chop off (with an axe) **отсека** [otseká]
to clean (e.g. kettle from scale) **пречиствам** [potʃístvam]

to clean (shoes, etc.) **обелвам** [obélvam]
to clean up (tidy) **подреждам** [podréʒdam]
to close (vt) **затварям** [zatvárʲam]

to comb one's hair	**сресвам се**	[srésvam se]
to come down (the stairs)	**слизам**	[slízam]
to come out (book)	**излизам**	[izlízam]
to compare (vt)	**сравнявам**	[sravnʲávam]
to compensate (vt)	**компенсирам**	[kompensíram]
to compete (vi)	**конкурирам**	[konkuríram]
to compile (~ a list)	**съставям**	[səstávʲam]
to complain (vi, vt)	**оплаквам се**	[oplákvam se]
to complicate (vt)	**усложнявам**	[usloʒnʲávam]
to compose (music, etc.)	**съчинявам**	[sətʃinʲávam]
to compromise (reputation)	**компрометирам**	[komprometíram]
to concentrate (vi)	**концентрирам се**	[kontsentríram se]
to confess (criminal)	**признавам се**	[priznávam se]
to confuse (mix up)	**обърквам**	[obə́rkvam]
to congratulate (vt)	**поздравявам**	[pozdravʲávam]
to consult (doctor, expert)	**консултирам се с …**	[konsultíram se s]
to continue (~ to do sth)	**продължавам**	[prodəlʒávam]
to control (vt)	**контролирам**	[kontrolíram]
to convince (vt)	**убеждавам**	[ubeʒdávam]
to cooperate (vi)	**сътруднича**	[sətrúdnitʃa]
to coordinate (vt)	**координирам**	[koordiníram]
to correct (an error)	**поправям**	[popravʲam]
to cost (vt)	**струвам**	[strúvam]
to count (money, etc.)	**броя**	[brojá]
to count on …	**разчитам на …**	[rastʃítam na]
to crack (ceiling, wall)	**напуквам се**	[napúkvam se]
to create (vt)	**създам**	[səzdám]
to crush, to squash (~ a bug)	**смачкам**	[smátʃkam]
to cry (weep)	**плача**	[plátʃa]
to cut off (with a knife)	**отрязвам**	[otrʲázvam]

253. Verbs D-G

to dare (~ to do sth)	**осмелявам се**	[osmelʲávam se]
to date from …	**датирам се**	[datíram se]
to deceive (vi, vt)	**лъжа**	[lə́ʒa]
to decide (~ to do sth)	**решавам**	[reʃávam]
to decorate (tree, street)	**украсявам**	[ukrasʲávam]
to dedicate (book, etc.)	**посвещавам**	[posveʃtávam]
to defend (a country, etc.)	**защитавам**	[zaʃtitávam]
to defend oneself	**защищавам се**	[zaʃtiʃtávam se]
to demand (request firmly)	**изисквам**	[izískvam]
to denounce (vt)	**доносничa**	[donósnitʃa]
to deny (vt)	**отричам**	[otrítʃam]
to depend on …	**завися от …**	[zavísʲa ot]
to deprive (vt)	**лишавам**	[liʃávam]

to deserve (vt)	**заслужавам**	[zasluʒávam]
to design (machine, etc.)	**проектирам**	[proektíram]
to desire (want, wish)	**желая**	[ʒelája]
to despise (vt)	**презирам**	[prezíram]
to destroy (documents, etc.)	**унищожавам**	[uniʃtoʒávam]
to differ (from sth)	**отличавам се**	[otliʧávam se]
to dig (tunnel, etc.)	**ровя**	[róvʲa]
to direct (point the way)	**направлявам**	[napravlʲávam]
to disappear (vi)	**изчезна**	[izʧézna]
to discover (new land, etc.)	**откривам**	[otkrívam]
to discuss (vt)	**обсъждам**	[obsə́ʒdam]
to distribute (leaflets, etc.)	**разпространявам**	[rasprostranʲávam]
to disturb (vt)	**безпокоя**	[bespokojá]
to dive (vi)	**гмуркам се**	[gmúrkam se]
to divide (math)	**деля**	[delʲá]
to do (vt)	**правя**	[právʲa]
to do the laundry	**пера**	[perá]
to double (increase)	**удвоявам**	[udvojávam]
to doubt (have doubts)	**съмнявам се**	[səmnʲávam se]
to draw a conclusion	**правя заключение**	[právʲa zaklʲuʧénie]
to dream (daydream)	**мечтая**	[meʧtája]
to dream (in sleep)	**сънувам**	[sənúvam]
to drink (vi, vt)	**пия**	[píja]
to drive a car	**карам кола**	[káram kolá]
to drive away (scare away)	**изгоня**	[izgónʲa]
to drop (let fall)	**изтървавам**	[istərvávam]
to drown (ab. person)	**давя се**	[dávʲa se]
to dry (clothes, hair)	**суша**	[suʃá]
to eat (vi, vt)	**ям**	[jam]
to eavesdrop (vi)	**подслушвам**	[potslúʃvam]
to emit (diffuse - odor, etc.)	**разпространявам**	[rasprostranʲávam]
to enjoy oneself	**веселя се**	[veselʲá se]
to enter (on the list)	**вписвам**	[fpísvam]
to enter (room, house, etc.)	**влизам**	[vlízam]
to entertain (amuse)	**забавлявам**	[zabávlʲavam]
to equip (fit out)	**оборудвам**	[oborúdvam]
to examine (proposal)	**разгледам**	[razglédam]
to exchange (sth)	**разменям си**	[razménʲam si]
to excuse (forgive)	**извинявам**	[izvinʲávam]
to exist (vi)	**съществувам**	[səʃtestvúvam]
to expect (anticipate)	**очаквам**	[oʧákvam]
to expect (foresee)	**предвиждам**	[predvíʒdam]
to expel (from school, etc.)	**изключвам**	[isklʲúʧvam]
to explain (vt)	**обяснявам**	[obʲasnʲávam]
to express (vt)	**изразявам**	[izrazʲávam]
to extinguish (a fire)	**загасявам**	[zagasʲávam]

to fall in love (with ...)	**влюбя се**	[vlʲúbʲa se]
to fancy (vt)	**харесвам**	[harésvam]
to feed (provide food)	**храня**	[hránʲa]
to fight (against the enemy)	**боря се**	[bórʲa se]
to fight (vi)	**бия се**	[bíja se]
to fill (glass, bottle)	**напълвам**	[napəlvam]
to find (~ lost items)	**намирам**	[namíram]
to finish (vt)	**приключвам**	[priklʲútʃvam]
to fish (angle)	**ловя риба**	[lovʲá ríba]
to fit (ab. dress, etc.)	**подхождам**	[podhóʒdam]
to flatter (vt)	**подмазвам се**	[podmázvam se]
to fly (bird, plane)	**летя**	[letʲá]
to follow ... (come after)	**вървя след ...**	[varvʲá slet]
to forbid (vt)	**забранявам**	[zabranʲávam]
to force (compel)	**принуждавам**	[prinuʒdávam]
to forget (vi, vt)	**забравям**	[zabrávʲam]
to forgive (pardon)	**прощавам**	[proʃtávam]
to form (constitute)	**образовам**	[obrazóvam]
to get dirty (vi)	**изцапам се**	[istsápam se]
to get infected (with ...)	**заразя се**	[zarazʲá se]
to get irritated	**дразня се**	[dráznʲa se]
to get married	**женя се**	[ʒénʲa se]
to get rid of ...	**избавям се от ...**	[izbávʲam se ot]
to get tired	**уморявам се**	[umorʲávam se]
to get up (arise from bed)	**ставам**	[stávam]
to give (vt)	**давам**	[dávam]
to give a bath (to bath)	**къпя**	[kəpʲa]
to give a hug, to hug (vt)	**прегръщам**	[pregrəʃtam]
to give in (yield to)	**отстъпвам**	[otstəpvam]
to glimpse (vt)	**видя**	[vídʲa]
to go (by car, etc.)	**пътувам**	[pətúvam]
to go (on foot)	**вървя**	[vərvʲá]
to go for a swim	**къпя се**	[kəpʲa se]
to go out (for dinner, etc.)	**излизам**	[izlízam]
to go to bed (go to sleep)	**лягам да спя**	[lʲágam da spʲa]
to greet (vt)	**приветствувам**	[privétstvuvam]
to grow (plants)	**отглеждам**	[otgléʒdam]
to guarantee (vt)	**гарантирам**	[garantíram]
to guess (the answer)	**отгатна**	[otgátna]

254. Verbs H-M

to hand out (distribute)	**раздам**	[razdám]
to hang (curtains, etc.)	**закачам**	[zakátʃam]
to have (vt)	**имам**	[ímam]

to have a bath	**мия се**	[míja se]
to have a try	**опитам се**	[opítam se]
to have breakfast	**закусвам**	[zakúsvam]
to have dinner	**вечерям**	[vetʃérʲam]
to have lunch	**обядвам**	[obʲádvam]
to head (group, etc.)	**оглавявам**	[oglavʲávam]
to hear (vt)	**чувам**	[tʃúvam]
to heat (vt)	**нагрявам**	[nagrʲávam]
to help (vt)	**помагам**	[pomágam]
to hide (vt)	**крия**	[kríja]
to hire (e.g. ~ a boat)	**наемам**	[naémam]
to hire (staff)	**наемам**	[naémam]
to hope (vi, vt)	**надявам се**	[nadʲávam se]
to hunt (for food, sport)	**ловувам**	[lovúvam]
to hurry (vi)	**бързам**	[bǝrzam]
to imagine (to picture)	**представям си**	[pretstávʲam si]
to imitate (vt)	**имитирам**	[imitíram]
to implore (vt)	**умолявам**	[umolʲávam]
to import (vt)	**внасям**	[vnásʲam]
to increase (vi)	**увеличавам се**	[uvelitʃávam se]
to increase (vt)	**увеличавам**	[uvelitʃávam]
to infect (vt)	**заразявам**	[zarazʲávam]
to influence (vt)	**влияя**	[vlijája]
to inform (e.g. ~ the police about …)	**съобщавам**	[sǝobʃtávam]
to inform (vt)	**информирам**	[informíram]
to inherit (vt)	**наследявам**	[nasledʲávam]
to inquire (about …)	**научавам**	[nautʃávam]
to insert (put in)	**слагам**	[slágam]
to insinuate (imply)	**намеквам**	[namékvam]
to insist (vi, vt)	**настоявам**	[nastojávam]
to inspire (vt)	**въодушевявам**	[vǝoduʃevʲávam]
to instruct (teach)	**инструктирам**	[instruktíram]
to insult (offend)	**оскърбявам**	[oskǝrbʲávam]
to interest (vt)	**интересувам**	[interesúvam]
to intervene (vi)	**намесвам се**	[namésvam se]
to introduce (sb to sb)	**запознавам**	[zapoznávam]
to invent (machine, etc.)	**изобретявам**	[izobretʲávam]
to invite (vt)	**каня**	[kánʲa]
to iron (clothes)	**гладя**	[gládʲa]
to irritate (annoy)	**дразня**	[dráznʲa]
to isolate (vt)	**изолирам**	[izolíram]
to join (political party, etc.)	**присъединявам се**	[prisǝedinʲávam se]
to joke (be kidding)	**шегувам се**	[ʃegúvam se]
to keep (old letters, etc.)	**съхранявам**	[sǝhranʲávam]
to keep silent, to hush	**мълча**	[mǝltʃá]
to kill (vt)	**убивам**	[ubívam]

to knock (on the door)	**чукам (на врата)**	[ʧúkam na vratá]
to know (sb)	**познавам**	[poznávam]
to know (sth)	**знам**	[znam]
to laugh (vi)	**смея се**	[sméja se]
to launch (start up)	**пускам, стартирам**	[púskam], [startíram]
to leave (~ for Mexico)	**заминавам**	[zaminávam]
to leave (forget sth)	**забравям**	[zabrávʲam]
to leave (spouse)	**изоставям**	[ostávʲam]
to liberate (city, etc.)	**освобождавам**	[osvoboʒdávam]
to lie (~ on the floor)	**лежа**	[leʒá]
to lie (tell untruth)	**лъжа**	[ləʒa]
to light (campfire, etc.)	**запалвам**	[zapálvam]
to light up (illuminate)	**осветявам**	[osvetʲávam]
to limit (vt)	**ограничавам**	[ograniʧávam]
to listen (vi)	**слушам**	[slúʃam]
to live (~ in France)	**живея**	[ʒivéja]
to live (exist)	**живея**	[ʒivéja]
to load (gun)	**зареждам**	[zaréʒdam]
to load (vehicle, etc.)	**натоварвам**	[natovárvam]
to look (I'm just ~ing)	**гледам**	[glédam]
to look for ... (search)	**търся**	[tərsʲa]
to look like (resemble)	**приличам**	[prilíʧam]
to lose (umbrella, etc.)	**губя**	[gúbʲa]
to love (e.g. ~ dancing)	**обичам**	[obíʧam]
to love (sb)	**обичам**	[obíʧam]
to lower (blind, head)	**спускам**	[spúskam]
to make (~ dinner)	**готвя**	[gótvʲa]
to make a mistake	**греша**	[greʃá]
to make angry	**сърдя**	[sərdʲa]
to make easier	**облекча**	[oblekʧá]
to make multiple copies	**размножавам**	[razmnoʒávam]
to make the acquaintance	**запознавам се**	[zapoznávam se]
to make use (of ...)	**ползвам**	[pólzvam]
to manage, to run	**ръководя**	[rəkovódʲa]
to mark (make a mark)	**отбелязвам**	[otbelʲázvam]
to mean (signify)	**знача**	[znáʧa]
to memorize (vt)	**запомням**	[zapómnʲam]
to mention (talk about)	**споменавам**	[spomenávam]
to miss (school, etc.)	**пропускам**	[propúskam]
to mix (combine, blend)	**смесвам**	[smésvam]
to mock (make fun of)	**присмивам се**	[prismívam se]
to move (to shift)	**премествам**	[preméstvam]
to multiply (math)	**умножавам**	[umnoʒávam]
must (v aux)	**дължа**	[dəlʒá]

255. Verbs N-R

to name, to call (vt)	**наричам**	[narítʃam]
to negotiate (vi)	**водя преговори**	[vódʲa prégovori]
to note (write down)	**отбележа**	[otbeléʒa]
to notice (see)	**забелязвам**	[zabelʲázvam]
to obey (vi, vt)	**подчинявам се**	[podtʃinʲávam se]
to object (vi, vt)	**възразявам**	[vəzrazʲávam]
to observe (see)	**наблюдавам**	[nablʲudávam]
to offend (vt)	**обиждам**	[obíʒdam]
to omit (word, phrase)	**пропускам**	[propúskam]
to open (vt)	**отварям**	[otvárʲam]
to order (in restaurant)	**поръчвам**	[porə́tʃvam]
to order (mil.)	**заповядвам**	[zapovʲádvam]
to organize (concert, party)	**организирам**	[organizíram]
to overestimate (vt)	**надценявам**	[nattsenʲávam]
to own (possess)	**владея**	[vladéja]
to participate (vi)	**участвам**	[utʃástvam]
to pass through (by car, etc.)	**минавам**	[minávam]
to pay (vi, vt)	**плащам**	[pláʃtam]
to peep, to spy on	**надниквам**	[nadníkvam]
to penetrate (vt)	**прониквам**	[proníkvam]
to permit (vt)	**разрешавам**	[razreʃávam]
to pick (flowers)	**късам**	[kə́sam]
to place (put, set)	**нареждам**	[naréʒdam]
to plan (~ to do sth)	**планирам**	[planíram]
to play (actor)	**играя**	[igrája]
to play (children)	**играя**	[igrája]
to point (~ the way)	**посочвам**	[posótʃvam]
to pour (liquid)	**наливам**	[nalívam]
to pray (vi, vt)	**моля се**	[mólʲa se]
to prefer (vt)	**предпочитам**	[pretpotʃítam]
to prepare (~ a plan)	**подготвя**	[podgótvʲa]
to present (sb to sb)	**представлявам**	[pretstavlʲávam]
to preserve (peace, life)	**съхранявам**	[səhranʲávam]
to prevail (vt)	**преобладавам**	[preobladávam]
to progress (move forward)	**напредвам**	[naprédvam]
to promise (vt)	**обещавам**	[obeʃtávam]
to pronounce (vt)	**произнасям**	[proiznásʲam]
to propose (vt)	**предлагам**	[predlágam]
to protect (e.g. ~ nature)	**опазвам**	[opázvam]
to protest (vi)	**протестирам**	[protestíram]
to prove (vt)	**доказвам**	[dokázvam]
to provoke (vt)	**провокирам**	[provokíram]
to pull (~ the rope)	**дърпам**	[də́rpam]
to punish (vt)	**наказвам**	[nakázvam]

to push (~ the door)	**блъскам**	[blóskam]
to put away (vt)	**скривам**	[skrívam]
to put in order	**подреждам**	[podréʒdam]
to put, to place	**слагам**	[slágam]
to quote (cite)	**цитирам**	[tsitíram]
to reach (arrive at)	**стигам**	[stígam]
to read (vi, vt)	**чета**	[ʧeta]
to realize (a dream)	**осъществявам**	[osəʃtestvʲávam]
to recognize (identify sb)	**опознавам**	[opoznávam]
to recommend (vt)	**съветвам**	[səvétvam]
to recover (~ from flu)	**оздравявам**	[ozdravʲávam]
to redo (do again)	**преправям**	[preprávʲam]
to reduce (speed, etc.)	**намалявам**	[namalʲávam]
to refuse (~ sb)	**отказвам**	[otkázvam]
to regret (be sorry)	**съжалявам**	[səʒalʲávam]
to reinforce (vt)	**укрепвам**	[ukrépvam]
to remember (Do you ~ me?)	**помня**	[pómnʲa]
to remember (I can't ~ her name)	**спомням**	[spómnʲam]
to remind of …	**напомням**	[napómnʲam]
to remove (~ a stain)	**премахвам**	[premáhvam]
to remove (~ an obstacle)	**отстранявам**	[otstranʲávam]
to rent (sth from sb)	**наемам**	[naémam]
to repair (mend)	**поправям**	[poprávʲam]
to repeat (say again)	**повтарям**	[poftárʲam]
to report (make a report)	**докладвам**	[dokládvam]
to reproach (vt)	**упреквам**	[uprékvam]
to reserve, to book	**резервирам**	[rezervíram]
to restrain (hold back)	**удържам**	[udə́rʒam]
to return (come back)	**завръщам се**	[zavrə́ʃtam se]
to risk, to take a risk	**рискувам**	[riskúvam]
to rub out (erase)	**изтрия**	[istríja]
to run (move fast)	**бягам**	[bʲágam]
to rush (hurry sb)	**карам … да бърза**	[káram … da bə́rza]

256. Verbs S-W

to satisfy (please)	**удовлетворявам**	[udovletvorʲávam]
to save (rescue)	**спасявам**	[spasʲávam]
to say (~ thank you)	**кажа**	[káʒa]
to scold (vt)	**ругая**	[rugája]
to scratch (with claws)	**драскам**	[dráskam]
to select (to pick)	**избера**	[izberá]
to sell (goods)	**продавам**	[prodávam]
to send (a letter)	**изпращам**	[ispráʃtam]
to send back (vt)	**върна обратно**	[və́rna obrátno]

to sense (~ danger)	**чувствам**	[ʧúfstvam]
to sentence (vt)	**осъждам**	[osə́ʒdam]
to serve (in restaurant)	**обслужвам**	[obslúʒvam]
to settle (a conflict)	**уреждам**	[uréʒdam]
to shake (vt)	**треса**	[tresá]
to shave (vi)	**бръсна се**	[brə́sna se]
to shine (gleam)	**светя**	[svétʲa]
to shiver (with cold)	**треперя**	[trepérʲa]
to shoot (vi)	**стрелям**	[strélʲam]
to shout (vi)	**викам**	[víkam]
to show (to display)	**показвам**	[pokázvam]
to shudder (vi)	**трепвам**	[trépvam]
to sigh (vi)	**въздъхна**	[vəzdə́hna]
to sign (document)	**подписвам**	[potpísvam]
to signify (mean)	**означавам**	[oznaʧávam]
to simplify (vt)	**опростявам**	[oproʃtávam]
to sin (vi)	**греша**	[greʃá]
to sit (be sitting)	**седя**	[sedʲá]
to sit down (vi)	**сядам**	[sʲádam]
to smell (emit an odor)	**мириша**	[miríʃa]
to smell (inhale the odor)	**мириша**	[miríʃa]
to smile (vi)	**усмихвам се**	[usmíhvam se]
to snap (vi, ab. rope)	**скъсам се**	[skə́sam se]
to solve (problem)	**реша**	[reʃá]
to sow (seed, crop)	**сея**	[séja]
to spill (liquid)	**проливам**	[prolívam]
to spit (vi)	**плюя**	[plʲúja]
to stand (toothache, cold)	**търпя**	[tərpʲá]
to start (begin)	**започвам**	[zapóʧvam]
to steal (money, etc.)	**крада**	[kradá]
to stop (for pause, etc.)	**спирам се**	[spíram se]
to stop (please ~ calling me)	**прекратявам**	[prekratʲávam]
to stop talking	**замълча**	[zaməlʧá]
to stroke (caress)	**галя**	[gálʲa]
to study (vt)	**изучавам**	[izuʧávam]
to suffer (feel pain)	**страдам**	[strádam]
to support (cause, idea)	**подкрепям**	[potkrepʲám]
to suppose (assume)	**предполагам**	[pretpolágam]
to surface (ab. submarine)	**изплувам**	[isplúvam]
to surprise (amaze)	**удивлявам**	[udivlʲávam]
to suspect (vt)	**подозирам**	[podozíram]
to swim (vi)	**плувам**	[plúvam]
to take (get hold of)	**взимам**	[vzímam]
to take a rest	**почивам**	[poʧívam]
to take away (e.g. about waiter)	**отнасям**	[otnásʲam]

to take off (aeroplane)	**излитам**	[izlítam]
to take off (painting, curtains, etc.)	**свалям**	[sválʲam]
to take pictures	**снимам**	[snímam]
to talk to …	**говоря с …**	[govórʲa s]
to teach (give lessons)	**обучавам**	[obuʧávam]
to tear off, to rip off (vt)	**откъсна**	[otkə́sna]
to tell (story, joke)	**разказвам**	[raskázvam]
to thank (vt)	**благодаря**	[blagodarʲá]
to think (believe)	**смятам**	[smʲátam]
to think (vi, vt)	**мисля**	[míslʲa]
to threaten (vt)	**заплашвам**	[zapláʃvam]
to throw (stone, etc.)	**хвърлям**	[hvə́rlʲam]
to tie to …	**завързвам**	[zavə́rzvam]
to tie up (prisoner)	**свързвам**	[svə́rzvam]
to tire (make tired)	**уморявам**	[umorʲávam]
to touch (one's arm, etc.)	**докосвам се**	[dokósvam se]
to tower (over …)	**възвисявам се**	[vəzvisʲávam se]
to train (animals)	**дресирам**	[dresíram]
to train (sb)	**тренирам**	[treníram]
to train (vi)	**тренирам се**	[treníram se]
to transform (vt)	**трансформирам**	[transformíram]
to translate (vt)	**превеждам**	[prevéʒdam]
to treat (illness)	**лекувам**	[lekúvam]
to trust (vt)	**доверявам**	[doverʲávam]
to try (attempt)	**опитвам се**	[opítvam se]
to turn (e.g., ~ left)	**завивам**	[zavívam]
to turn away (vi)	**обръщам се**	[obrə́ʃtam se]
to turn off (the light)	**изключвам**	[isklʲúʧvam]
to turn on (computer, etc.)	**включвам**	[fklʲúʧvam]
to turn over (stone, etc.)	**обърна**	[obə́rna]
to underestimate (vt)	**недооценявам**	[nedootsenʲávam]
to underline (vt)	**подчертая**	[podʧertája]
to understand (vt)	**разбирам**	[razbíram]
to undertake (vt)	**предприемам**	[pretpriémam]
to unite (vt)	**обединявам**	[obedinʲávam]
to untie (vt)	**отвързвам**	[otvə́rzvam]
to use (phrase, word)	**употребявам**	[upotrebʲávam]
to vaccinate (vt)	**ваксинирам**	[vaksiníram]
to vote (vi)	**гласувам**	[glasúvam]
to wait (vt)	**чакам**	[ʧákam]
to wake (sb)	**събуждам**	[səbúʒdam]
to want (wish, desire)	**искам**	[ískam]
to warn (of a danger)	**предупреждавам**	[predupreʒdávam]
to wash (clean)	**мия**	[míja]
to water (plants)	**поливам**	[polívam]

to wave (the hand)	**махам**	[máham]
to weigh (have weight)	**тежа**	[teʒá]
to work (vi)	**работя**	[rabótʲa]
to worry (make anxious)	**безпокоя**	[bespokojá]
to worry (vi)	**вълнувам се**	[vəlnúvam se]
to wrap (parcel, etc.)	**опаковам**	[opakóvam]
to wrestle (sport)	**боря се**	[bórʲa se]
to write (vt)	**пиша**	[píʃa]
to write down	**записвам**	[zapísvam]

Printed in Great Britain
by Amazon